DATE DUE

Unless Recalled Earlier

JUN - 4 1993

The Economics of
Household Consumption

The Economics of
Household Consumption

Frances M. Magrabi,
Young Sook Chung,
Sanghee Sohn Cha,
and Se-Jeong Yang

PRAEGER

New York
Westport, Connecticut
London

Library of Congress Cataloging-in-Publication Data

The Economics of household consumption / Frances M. Magrabi . . . [et al.].
   p. cm.
  Includes bibliographical references and index.
  ISBN 0–275–93406–3 (alk. paper).— ISBN 0–275–94113–2 (pbk. :
alk. paper)
   1. Consumption (Economics) 2. Households. I. Magrabi, Frances M.
HB820.E26 1991
339.4'7—dc20   91–20302

British Library Cataloguing in Publication Data is available.

Library of Congress Catalog Card Number: 91–20302
ISBN: 0–275–93406–3
    0–275–94113–2 (pbk.)

First published in 1991

Praeger Publishers, One Madison Avenue, New York, NY 10010
An imprint of Greenwood Publishing Group, Inc.

Printed in the United States of America

The paper used in this book complies with the Permanent
Paper Standard issued by the National Information Standards
Organization (Z39.48–1984).

10 9 8 7 6 5 4 3 2 1

Contents

Figures and Tables

FIGURES

TABLES

Preface

This book examines household consumption patterns and provides an understanding of how to use such knowledge. It has three general purposes, corresponding to the three major parts of the book: (1) to provide the tools students need in order to use information about household consumption, including major concepts and theories used in the study of consumption, empirical methodologies, and sources of data; (2) to describe current patterns, trends, and problems in household consumption in the United States and in other countries; and (3) to show how information about household consumption is used. Part II contains an original analysis of data from the Bureau of Labor Statistics Survey of Consumer Expenditures, as well as information from published research.

Most of the data on consumption expenditures in the United States are for 1988 and are the most recent data available at the time this book was written. Data on income, prices, and other variables related to household consumption are also for 1988 where possible. Otherwise the most recent data available are reported. Much of the information is based on published analyses of data from surveys earlier than 1988.

The book is intended for upper-division undergraduate and graduate students who have career plans involving market analysis, government policy-making, or consumer education. Students are assumed to have a prior understanding of microeconomic theory and statistics. Upon completing the book, students should have a working knowledge of the role that income and prices play in determining consumption behavior; be able to identify the effects of tastes and preferences, as well as other noneconomic factors, on patterns of consumption; understand and be able to manipulate measures of income and prices so as to account for effects of inflation on consumption; be familiar with consumption life-style groups in the United States and be able to identify sources of differences among them; be aware of the nature and scope of differences in consumption between the United States and other countries; understand the relationship between consumption and economic growth; and be aware of the major consumption problems confronting the world.

We are grateful to the University of Illinois at Urbana-Champaign, especially to the School of Human Resources and Family Studies, the Illinois Agricultural Experiment Station, and the Research Board, for some of the time and research resources used in writing the book. We hope that our work will provide a needed service to the public and to scholars concerned with the economic behavior of families.

Part I

Concepts, Theories, and Empirical Measurement

WHAT IS CONSUMPTION ECONOMICS?

What is consumption economics? And how does it differ from production economics or from economics in general?

Samuelson describes economics as "the study of how men and society choose, with or without the use of money, to employ scarce productive resources to produce various commodities over time and to distribute them for consumption, now and in the future, among various people and groups" (1961, p. 6). It is, then, a study of choice. Who chooses? Some choices are made by individuals, some by business firms or households or by larger social groups, some by the nation as a whole. Why do they choose? Because resources are scarce and because they seek something economists call "utility," which can be obtained only through use of resources. How they choose is the subject of economics.

Choices have to be made (by people and societies) regarding what shall be produced and how resources will be used in that production. Choices also have to be made about how the goods and services that are produced shall be allocated among the ultimate consumers—households and individuals. Consumption economics is concerned with the latter set of choices and with the factors that influence those choices.

Although consumption was recognized as a legitimate area for study at least as early as the period of Adam Smith, the first major effort to establish a formal theory of household consumption was Kyrk's 1923 book, *The Theory of Consumption*. Kyrk claimed for this new area of study a broad, interdisciplinary scope, pointing out that "consumption habits vary with time and place . . . [and cover] numerous modes of human activity . . . , [and that the] motives, interests, and impulses behind it are of infinite variety, and are molded, shaped, and organized by the whole environment in which the individual is placed" (pp. 6–7).

Hoyt, a contemporary of Kyrk, described consumption economics as an area of study concerned with the use of economic resources by ultimate consumers and stressed that it is concerned not only with goods and services actually offered on the market but also with those that might be available if the resources of society were put to different uses (1938, pp. 4–6). Hoyt also believed that consumption economics should be concerned with all goods and services consumed by households regardless of source, including those produced at home, received as gifts or in-kind income, or provided by government. Cochrane and Bell formally defined consumption economics as "the study of decision making by households with respect to the choice of goods and services used in living, together with the relationships growing out of, and the activities surrounding, that decision making" (1956, p. 6).

The multidisciplinary character of the field and its focus on use of goods and services, as well as their acquisition, was recognized and stressed by both Kyrk and Hoyt and by other consumption economists since. Burk stated that consumption economics is an interdisciplinary area of study concerned with allocation of resources to satisfy wants, accomplished through the choice and use of commodities by households (1968, pp. 3–13). She identified five dimensions of consumption economics: (1) behavioral, drawing on concepts and variables of the behavioral sciences; (2) economic, with a focus on the economic problems of maximizing utility or minimizing cost; (3) technical, in that it must take into account technological relationships involved in production and distribution as well as the technical characteristics of the goods themselves as inputs in the process of producing utility; (4) temporal, in that it is concerned with both relationships in a static situation and change; and (5) aggregative, in the sense of being concerned both with the individual household and with aggregate data about population groups.

In 1977 a committee of professionals working in the field (North Central Regional Research Committee on Family Economics, NCR–52) differentiated consumption economics, which they defined as macro- and microanalysis of household consumption patterns and behavior, from family economics, which they defined as the study of determinants of level of living and possibilities for change, and consumer economics, the study of economic interactions of consumers with their external environments (Magrabi, 1984).

We will regard consumption economics as encompassing the acquisition, use, and disposal of goods and services by households. We recognize it to be a stage in a process, which means that we must be concerned with its relation to adjacent stages. Samuelson's definition implies a three-stage process, in which resources (human resources or labor, technology, land, and capital goods) are used to produce goods and services, which in turn are acquired by households and then consumed. The technical relationship among these stages is clear. Adam Smith described an economic and moral relationship when he wrote, "Consumption is the sole end and purpose of all production; and the interest of the producer ought to be attended to, only so far as it may be necessary for promoting that of the consumer" (1937, p. 625).

If we held strictly to the view expressed by Adam Smith and implicit in the writings of many economists, that is where the process would stop, with consumption. But some economists (e.g., Schultz, 1961) have recognized that human resources must themselves be produced. The inputs into the production of human resources include consumption goods and services. Thus, the process we are concerned with is not linear but circular. We are concerned not only with the consumption behavior of households and its determinants but also with the impact of consumption behavior on human and other resources of a society.

WHY STUDY CONSUMPTION?

We can identify several reasons for seeking to understand household consumption behavior: to estimate present or future demand and to estimate present or future need. Consumption economics is an applied field, and those are types of problems to which it is applied. But to understand the field fully, we need to understand how such information might be used. The following are some general types of applications. We might want to estimate present or future demand or need in order to make a number of decisions.

1. Decide on quantities to produce or offer for sale to maximize profits. The client for such an application would be a producer or distributor of goods and services to be sold to consumers. Since nearly all goods are purchased by the consumer from an inventory maintained by the seller, the seller needs to be able to anticipate demand, sometimes months or years or even decades in advance. Thus, an important application of consumption economics is to estimate demand in the long and short run.

2. Determine quantities required to meet the needs of the population. The client in this application is likely to be a government or similar body with responsibility for the well-being of a population. One example is actions taken by the British government during World War II, when much of the civilian food supply and other goods needed to be shipped in, competing with war materiel for scarce shipping space. Planning and allocation were centralized during that emergency. Estimates were developed of the quantities of consumer goods necessary to maintain the health of the population, tonnage was allocated accordingly, and a rationing system was established to ensure that the limited supplies were distributed fairly and according to need.

Centrally planned economies go through similar exercises when they develop their five- and ten-year plans. The resources available to the country must be allocated in a way that will satisfy the wants of the population while reserving resources for investment in capital goods for future production, the military, or other national purposes. Even in free-enterprise societies, governments need to do some monitoring of consumption needs of the population and the degree to which these needs are met, since voters expect government to intervene, directly or indirectly, when the private sector fails to perform in a way that fulfills the goals of the society.

3. Change demand for some commodity. Business firms direct their efforts toward this end constantly, mostly through advertising. An understanding of the consumption behavior of households can help firms focus their advertising on the population groups most likely to be interested in the product, formulate effective messages, and otherwise make their advertising activities as efficient and effective as possible.

4. Change the consumption of some commodity. Groups concerned with the well-being of consumers or society, such as nutrition scientists, health care professionals, law enforcement agencies, and other protective agencies or national policy-making bodies, often see the root causes of problems in consumption patterns and see changing those patterns as a logical and cost-effective means of solving the problems. Thus, we see educational campaigns aimed at curbing smoking and alcohol use, stopping the consumption of drugs such as cocaine, and changing dietary patterns. We also see campaigns aimed at changing the way we use commodities, for example, education to encourage safer driving, conserve energy, or promote the disposal of consumption waste (containers and leftovers) in ways that will not pollute the environment. During the 1970s, when conservation of energy became a national concern, the federal government not only formulated an energy policy but supported research and education aimed at learning how households use fuels and how their usage might be reduced.

5. Assess the effects of government policies, laws, and regulations on different sectors or groups. One example concerns the enactment of new taxes or changes in the tax code. Such changes affect the disposable income or purchasing power of households and are, moreover, likely to affect different population groups differently, either because the changes are regressive or progressive in their impact on real income or because of the differences that exist in the consumption patterns of different population groups. Public interest groups therefore ask such questions as the following: Will the proposed taxes result in greater hunger and malnutrition among the poor? cause the elderly to suffer from inadequate heating? increase the numbers of homeless? place an undue burden on middle-income families? Answering these questions requires an understanding of current consumption patterns of the various population groups and of how those patterns are likely to change when the factors that influence them, such as income or price of the commodity, change as a result of government policy.

1

The Household as an Economic System

Human well-being is the ultimate goal of most human activity. Consumption, that is, the use of goods and services by households, is a determinant of well-being, a builder of human capital, and a major input into the social and economic functioning of the nation.

Consumption goods and services are acquired by households through the use of resources. Thus, the amount and kind of available goods and services consumed by households are determined by the amount and kind of resources at their command, how they use those resources, the amount of resources needed to obtain goods and services, and the tastes and preferences of the household. Each of these factors is, in turn, influenced by the environment (natural and man-made) of the household.

PRODUCTION AND CONSUMPTION IN THE HOUSEHOLD

A simple model of the market economy includes the business sector, in which goods and services are produced and distributed to households, and the household sector, in which goods and services are consumed for the sake of the utility yielded by consumption. Both sectors are influenced by other institutions of the larger society, especially government, which regulates and protects both the business and the household sectors. There are two circular flows between the business sector and the household sector: a flow of goods and services to households in exchange for money and a flow of labor from households to the business sector in exchange for salary or wages. This model is valid but fails to exhibit intrahousehold activities, practices, and relationships that have an impact on household consumption.

Within the household sector, the unit chosen for study might be any of several alternatives: the individual, the family, the household, the consumer unit, or some other unit, such as a commune, group home, or other institution. A household is

all persons who occupy a housing unit. A house, an apartment or other group of rooms, or a single room is regarded as a housing unit when it is occupied or intended for occupancy as separate living quarters; that is, when the occupants do not live and eat with any other persons in the structure and there is direct access from the outside or through a common hall. (U.S. Bureau of Census [Census], 1990e, p. 109)

A consumer unit, as defined by the Bureau of Labor Statistics,

comprises either: (1) all members of a particular household who are related by blood, marriage, adoption, or other legal arrangements; (2) a person living alone or sharing a household with others or living as a roomer in a private home or lodging house or in permanent living quarters in a hotel or motel, but who is financially independent; or (3) two or more persons living together who pool their income to make joint expenditure decisions. Financial independence is determined by the three major expense categories: housing, food, and other living expenses. To be considered financially independent, at least two of the three major expense categories have to be provided by the [person or persons regarded as a consumer unit]. (U.S. Bureau of Labor Statistics [BLS], 1989, p. 1422)

A family is "a group of two or more persons (one of whom is the householder) related by birth, marriage, or adoption and residing together" (Census, 1990e, p. 109). In this book, we will frequently use the term *household* to mean "consumer unit" since that is the most generally used term. In referring to data from the Bureau of the Census, we will use its terminology.

The household as a system for production and consumption is shown in Figure 1.1. In this model, consumption is viewed as a stage in a process that begins with the acquisition of inputs to household production—goods and services and various raw materials purchased or rented from market sources or provided by the community, real property and durables owned by the household, and the time, skills, and knowledge of household members. These inputs are used primarily to produce commodities for consumption in the household: food that is prepared and ready to eat, the bed ready to sleep in, the clean, comfortable house that shelters household members, care and nurturing of a child or other household member. These inputs may also be used to produce inputs for future household production: tools, stocks of durable and nondurable goods, and other forms of wealth. In some cases goods and services are produced for sale or barter to individuals outside the household.

Two kinds of output result from the consumption of household commodities: (1) satisfaction and feelings of well-being experienced by members of the household and (2) productive resources—paid and unpaid labor used in other sectors of society, participation in public decision making and other essential functions of the larger society, and children, who will provide both labor and leadership

Figure 1.1
Model of Household Production/Consumption System

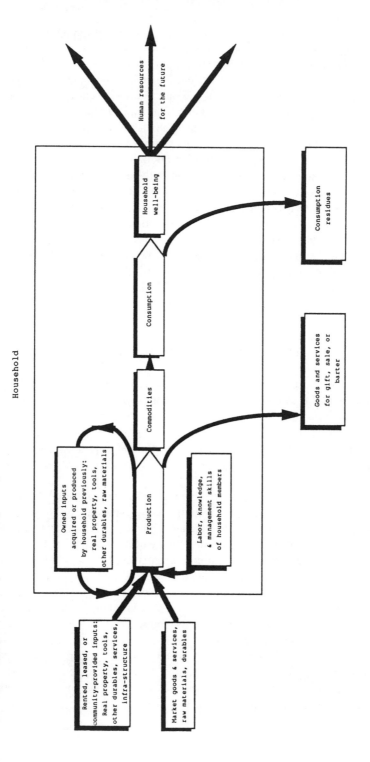

in the future. Consumption is not merely a means of obtaining satisfaction; it is also a means of developing human resources for use in other sectors of society.

Individual household members are not undifferentiated, interchangeable elements of the household. Rather, each member has a set of roles to perform, assigned in part on the basis of biological considerations, in part on the basis of what is deemed appropriate within that society and culture for an individual of a given age, gender, and kinship to other household members, and in part on the basis of the preferences and capabilities of the individual. Roles tend to be differentiated with respect to both production and consumption. Role differentiation in production is reflected in the allocation of responsibility for making purchasing decisions and performing household tasks. The amount and kind of goods and services consumed is also determined in part by role. Thus, neither efficiency nor need completely accounts for the way work is actually assigned and commodities shared.

Several implications for the analysis of household consumption stem from the nature of the household consumption system. First, it is not sufficient to measure the goods and services that are acquired from market sources by the household. Another entity of interest is the household commodity—that which is available for consumption within the household. Because much productive activity takes place within households, the value of the household commodities consumed is likely to be greater than the value of the market goods and services acquired by the household.

Second, to assess well-being accurately, one must measure the actual consumption of commodities by each household member. Much waste occurs. Also, commodities may be allocated among household members on bases other than need, as need is defined by scientific or public opinion or by other standards external to the household. To take one example, a pregnant or lactating woman has special needs for nutrients, yet her food needs may be the last in the household to be satisfied.

Third, for accurate prediction of household behavior, the existence, magnitude, technical relationships, and role assignments pertaining to household production must be known and taken into account. For example, new, improved products, such as an improved appliance, may not be utilized if they are unsuited to existing raw ingredients, methods, and equipment used by households. Information or other resources intended to change household consumption are likely to have little effect if they are not directed to the person in the household who controls the production and/or allocation of household commodities.

Finally, to understand how consumption, and thus well-being, can be improved, one must understand the process by which household commodities become available. What technical operations are performed in the household production process? Which operations lend themselves to improvement and change? What new technologies and methods could be introduced with beneficial result? What are the practices of the household with respect to intrahousehold allocation? Are those practices beneficial to the household or to social goals? How might they be changed?

CONSUMPTION CONCEPTS

Consumption is the use of commodities by households. It is a three-stage process, encompassing acquisition of goods and services from all sources, their use to maintain household well-being, and the disposal of consumption residues. Although purchase of goods and services has received and continues to receive by far the most attention, many goods and services are actually obtained from nonmarket sources. Such items include the use of parks and other recreational areas, streets and highways, subsidized transportation systems, fire and police protection, public education and educational services, and free or subsidized health care. Disposal of consumption residue is another neglected aspect of consumption that is being forcefully brought to our attention by growing problems of solid waste disposal and environmental deterioration.

Consumption Pattern and Standard of Living

Davis (1945) proposed a useful distinction between consumption and living. Consumption is the use of goods and services—food, clothing, child care, and so on—by households. Living, according to Davis, includes consumption but also community services, working conditions, freedoms of various sorts, something Davis calls "atmosphere," and other intangibles that contribute to the household's well-being. Davis also differentiated between level of living or consumption (the collection of goods and services and other elements that is actually used or experienced by the household) and standard (that which is regarded as a goal and earnestly strived for). Higher levels of consumption or living yield higher levels of satisfaction or well-being.

Consumption pattern is the way elements of consumption are combined to form level of consumption as a whole. According to Kyrk (1933), there are three ways of describing level of consumption: by the kinds and amounts of goods and services consumed in the household (how many pounds of butter, pairs of shoes, and so forth); by the way these commodities are organized for use (the tendency for products to be chosen in clusters, with choice of one product leading to choice of others of the same style, and the activities and rituals associated with product use); and by the values that underlie the choices of a household. Kyrk believed that to understand consumption fully, one should examine all of these aspects (pp. 377–379).

Kyrk believed that elements of consumption are incorporated into the standard of living because of specific consumption values. According to her, a household's needs and wants are the basis from which consumption values—which include survival value, prestige value, and group-created value—arise. They are related to needs for physiological requirements; needs for social prestige, distinction, and recognition; and aesthetic, creative, and religious interests. According to Kyrk, most irrational consumption patterns are fostered by prestige values, by which expenditure is incorporated into standards of living as symbols of a certain social class.

Cochrane and Bell (1956) viewed wants as a fundamental factor influencing consumer choice. According to them, the consumption process has two stages. First, the consumer decides which want is to be satisfied and to what degree; then he or she decides which combination of goods and services shall be acquired to satisfy the pattern of wants already determined. Cochrane and Bell considered consumption-related human wants to include physiological requirements and social-made wants. Physiological requirements refer to wants for food, the protection provided by shelter and clothing, family, and social activities. Social-made wants refer to the wants resulting from group and social activities. They classified social-made wants according to their source or motivation: custom-made wants, derived from custom; conspicuous consumption wants, which stem from the desire for display; fashion-made wants, for conforming to the prevailing style in consumption; imitative wants, for copying neighbors and others; and producer-made wants, created by advertising and by technological development. Cochrane and Bell argue that social-made wants are limitless and hence have a great impact on consumers' decisions.

Consumption Categories Based on Human Needs and Wants

Conventional categories of goods and services include food, housing, clothing, education, health, and recreation. These categories, however, have limited power to provide an appropriate explanation of why households consume such items. They do not have a clear and unambiguous relationship to the underlying needs and wants. To take food as an example, people are usually considered to consume food to satisfy basic needs, such as physiological requirements, but this does not hold true for all subcategories of food.

Several attempts have been made to categorize goods and services based on the source and intensities of needs and wants of a household. A common way of categorizing goods and services is to classify them as necessities, usually thought of as goods that one ought to have, and luxuries, defined variously as those goods that bring about a desirable state of affairs, those one ought not to possess, or those that do not increase productive efficiency (Kyrk, 1933).

Hawtrey (1925) identified two classes of objects of consumption: "defensive products," intended to prevent or alleviate physical discomfort, and "creative products," which supply some positive gratification or satisfaction. Hawtrey regarded each class of product as meeting a need:

In the case of the defensive product the need arises from the distress caused or threatened by some physical condition. . . . In the case of the creative product, on the other hand, the need can only arise from a knowledge of the possibility of the product. (pp. 189–190)

The distinction between pleasure and comfort was discussed also by Scitovsky (1976, pp. 59–63). Comfort, according to Scitovsky, includes such gratifications as belonging, being useful, and sticking to our habits. It hinges on our level of arousal being at or close to its optimum. Pleasure accompanies changes in the level of arousal toward the optimum. When we are comfortable, we do not experience pleasure. Pleasure occurs when our needs for physical and mental stimulation are satisfied.

Hoyt (1938) analyzed standard of living in terms of three types of consumption elements: physiological, conventional, and personal and individual elements. Physiological elements include proper food, clothing, and other things that enhance physical health and vitality (air-conditioning, for instance). Conventional elements include consumption items that satisfy needs for social approval. Hoyt believed that the relative amounts of satisfaction received from social approval may differ among people, as does the kind of consumption items belonging to conventional elements. Personal and individual elements include consumption items one chooses because one likes them.

Hoyt (1938) examined the relative importance of the three types of elements using actual data. She conducted an experimental study, giving each member of a group of 100 students a sum of money to cover total expenditures for one college year. Each of the students was asked to record dollar expenditures for main consumption categories (food, room, clothing, etc.) and estimate the importance of different elements in dollar terms. In a typical student estimate, nearly half of the total expenditure was attributed to conventional, one-third to physiological, and one-sixth to personal elements. Among health expenditures, physiological elements were considered to be most important. Conventional elements were most important in expenditures on barber and beauty shop services, clothing, recreation, and church and charity. Personal elements were most important for expenditures on candy, beverages, books, and reading. Hoyt concluded that the students differed with respect to which needs were of greater importance in determining a given expenditure.

In a later analysis, Hoyt (1959) categorized consumption items in terms of their influence on total welfare of a household. She classified them as protective, expansive, and destructive elements. Protective elements give security to the current level of welfare of a household, while expansive elements raise and destructive elements lower the household's level of living. Protective elements satisfy individual and conventional needs and include physical necessities, social necessities, and compensatory elements. Compensatory elements are the consumption items a consumer chooses in the place of unmet needs; for example, a need for a conventional standard of housing could be compensated for by a better car or clothes when the consumer could not obtain the desired housing. Expansive elements serve to raise the standard or level of living. They include education, travel, some kinds of recreation, and religion. Destructive elements, which include recreational drugs and alcoholic beverages, tend to lower the standard or level of living. When compensatory elements are carried too far and displace protective or expansive elements (as when interest in car or clothing becomes obsessive) or lead to health problems (as when eating to reward oneself becomes overeating), they also become destructive.

Roberts and Dant (1988) attempted to categorize expenditure items so that a household's budget allocation among categories would reflect its consumption needs. They defined five categories of expenditure:

1. Rent, including taxes and some obligatory payments.
2. Subsistence funds: Expenditures spent to satisfy minimal needs for survival.
3. Replacement funds: Expenditures on contemporary cultural necessities. For example, personal computers and word processors are examples of cultural necessities of contemporary society because they are commonly used as substitutes for typewriters.
4. Ceremonial funds: Expenditures for the purpose of maintaining and cultivating social relationships, for example, expenditures on family parties, vacations, celebration of holidays, participation in sporting, religious, and cultural events, and symbolic gift giving in the case of marriage and graduation.
5. Personal funds: Expenditures devoted to self and that serve personal goals.

Roberts and Dant pointed out that replacement, ceremonial, and personal funds are relatively more important for modern consumers than are rent and subsistence funds. They argued that the rapid development of technology and cultural change make some products unavailable, while other products become essentials in everyday life and thereby stimulate need for replacement and ceremonial funds.

CONSTRAINTS ON CONSUMPTION

The basic model for studying consumption choices can be summarized as follows: Choice is influenced by two types of determinants: the resources commanded by the household, which enable it to acquire commodities for consumption, and the factors that affect or make up the household's tastes, preferences, and needs for consumption commodities. The environment within which choice occurs may affect both household resources and tastes and preferences. Consumption results in well-being, which, in turn, affects the pool of resources.

Constraints on consumption include the price or cost of goods and services, the amount of resources (especially money income, wealth, and the household's own labor) available to the household for use in acquiring household commodities, and characteristics of the environment or choice situation.

Resources are generally categorized as human and nonhuman resources. Nonhuman resources include income, that is, the flow of resources received by the household during a given time period, and wealth, the stock of accumulated resources that might be drawn upon.

Human Resources

Human resources consist of the labor available to the household that can be used to earn income through paid employment or be used in household production. Productivity of human resources in either use depends partly on the innate endowment of the individual; partly on acquired knowledge, skills, and managerial ability; partly on motivation; and partly on the tools and other nonhuman resources used by the laborer. Quality of human resources is influenced by the kind and quality of consumption. For example, research indicates that the physical and intellectual capacity of adults may be influenced by their nutritional status in infancy and even by the nutritional status of their mothers during and prior to the pregnancy (e.g., Rhodes, 1979).

Income

It is useful to differentiate between money income and real income. Money income is money received from earnings, interest or dividends, rent, pensions, or other sources. Real income is the flow of goods and services consumed (or available for consumption) by the household. Although the underlying concept of real income is an actual flow of goods and services, it is in practice measured by the purchasing power of money income.

Household consumption choices are influenced not only by the amount of income available to it but by other characteristics of income as well. The regularity and certainty of income may affect the proportion of income used for current consumption. Expectations regarding future income may also affect the savings rate and willingness to use credit to pay for current consumption. Source of income and number of earners may affect decisions about income use.

Wealth

Wealth and consumer credit provide means of acquiring commodities without the use of income. Wealth includes financial assets, which might be liquidated and used for consumption. It also includes durable goods, which provide services to the household. Dwellings, furnishings and equipment, and automobiles are the durables most commonly owned. The use of wealth and consumer credit for current consumption affects future consumption, since financial assets can be used up, durables deteriorate, and debts must be repaid out of future income. On the other hand, saving out of current income can be used to build up wealth and increase total lifetime consumption.

Price

Resources influence consumption in combination with price—the quantity of a resource needed to acquire a unit of commodity. Although we are most familiar with money price, we should also recognize that time is another resource needed for consumption of commodities. In some cases, we need to take account of the time, as well as the money cost, of consumption.

Other Constraints

Availability of market goods and services is an environmental constraint on consumption choices; households cannot purchase products that are not offered for sale. Availability depends in part on the state of technology, which determines the kinds and characteristics of goods produced, and on the distribution system, which makes items accessible to potential consumers. Consumer knowledge of the availability of goods and services, their price, and their quality is also a constraint.

HOUSEHOLD WELL-BEING

Well-being is an outcome of consumption. It is the state of health, comfort, or happiness that results from (among other things) the consumption of goods and services. Individuals and households have numerous needs and desires, many of which require consumption of goods and services to satisfy. Some of those needs are essential for maintaining life, some are based on culturally determined prescriptions of how to live, and some are rooted in individual tastes and preferences. All yield satisfaction to the individual when they are satisfied.

Given this close association between consumption and well-being, it is reasonable to assume that measures of consumption are good indicators of well-being, and they are generally accepted as such. Access to goods and services (as opposed to the actual acquisition or possession of them) is also used as an indicator of well-being. Often access to goods and services is defined as having the means to acquire them.

Although the actual relationship between consumption and well-being is difficult, perhaps impossible, to measure directly with any degree of accuracy, several theories have evolved concerning the nature of that relationship. The simplest theory is that more is better, and hence the more that is consumed, the higher is the level of well-being. This theory, widely used in both research designed to aid policymakers and by consumers themselves, is a useful simplification, although it has many well-known exceptions.

Another theory is that satisfaction, and hence well-being, is a function of the magnitude of the gap between one's actual level of consumption and one's standard. The further below the standard one is, the lower is one's level of well-being. An example is the gap between actual food consumption and recommended standards for nutrient intake. Diets are often assessed with respect to the percentage of the nutritional standard provided. The higher the percentage is, the higher is the well-being.

Gaps may also be interpreted in terms of other comparisons, such as a standard based on scientific evidence regarding what is essential for well-being. An alternative to using scientifically based standards is the use of level of consumption (or income) of a reference group as a standard for assessing well-being. If the household's level of consumption (or income) is below that of the reference group, its level of well-being is regarded as being correspondingly low; if the household is at the same level as the reference group, regardless of how low that level may be in absolute terms, then the household is deemed to be at a satisfactory level of well-being (Duesenberry, 1959, p. 32).

Still another theory is that well-being is a function of the gap between current consumption and previous levels experienced by the household. If level of consumption is rising, then the household perceives itself as having a high level of well-being, although its absolute level may be low. If its level of consumption is declining, the household perceives itself to be at a low level of well-being, although its consumption level may still be high in absolute terms.

Well-being is also believed to be influenced by the balance among the elements or categories of consumption. For example, the household whose consumption consists mostly of necessities can be inferred to be less well off than a household with a substantial proportion of its consumption allocated to luxuries. An implication of Hoyt's classification of commodities as protective, expansive, and destructive is that an optimum consumption pattern might be one in which there is an appropriate balance between protective and expansive elements, with destructive elements kept to a minimum. Both Hawtrey and Scitovsky suggested that a desirable pattern is one in which there is a high ratio of pleasure-producing products to those that merely provide comfort.

2

Theoretical Approaches to the Study of Household Consumption

A theory may be described as a set of concepts and relationships—a network in which each node is a concept and the links between nodes are relationships. If, for example, we say that the amount consumed of a commodity by a household is determined by its price, income of the household, the household's tastes and preferences, and environmental factors, we have specified four concepts (amount consumed, price, income, tastes and preferences, environment) and a relationship (determination) between amount consumed and the remaining concepts. A relationship may be a definition (A includes C, D, and E) or a hypothesis (if A increases, then B will decrease). A theory is expected to be logically coherent.

Facts, on the other hand, are data about the observable world, about what in reality exists. A theory is related to the observable world but not a part of it. Hempel (1952, pp. 29–39) spoke of theory as floating above the observable world, linked to it at specific points by rules of interpretation that enable us to equate concepts with real-world phenomena. It is these linkages to the real world that enable us to test hypotheses that form part of the theory to see if they are true in an empirical as well as a theoretical sense. The linkages also enable us to apply the theory to real-world situations and make predictions about events that can be expected to occur based on observations of other phenomena.

Not all the relationships pertaining to a theory need to be tested or even testable for a theory to be useful. Some may be deductively derived. Other relationships that are accepted without (or in spite of) testing are referred to as assumptions. Many assumptions consist of definitions or rules identifying concepts with real-world phenomena.

In the study of household consumption, economic theories help shape the empirical work that is done. They substantially determine what questions are studied, what data are collected, and what methods of analysis are used. Policymakers and researchers alike pose questions that arise from their understanding of the world, and that understanding is shaped and, to a large extent, limited by the theories they learned in school or later. Also, they tend to ask only those questions for which they have a reasonable hope of receiving acceptable (and accepted) answers. Those questions are likely to be ones that can be answered within a theoretical context. Thus, one reason for becoming familiar with the theories used in the study of household consumption is that they have shaped and to a degree limited the empirical literature available to us. Were it not for the influence of theory, different or a wider variety of questions might have been researched. In order to understand the information available, we need to know what has not been studied and why it has been neglected.

Theories also perform the essential function of enabling us to generalize from specific instances to general classes of phenomena. When we read information based on statistical data, we want to know answers to several questions. Is it likely that this is true now, as it was in the year the data were collected? Will it continue to be true in the future? Is it likely to be generally true in other populations and groups? To answer these questions, we need to understand why the specific instance occurred and under what circumstances it is likely to occur again. If the statistical information were based only on common sense or a general knowledge of the world, then our only basis for deciding whether it is safe to generalize is common sense or general knowledge. If it were based on a theory, then the theory, and previous tests of it, provide guidance for determining how far it is safe to generalize.

This chapter provides a brief synopsis of the main theories that have been applied to the study of household consumption. No comprehensive, integrated theory exists. What we do have can best be described as a set of loosely related formulations that constitute approaches to the empirical study of household consumption. Some of these approaches address the general problem of consumption choices; others focus on specific aspects of consumption behavior. Each approach has strengths and limitations, but which is best depends on the empirical question to be addressed.

UTILITY FUNCTIONS

Concepts and Relationships

The utility function may be represented as:

$$U = u(A)$$

where U represents the total utility (satisfaction) received by an individual in a given time period or on a given occasion and A is a set of alternatives from which he or she may choose. The decision maker is assumed to seek the maximum total utility.

This functional relationship is a central element of decision theory, where the focus of attention is on how choices are made and on the improvement of that process. It is also a central element of neoclassical demand theory, including its variations and extensions. It is mentioned here separately because some attempts have been made to measure utility directly, identify the form of the functional relationship, or identify the procedures and decision rules applied by the decision maker in choosing among the alternatives. Examination of the nature of the utility function provides useful insights that can enrich our understanding of other theoretical approaches.

Generally the utility function is part of a larger theoretical construct that usually includes constraints on choice, such as a budget constraint. The terms in the utility function have been variously defined. For example, alternatives may be regarded as having multiple attributes, with each attribute affecting the amount of utility derived from the alternative. Two lines of study have especial relevance to consumption decisions: decision rules and decision making under uncertainty.

Decision Rules. While it may be reasonable to assume that consumers seek to maximize their utility, the process of actually identifying the alternatives that will provide maximum utility is generally acknowledged to be exceedingly complex. One difficulty is lack of complete information on which to base choice. The number of alternatives potentially available to the purchaser of consumer products is extremely large, and the consumer is unlikely to have complete and accurate information about more than a fraction of them. Even the availability of some alternatives may be unknown. While additional (but not necessarily complete) information may be obtainable, the search for it requires time, effort, and perhaps monetary expenditure and may not be worthwhile in terms of potential gain in utility. Another difficulty is the complexity of processing the large amounts of potentially relevant information.

Given the complexity of making decisions, how do consumers actually choose? An example of a study that addressed this problem is one by Hauser and Urban (1986). They assumed an additive utility function:

$$U = u_1 a_1 + \ldots + u_n a_n.$$

The consumer was assumed to have a budget constraint and to be able to measure the quantity of utility he or she would obtain from each alternative (a commodity, such as an automobile or a vacation, representing a substantial expenditure). They tested two alternative hypotheses. One was that the consumer would choose on the basis of the ratio of utility from a given purchase to its price, that is, the quantity of utility obtained per dollar. It was hypothesized that the consumer would choose the alternatives that provided the most utility per dollar. The alternative hypothesis was that the consumer would choose the alternatives that provided the greatest net utility, considered to be the opportunity cost of selecting the alternative (the difference between the utility provided by the given alternative and the utility that could have been obtained had the price of the item been used to purchase a different set of commodities). Thus, the second hypothesis recognized the "lumpiness" of alternatives. One cannot buy a dollar's worth of automobile; one must invest the entire purchase price or nothing. Both hypotheses were found to be consistent with data from a small sample of consumers, who were asked about their current ownership of items, plans to purchase, and priorities for purchase.

In studies such as the one by Hauser and Urban, the number of alternatives and information considered by the decision maker is artificially limited. In real-world decision making, consumers often deal with large numbers of potential alternatives and have access to large quantities of information—some highly technical and much of doubtful validity or applicability to their situation. A practical solution to the complexity problem is for the decision maker to use choice heuristics—rules for selecting alternatives that, although not guaranteeing that utility will always be maximized, do enable the decision maker to identify good alternatives with relatively little expenditure of effort for obtaining or processing information.

Suppose each alternative has several attributes and that the amount of utility provided depends on the nature of the attributes. One way to choose, called the conjunctive rule, is to establish a minimum cutoff for each attribute. An alternative below the cutoff for one or more attributes is eliminated from consideration, and a choice is made from the reduced set. Another example of a heuristic is the lexicographic rule. In applications of this rule, it is assumed that attributes can be ranked in order of their importance to the decision maker. The most important attribute is considered first (and may be the only attribute considered). The alternative that provides the most of that attribute is the one chosen. If there is a tie, choice is made on the basis of the next most important attribute, and so on. A number of other choice heuristics have been formulated (Bettman, 1979, pp. 179–185).

Decision Making under Uncertainty. Choices are necessarily made on the basis of expected utility rather than the utility actually experienced. Thus, utility may be conceived of as resulting from the outcome of the alternative chosen. If each alternative has only one possible outcome and if this outcome and its associated utility are known to the decision maker, then the decision can be made with certainty; however, a given alternative might have several possible outcomes. Which outcome will actually occur might depend on the state of the world (elements in the environment). State of the world, in combination with the chosen alternative, would determine the outcome, that is, the events that ensued from choice of a given alternative or the utility experienced.

In order to choose rationally, the decision maker needs information about two aspects: the utility attached to each possible outcome and the probability that each given outcome will occur for each given alternative. Even then this person cannot choose with the assurance that he or she will maximize utility. A strategy will be needed, similar to the decision rules mentioned above. The consumer may decide to maximize expected utility, although there is a risk of incurring an outcome that, although having a low probability of occurrence, would be intolerable. Among the alternative strategies proposed is the maximin rule, in which the decision maker chooses the alternative whose worse outcome is least undesirable, thereby ensuring that intolerable outcomes do not occur (although perhaps giving up any chance of getting highly desirable outcomes).

Assessment of Approach

One obvious limitation of the study of consumer utility functions is the restrictive nature of assumptions that appear to be needed in order to apply the theory empirically. We must assume that consumers seek to maximize their satisfaction. Assumptions are also needed about the nature of utility. Is it simple satisfaction experienced from a given outcome, not conditioned by circumstances? Is it homogeneous in that the satisfaction experienced as a result of, say, eating is not different in kind from the satisfaction from, say, listening to music or owning a fine automobile? We may need assumptions about the form of the utility function and about the meaning of observed behaviors. If these assumptions are unrealistic in particular situations (as they may often be), then empirical results based on the theory are of doubtful validity. This limitation applies to a greater or lesser extent to all of the approaches we will examine.

The major strength of the utility function approach is that it does direct attention to the crux of the consumption problem: How do households actually choose and on what basis? As we try to answer that question, we may get a better understanding of the limitations of other approaches, in which the existence of a utility function is assumed but not examined.

NEOCLASSICAL DEMAND THEORY

Concepts and Relationships

Let us express the utility function as

$$U = u(Q)$$

where Q is a set of goods and services (commodities) purchased in the market. Each q_i has an associated price, p_i, and total purchases cannot exceed the consumer's income, Y:

$$\Sigma \ q_i p_i = Y.$$

From these relationships, given certain assumptions, we can derive the conditions under which the consumer will maximize utility and his or her demand schedule for any given good or service. Among the necessary assumptions are that the consumer seeks to maximize utility, is rational, has complete and accurate information about the availability of commodities, their prices, and their ability to satisfy his or her wants; that utility is measurable and homogeneous with respect to all commodities consumed; that the consumer's tastes and preferences are stable over the time period of interest; that the time during which commodities are consumed is irrelevant to the purchase decision; that the consumer makes purchasing decisions independently of others (no group decision making); and that commodities are uniform in quality and highly divisible.

Assumptions about the nature of the utility function are needed as a basis for identifying the conditions under which utility will be at its maximum.

Cardinal Utility Approach. The simplest assumption is that utility can be measured cardinally, in other words, that the ability or power of a commodity to satisfy a want can be measured in units (sometimes called utils) that can be meaningfully added, subtracted, multiplied, or divided. It is not necessary to assume that a given commodity provides the same number of utils to every consumer, but it is necessary to assume that the consumer knows how much utility he or she would obtain from any commodity.

The consumer seeks to maximize total utility from all goods and services in a given period of time. Three measures of utility are relevant to the calculation: *total utility*, the entire amount of satisfaction obtained from consuming a given quantity of a commodity per unit of time; *marginal utility*, the change in total utility resulting from a one-unit change in consumption of the commodity per unit of time; and *weighted marginal utility*, marginal utility divided by the price of the marginal unit.

Marginal utility can be expected to vary depending on the quantity previously consumed. The first potato chip tastes wonderful, and so does the second (they have a high marginal utility), but after half the bag has been consumed, eating an additional potato chip will yield little additional utility, and at some point (when you begin to feel a bit sick) the marginal utility may be negative. This relationship is sometimes called the *law of diminishing marginal utility*: If successive units of a commodity are consumed (all other consumption being constant), a point is reached at which the utility associated with each additional unit begins to diminish. Several causes contribute to this phenomena: (1) consumers have many wants, none of which are insatiable, at least within a given time period; (2) commodities are generally not perfect substitutes for one another, although a given commodity may contribute to satisfying several different wants and several commodities may satisfy the same want; and (3) consumers have a high regard for variety. Thus, as successive units of the commodity are consumed and some wants are fully satisfied, other wants, which the commodity has little ability to satisfy, become the focus of the consumer's attention. In general, the more wants a commodity is capable of satisfying and the higher its degree of substitutability for other commodities, the slower will its marginal utility decline.

The condition for maximizing utility, sometimes called the *equimarginal principle* or *equilibrium condition*, can be stated as follows: If a fixed amount of income is to be divided among a set of commodities, utility will be maximized if (1) the quantities purchased are such that the weighted marginal utilities of all commodities are equal,

$$MU_A/p_A = MU_B/p_B = \ldots = MU_M/p_M,$$

and (2) all income is spent. This is the equilibrium point for the consumer because, if utility is at a maximum, he or she has no incentive to shift funds from one commodity to another.

Suppose that the consumer has chosen a market basket of commodities that just exhausts this person's income, that the quantity to be purchased of each is in the diminishing marginal utility range, and that their weighted marginal utilities are equal. Is this the utility-maximizing selection? He can determine this by making comparisons at the margin. Since all his income is exhausted, if he wants to increase his consumption of commodity A by one unit, he must reduce his expenditure on some other commodity B by an amount that will offset the cost of the one-unit increase in A. If an additional dollar spent on A will yield a gain in utility that is larger than the utility lost by reducing expenditure on B, then his utility is not at its maximum, and he should make the trade; otherwise he should not. But because marginal utility is diminishing, we know that the utility associated with the additional dollar spent on A must be less than that associated with the previous dollar, and hence less than the B utility he must give up. If he makes the shift, he will lose more utility than he gains, and the same will be true of any possible shift in expenditure. But suppose he begins by selecting a market basket in which one or more commodities are not in the diminishing marginal utility range. He will find that when he has made all the shifts that are advantageous to him, the quantities purchased of all commodities will then be in the diminishing marginal utility range. This reasoning is illustrated in Table 2.1. If the consumer has $1.20 to spend on bananas and oranges and each costs $.20 per piece, his best combination is four bananas and two oranges (the point at which the weighted marginal utility of each is equal to 3.0). This can be demonstrated by calculating the total utility from each feasible combination (illustrated in the table) or by comparing marginal gains and losses from shifting from one feasible combination to another.

Indifference Analysis. Suppose we prefer not to make the unrealistic assumption that utility is measurable cardinally. The utility-maximizing combination can still be identified, provided that we are willing to assume that (1) commodities are substitutable for each other, (2) the consumer can always decide whether she prefers A (a set of commodities in given quantities) to B (an alternative set of quantities), B to A, or is indifferent between them, (3) the consumer always prefers more to less, and (4) her preferences are transitive (i.e., if she prefers A to B and B to C, then she will always prefer A to C).

In principle, then, a consumer's relative preferences could be plotted, in the case of two commodities, on an indifference map (Figure 2.1). Each curve—I_1, I_2, I_3—identifies different combinations of quantities of A and B among which the consumer is indifferent. She does, however, always prefer a combination of A and B on a higher indifference curve to one on a lower curve. Indifference curves have the following characteristics: they have a negative slope, because

Table 2.1
Utility Maximizing Using a Cardinal Measure of Utility

Quantity	Bananas (20 cents/unit)			Quantity	Oranges (20 cents/unit)		
	TU	MU	WMU		TU	MU	WMU
0	0	0	0.0	0	0	0	0.0
1	100	100	5.0	1	44	44	2.2
2	226	126	6.3	2	104	60	3.0
3	322	96	4.8	3	160	56	2.8
4	382	60	3.0	4	208	48	2.4
5	416	34	1.7	5	246	38	1.9
6	436	20	1.0	6	268	22	1.1

Key: TU = total utility; MU = marginal utility; WMU = weighted marginal utility (marginal utility divided by price per unit), the amount of utility obtained from the last penny spent.

Total utility obtainable from $1.20 expenditure:

Bananas	Oranges	TU
0	6	268
1	5	346
2	4	434
3	3	482
4	2	486
5	1	460
6	0	436

Figure 2.1
Utility Maximizing Using an Ordinal Measure of Utility: Indifference Curves

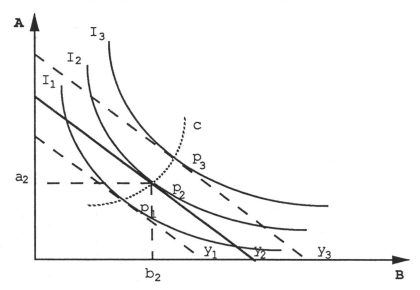

more is preferred to less and the level of utility is constant on any given indifference curve; higher curves represent higher levels of utility; curves do not intersect because of transitivity; and the set of indifference curves is unique to the consumer and to a specified time period, during which her tastes and preferences do not change.

The slope of the indifference curve $(-\Delta Q_B/\Delta Q_A)$ is called the marginal rate of substitution of B for A. In cardinal utility terms, it is equal to the ratio of the marginal utility of A to the marginal utility of B and is the amount of B the consumer would be willing to give up in order to gain an additional unit of A.

Suppose a consumer has a fixed budget to spend for the two commodities. The budget restraint line (y_2), which identifies the various combinations of A and B that could be purchased, can also be plotted, provided the prices of the commodities are known. The slope of the budget restraint line is equal to the ratio of the prices. If the budget for A and B is fixed and must be spent and if tastes and preferences (represented by the indifference curves) are stable, then the combination that provides maximum utility (a_2 and b_2) is that identified by the point (p_2) where the budget restraint line is tangential to an indifference curve. This is also the point at which the marginal rate of substitution is equal to the ratio of the prices.

The utility-maximizing combination of commodities p_2 can be seen to depend on three factors: their prices, the consumer's budget (income), and the consumer's tastes and preferences. As long as all three factors remain constant, she is at equilibrium at p_2. But suppose her income increases or declines. She would have

Figure 2.2
Consumer Response to a Price Change

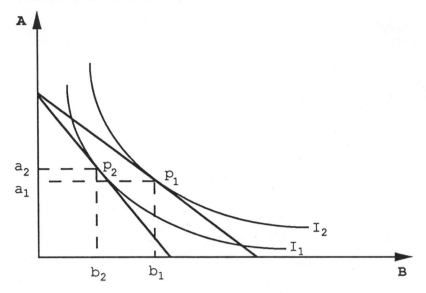

a new budget constraint line (y_3 or y_1), which would put her utility-maximizing combination on a higher (I_3) or lower (I_1) indifference curve. If we were to identify the utility-maximizing combinations at a range of income levels and connect them, we could form a new curve, called the income-consumption curve, which would identify quantities of commodities A and B that would be consumed at different income levels, holding prices and tastes and preferences constant.

Suppose the price of commodity B increases while income and the price of commodity A remain the same (Figure 2.2). The consumer then has a new budget constraint line and a new utility-maximizing combination (p_2), which, because of the price increase, is on a lower indifference curve.

Not only did the amount purchased of commodity B decline (from b_1 to b_2) in response to the increase in its price, but the amount purchased of commodity A also changed, although its price did not change. There are, in fact, two forces at work: the income effect and the substitution effect (Figure 2.3). The income effect is the change in quantity demanded resulting from the change in total purchasing power (real income). It is the change associated with the move from a higher to a lower indifference curve before we account for the effect of the change in the price ratio ($b_1 - b_3$). The substitution effect is the change in quantity demanded resulting from the change in relative prices after we have adjusted to the change in total purchasing power ($b_3 - b_2$). Total response to the change in the price of B is the sum of the two effects.

Demand Curves. Consumer demand is the quantity of a given commodity that

Figure 2.3
Income and Substitution Effects

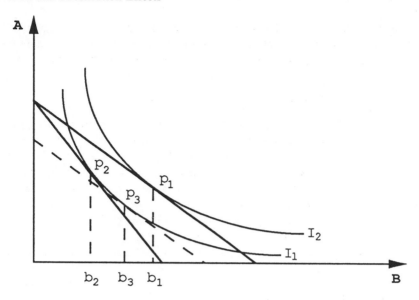

a consumer would buy at various prices, assuming that his income, tastes and preferences, and the prices of other commodities do not change,

$$q_i = f(p_i, p_j, \ldots, p_n, Y, U')$$

where q_i is the quantity purchased of good i, p_i is the price of i, $p_j, \ldots, p_n$ are the prices of substitute goods and services, Y is the budget constraint, and U' represents the tastes and preferences of the consumer. The demand schedule or curve for an individual can be derived through the cardinal utility approach or the indifference curve approach.

To derive the consumer's demand curve for a given commodity A using the cardinal utility approach, we need to know the unit cost of A, the marginal utility he would receive from each successive unit of A, and the cost and marginal utility of another commodity, which we will call money. The "cost" of money is identical with the amount; one dollar costs one dollar. The marginal utility of money is the amount of utility that could be obtained per unit of money if it were spent on commodities other than A (e.g., 50 utils per dollar). The "price" of 1 util is therefore the dollar cost of obtaining it: the unit of money (one dollar) divided by its marginal utility (50) or, in this example, $.02. The "cost" in utility forgone of purchasing each successive unit of A is its marginal utility times the price of 1 util. For example, if the first unit of A that is purchased yields a marginal utility of 20, the opportunity cost of purchasing that first unit is $.40. The consumer will buy the unit of A only if its price is no greater than

$.40, the value of the marginal utility gained. If we plot the opportunity cost of purchasing each successive unit of A, we have the consumer's demand curve for A.

The indifference approach derivation is even simpler. We simply identify the utility-maximizing quantity of the commodity at different prices, holding other factors constant, and plot them or record them as a demand schedule.

Assessment of Approach

Major limitations of the theory stem from its assumptions. Because it ignores time as an aspect of consumption, it is not well adapted to the study of durable goods. It is also limited to the study of goods and services currently on the market and has nothing to say about demand for new products that may be introduced. It ignores the role of habit in consumer choice, the existence of multiple motives, and the problems presented by group decision making. Its assumptions are unrealistic (e.g., that goods are infinitely divisible and that the consumer has complete information) (Morgan, 1978).

Offsetting these limitations is the simplicity of the theory, a major advantage. Moreover, it appears to provide useful results, even when its assumptions are not satisfied. Its limitations have been partially overcome by variations and extensions of the basic theory.

CONSUMPTION AND SAVINGS FUNCTIONS

One body of consumer theory has been particularly concerned with the allocation of household income between consumption expenditure and savings. The original concern was macroeconomic; however, concepts from this approach have been frequently borrowed to help explain the microeconomic behavior of households. None of the hypotheses has been found to be completely consistent with empirical data (Ferber, 1973, pp. 1303, 1332).

Concepts and Relationships

In their most basic form, consumption and savings functions are concerned with only three elements: total income (Y), total consumption expenditure (E), and total investment or savings (S). Total income is assumed to be equal to the sum of consumption and savings; that is, it is assumed that households have only those two ways of disposing of their income. Allocation of income to consumption is called the propensity to consume. Average propensity to consume is the fraction (k) of income spent on consumption; thus, $E = kY$. Marginal propensity to consume is the proportion of an income change spent on consumption. Marginal propensity to consume is of interest to economists because it provides a basis for predicting consumer behavior.

Absolute Income Hypothesis. Keynes, in his *General Theory of Employment,*

Interest and Money (1936, pp. 113–131), hypothesized that as income increases, consumers increase their expenditures but that the rate of increase in expenditures is lower than the rate of increase in income; that is, the marginal propensity to consume is less than one and also less than the average propensity to consume. Subsequent research has provided estimates of average and marginal propensities to consume, but their results suggest that marginal propensity to consume is not completely stable over time. Among the factors that affect the magnitude of the marginal propensity to consume in the aggregate are the distribution of income (high-income consumers save a larger proportion of their incomes than do lower-income consumers, on the average), taxation (which changes the income distribution), consumer credit (which changes the income constraint on current spending), price changes, and consumer confidence (which might induce consumers to change the timing of purchases or change their preference for assets).

Intertemporal and Life-Cycle Models. A limitation of neoclassical demand theory as we have described it is that it ignores time. In fact, consumers must decide how to allocate their incomes over multiple time periods because of short-run variations in income, caused perhaps by irregularity of employment or irregularity of some income receipts (e.g., from bonuses or commissions). Such variations would result in undesirable variations in expenditure unless compensated for by saving or borrowing. Income also varies over the life cycle of the individual. While the shape of the income curve varies with occupation and other factors, income is typically low in early adulthood, rises to a peak in late middle age, and usually declines drastically at retirement. Consumption needs, on the other hand, although they may vary somewhat from year to year and over the life cycle, do not increase or decrease in accordance with income. In order to maximize satisfaction over periods longer than a year, the consumer needs to allocate income over time, using a strategy of borrowing or saving.

At the heart of this approach is the recognition that consumers have a time preference regarding consumption. They may prefer to maintain the same level of consumption over time. Alternatively, they may prefer high consumption in the current time period, although this means reduced consumption in later periods. Or they may prefer high consumption in a later time period at the expense of lower consumption now. Assuming that time preference is measurable, the problem is to identify the amount of income a consumer should allocate to consumption in each time period in order to maximize utility.

Allocation over a two-year time period can be analyzed using indifference curves to represent relative preference for consumption in year 1 versus year 2 (Figure 2.4). Each indifference curve represents different allocations of year 1 and year 2 income, which are all at the same level of utility. (Note that by utility we mean total utility, aggregated over the entire time period.) The budget constraint line shows feasible allocations, given the amount of income received in each year and the rate of interest on borrowing or saving. In year 1, total amount available for consumption is y_1 (the income in year 1) plus y_2 minus y_1 (the income in year 2 minus interest paid for borrowing it). In year 2, total amount

Figure 2.4
Utility Maximizing over Time

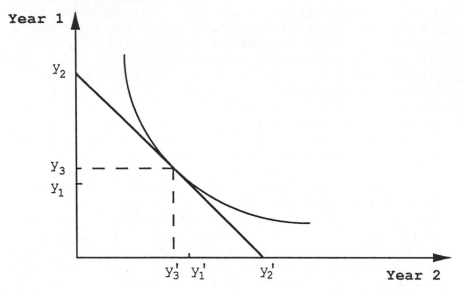

is y_1' (income in year 1 plus interest earned) plus y_2' minus y_1'. In the case in which the consumer prefers equal consumption in each year and year 2 income is higher than income in year 1, the consumer will maximize utility by borrowing a portion of year 2 income ($y_3 - y_1$) for use in year 1. If year 1 income were higher than year 2 income, the best allocation would be to save in year 1. Notice that total real income in the two-year period will vary, depending on whether the strategy includes borrowing or saving. Low income in the first year, combined with a preference for equal consumption in both periods, means that the consumer gets more utility by borrowing in year 1, although total real income is lower. Note also that a change in the interest rate on borrowing or lending will change the utility-maximizing allocation.

The problem of maximizing utility over the consumer's remaining life span from a given age is somewhat more complicated. Utility may be regarded as being a function of consumption (expressed in dollars) in each ensuing period of the life span, plus any utility the person receives from leaving an estate (expressed in dollars) at the end of life (Modigliani & Brumberg, 1962, pp. 395–396). The budget constraint in any given year is the net value of assets at the beginning of the year (assets minus amount owed) plus current-year income plus the discounted value of income to be received in each ensuing time period (how much the consumer could borrow and repay during his remaining lifetime, given the interest rate on consumer borrowing). In order to identify the utility-maximizing allocation of income, we must know (1) how long the consumer will live, (2) the age at which he will retire from active employment, (3) his preferences for consumption in each time period and for leaving an estate, (4) his current assets, (5) the amount of earnings he will receive in each period of the ensuing life span, and (6) the interest rate.

It should be noted that the utility the household is concerned with maximizing comes from consumption, not expenditure. Thus, even if we assume that the household prefers to maintain the same level of consumption in each time period, that does not mean that expenditures need to be equal. Durables paid for in preceding years contribute to the flow of consumption without adding to expenditure.

Permanent Income Hypothesis. Friedman (1957, pp. 20–31) proposed a somewhat different approach to the problem of allocation over time. He hypothesized that consumption and income can each be divided into a permanent and a transitory component. Permanent income may be regarded as the level of income anticipated over an extended period of time. Consumption is to be regarded as a flow of services rather than expenditure, with permanent consumption being expected and transitory being unanticipated. Permanent consumption of a household is hypothesized to equal a fraction (k) of the household's permanent income, with this fraction being a function of the interest rate, the ratio of nonhuman wealth owned by the household to its total wealth, and other objective factors that affect the household's expectations. Friedman hypothesized that there is no correlation between permanent and transitory income, between permanent and transitory consumption, and between transitory income and transitory consumption.

The concept of permanent income has been used in a number of studies of household expenditures. One study tested whether marginal propensity to consume from windfall (transitory) income varies, depending on the size of the windfall income in relation to the household's permanent income (Abdel-Ghany, Bivens, Keeler & James, 1983). The results indicated that this is in fact the case; households are likely to spend small windfalls but save a large proportion of windfalls that are large in comparison with the household's estimated permanent income.

Relative Income Hypothesis. The relative income hypothesis, formulated by Duesenberry (1959, pp. 32–37), conceptualizes a somewhat different utility function in which the utility that a household derives from its consumption (E) depends on the household's level of consumption in relation to a weighted average of the consumption of a reference group (G). Since he also viewed assets (W) as a direct source of utility, the lifetime utility function of the ith household is

$$U_i = u(E_{i1}/G_1, \ldots, E_{in}/G_n, W_{i1}/G_1, \ldots, W_{im}/G_m).$$

Thus, the proportion of income saved by a household was hypothesized to be a function of the ratio of the household's income to the average income of the reference group. A household above the mean will save a substantial part of its income since it has little incentive to increase its consumption level higher than the mean of its reference group. If its income is lower, it will save little or nothing since it seeks to bring its consumption level up to that of the reference group. If the reference group is regarded as the entire population of households, this hypothesis would account for the observed fact that high-income households save a larger proportion of their income than do low-income households.

An alternative formulation substitutes the household's previous income peak for reference group. Households are hypothesized to seek to maintain previous levels of consumption and adjust to income fluctuations only slowly.

Assessment of Approach

The problems addressed by these theories, especially that of allocation of income over time, are of great importance in the study of household consumption. Each of the hypotheses has some merit as an intuitively plausible explanation of household behavior. Major limitations are the complexity of the allocation-over-time model and the difficulty of obtaining valid measures of such concepts as time preference, permanent income, and reference group.

DURABLE GOODS MODELS

Concepts and Relationships

Consumer demand for durable goods (those consumed over several time periods) differs from demand for nondurables in several respects. The most basic distinction lies in the form of the utility function. The utility derived from goods and services stems from their consumption, not from their acquisition. The neoclassical demand model specified the form of the utility function as $U = u(Q)$, with Q being the set of quantities of goods and services purchased. To justify this form, we had to assume that time was not a factor. In order to conceptualize demand for durable goods accurately, time must be taken into account. The set of goods and services might be partitioned into two subsets: with Q representing nondurables only and S representing the stock of durables owned by the household. The modified utility function is $U = u(Q, S)$.

There are other differences between demand for durables and nondurables:

- Timing of purchases. Many purchases of durables are replacement purchases. Most durables deteriorate gradually over time rather than becoming unusable abruptly and completely. Thus, households have a good deal of latitude in choosing the timing of purchases. An automobile may be replaced when a new model comes out, when major repairs are needed, when the consumer judges it has become too unsafe or unreliable to use, when financing becomes available, or at any other time the consumer chooses.

- Complexity of decisions. Purchase decisions regarding durable goods, from the point of view of consumers, are especially complex and entail a high degree of risk. Consumers must anticipate future needs and possible changes in their tastes and preferences. They must take into account future costs of owning, operating, and repairing the item, often a significant part of the total cost. Since such purchases are made infrequently, consumers must acquire new information as a basis for choice rather than relying entirely on previous experience, as may be possible in the case of nondurable purchases. Needed information includes expected trends in the price of the durable, technical features that are currently available or are likely to be introduced, and the availability of the item second hand. Since many durables are relatively costly, the risk of financial loss from a bad choice may be great.

• Importance of decision. Acquisition of a durable is likely to have a substantial impact on other purchase decisions and on the consuming unit's total way of life. Like non-durables, owned durables may affect the health and safety of household members; because they are durables, the impact is felt over an extended period of time. Also, owned durables are assets, as well as means of consumption, and may constitute a major share of the household's wealth.

Several forms of the demand function have been proposed. Deaton and Muellbauer (1980, pp. 345–358) listed three.

Neoclassical Model. According to Deaton and Muellbauer, demand for a durable good can be conceptualized as a problem of maximizing utility over time. Quantity demanded is a function of four factors:

1. S_i: The depreciated value of the stock of durable i, owned in the previous period. The nearer this depreciated value is to the value of the item when new, the lower is the demand.

2. B: A budget constraint similar to that used in the life-cycle model, which inclules current value of owned assets, current income, and the discounted value of future income.

3. P_n: Prices of nondurables in the current and future time periods, discounted to their present value.

4. V: The user cost of durables, discounted to present value. User cost is the cost of owning one unit of the durable for one time period. It might be regarded as the purchase price of the durable divided by the total number of years owned (assuming that nothing is recouped through resale of the item at the time of disposal). Deaton and Muellbauer equated user cost with its rental equivalence price, that is, the cost of renting an equivalent item for a year.

Demand for a given durable (d_i) at a given time can be represented as

$$d_i = f(B, P_n, V) - S_i.$$

Stock Adjustment Model. Two motivations for purchases of durables can be identified: the wish to increase the quality or quantity owned of the durable to some desired level and replacement of depreciated items in order to maintain the stock of durables at its previous level.

Replacement demand depends solely on the annual rate of depreciation. In the case where the stock of durables is at the desired level, the number of items in inventory will be maintained at a constant level. If we assume a constant rate of depreciation, then total depreciation is allocated equally over the number of years the durable is kept in service (its service life, or SL). The number to be acquired each year (replacement demand or d_i^R) will be equal to the ratio of number owned in the previous year (S_{t-1}, in this case the desired stock) to service life ($d_i^R = S_{t-1}/SL$).

Demand due to desire for upgrading the inventory depends on the gap between desired stock, S^*, and inventory in the previous year (S_{t-1}). The consumer may, however, prefer or be unable to do all the desired upgrading in a single year. In that case, upgrading demand would be a fraction (k) of the gap:

$$d_i^U = k(S^* - S_{t-1}).$$

Total demand would be the sum of the two:

$$d_i = k(S^* - S_{t-1}) + S_{t-1}/SL.$$

Discretionary Replacement Model. Suppose that all demand for the durable good is replacement demand. Consumers may not maintain a rigid replacement schedule. They may exercise discretion, sometimes postponing replacement for a year or two and sometimes replacing earlier than normal, thus extending or shortening the service life of the item. Many factors may influence these adjustments; for example, consumers often replace durables when they change residence, especially if they purchase a new home. Replacement demand therefore can be conceptualized as normal demand (d^N) and deviations from normal demand (k'). Demand, then, would be

$$d_i = k'd^N.$$

Assessment of Approaches

Estimating demand for durables entails estimating values for one or more additional concepts: user cost of durables, depreciation rate, normal replacement rate, desired and actual stock. Additional factors, such as technological, demographic, and life-style changes, are almost certainly relevant. The difficulty of obtaining accurate data on these variables and the complexity of functional relationships probably account for shortcomings of demand predictions regarding durable goods.

CHARACTERISTICS THEORY

A severe limitation of the neoclassical theory of demand is its inability to explain why consumers derive utility from commodities. A related limitation is its inability to predict demand for new products. Characteristics theory, proposed by Lancaster (1971), addresses these limitations.

Concepts and Relationships

The basic departure from neoclassical theory is in the utility function. Utility is regarded as being a function of the characteristics (C) of commodities rather than of the commodities themselves:

$$U = u(C).$$

Lancaster assumed that characteristics of commodities can be measured objectively and thus would be the same for all consumers. A given characteristic might be obtained from several goods or services; thus, we can think of commodities as having natural groupings, that is, groups of commodities that are the source of the same characteristics. Food might be regarded as a natural grouping. All food provides nutrients, although the amount of nutrients provided varies widely among foods.

Characteristics are related to commodities through a production function, which defines the household technology used to produce the characteristic. Several commodities (q_i) may be used in combination to obtain a given characteristic. An input of household time (T_h) may also be required. The relationship might be represented by

$$c_i = f(q_1, \ldots, q_n, T_h).$$

This technology is assumed to be uniform for all households.

The household's choice problem therefore is one of choosing among bundles of characteristics in the light of its tastes and preferences for characteristics. It can be analyzed using the indifference curve approach. Assume that the consumer is choosing among foods and that only two characteristics are of importance: flavor and nutritional quality. Assume further that an objective measure of flavor is available (perhaps the result of taste panel studies) and that nutritional quality can also be represented objectively on a single scale (perhaps by the amount of calcium provided per calorie). Other assumptions of indifference curve analysis also apply.

Two characteristics, which we will call "taste" and "nutrition," are represented by the coordinates in Figure 2.5. The commodities, whole milk (W) and skim milk (S), are represented with solid lines as rays from the origin. The coordinates are calibrated to represent amounts of the characteristic, and the rays

Figure 2.5
Utility Maximizing Using Characteristics Theory

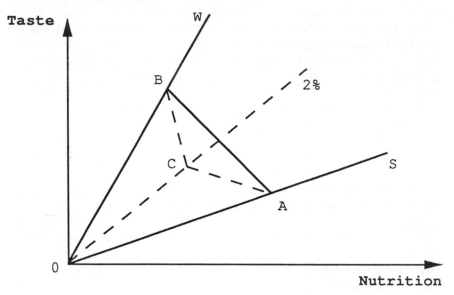

are calibrated to represent quantities of the commodity. Point A represents 2 quarts of skim milk. Assuming that the household has a budget for milk, a budget constraint curve (AB) can be plotted, based on the budget and prices of the commodities. The triangle 0AB contains all combinations of whole or skim milk that could be purchased.

To identify the combination the household should choose in order to maximize its utility, we need to know the tastes and preferences of the household for flavor and nutritional quality, which might be represented in the usual way by a set of indifference curves. Even without knowing the household's tastes and preferences, however, we have some information about the utility-maximizing choice. We know that it must lie somewhere on the line AB. This line, which we will call the efficiency frontier, identifies maximum amounts of the characteristics that may be obtained with a given expenditure of money. If we add a third commodity, 2 percent milk (represented by a dotted line), the efficiency frontier becomes a plane, ABC (with the portions pertaining to 2 percent milk in dotted lines). Given the relatively high price of 2 percent milk, it is not an efficient choice since by selecting some combination of whole and skim milk, more of one or both characteristics could be obtained with the same expenditure of money. If the price of 2 percent milk should decline, however, it might become more efficient than any combination of the other two.

Technical Efficiency Approach. The concept of the efficiency frontier can be used in developing normative information to help consumers make wise decisions. Through the application of the approach, subsets of efficient choices may be identified and inefficient choices eliminated. Since the characteristics and household technology are assumed to be the same for all households, all households will find their utility-maximizing choices within the same subset.

Geistfeld (1977) applied the concept in designing a type of decision-making aid. The information to be provided to the consumer would be in the form of a range of prices for each commodity, which would indicate the upper and lower price bounds within which the commodity is efficient, relative to an alternative commodity.

Hedonic Prices. The concept of hedonic prices (the prices associated with characteristics of commodities) actually predated the work of Lancaster and has been used in constructing housing price indexes (Ratchford, 1975). Suppose that the price of a commodity (p_i) is regarded as being a function of the amounts of various characteristics provided by the commodity ($p_i = g(c_{ji})$). The price of characteristics may be estimated using regression methods from data on household purchases of commodities within a set, for example, by

$$\log p =' a + b_1 \log c_{1i} + \ldots + b_n \log c_{ni},$$

where the C variables represent the amounts of each given characteristic purchased in a given transaction and the b coefficients are the implicit marginal prices of the characteristics.

A major problem in constructing housing indexes is the variability of the product. Houses vary widely in size, design, construction, and other aspects. Much of the price difference among houses is likely to be due to differences in these characteristics. Use of the hedonic approach enables one to estimate the marginal price of housing characteristics in different time periods, using the method described. The price index may be constructed by establishing a "standard house" with a specified set of characteristics, estimating its total price in each time period, and using the estimated total prices to construct the index.

Assessment of Approach

Application of characteristics theory has enabled social scientists to study consumer choices in a way that provides insight into reasons for choice and not merely on the fact of choice itself. Some variation of the approach is frequently used in studies of consumer behavior, an indication that it has been a fruitful source of new insights.

A major limitation of the approach is the difficulty of identifying appropriate sets of characteristics and measuring them objectively. One problem has to do with number of characteristics to be considered. Empirical choice models can generally handle only a small number of characteristics, far fewer than available on a given product. Thus, a small number of characteristics must be identified that capture the aspects that most consumers take into consideration. Another problem has to do with what might be called the form of the characteristic. The characteristics of an automobile, for example, might include shape of seats, fabric used to cover the seats, amount of legroom, and range of seat adjustments possible. Alternatively, these and other characteristics might be synthesized and evaluated as a single characteristic, "comfort." The first set of characteristics is easy to measure objectively, but the composite characteristic comfort, although not objectively measurable, is probably much closer to the idea on which consumers base choices.

HOUSEHOLD PRODUCTION THEORY

Household production theory addresses two aspects of consumption not addressed in neoclassical theory: the fact that goods and services are often used in combination (e.g., food and eating utensils) and that time is required for consumption. The solution offered by household production theory centers on the existence of household production functions, functions that describe the technology by which purchased goods and services are used in combination with owned durables and inputs of the household's time to produce a commodity that the household consumes.

Concepts and Relationships

The concept and practice of household production was identified and studied as early as 1934 when Reid formally identified it as "unpaid activities which are carried on, by and for the members, which activities might be replaced by market goods, or paid services, if circumstances such as income, market conditions, and personal inclinations permit the service being delegated to someone outside the household group" (p. 11). Interest has centered primarily around estimating the value of household production. Peskin (1982), for example, estimated the total value of household work in the United States in 1976 as $752.4 billion, 44 percent of the gross national product. This was an average of $6,694 for women and $3,475 for men.

In household production theory, utility is conceived as resulting from the consumption of home-produced commodities, the output of a household production function,

$$U = u(Z_i),$$

where Z_i is a commodity produced and consumed by the household. The household production function is a relationship between inputs and outputs. It identifies the quantity of a commodity that can be produced per unit of time with specific combinations of inputs. It may be represented by

$$Z_i = f(Q_i, S_i, T_{hi}, O),$$

where Q_i is a set of nondurable goods and services purchased for and used in the production of the commodity Z_i, S_i is a set of owned durables used to produce the commodity, T_{hi} is time spent by household members in producing Z_i, and O represents environmental factors that affect the production process.

The budget constraint must take into account limitations on both income and time. It may be represented by the household's monetary budget (Y) plus the amount of household time available for household production (T_h), valued in monetary terms. One possibility used to obtain an estimate of the value of household production is the opportunity cost of using time in this way, that is, the wage rate (w) that the individual would be assumed to be able to earn if the time were available for paid employment. The full budget constraint would be

$$S = Y + wT_h.$$

The full price of a given commodity (p'_i) would be the cost of purchased non-durable goods and services (Q_j) and durables (S_k) in the amounts used, plus the cost of household time:

$$p'_i = \Sigma p_j(Q_j/Z_i) + \Sigma p_k(S_k/Z_i) + w(T_{hi}/Z_i).$$

The full price of commodities is sometimes estimated.

If time is included as a cost, the equilibrium conditions must take into account alternative uses of time and the possibility of substituting household production time for purchased services or convenience products; that is, for each use of time (t_j and t_k) and each purchased good or service q_i, the following relationships must hold:

$$MUt_j/p_t = MUt_k/p_t \text{ and } MUt_j/p_t = MUq/p_q.$$

Households may be conceived of as consuming two kinds of commodities: those produced through household production and those obtained from market sources. This way of looking at household production is the one most commonly used. In an alternative form, proposed by Beutler and Owen (1980), a home-produced commodity is a good or service that has use value; it is in a form that is directly and immediately available for use by household members to produce utility. Home-produced commodities, so defined, are the only goods and services consumed by households. All home-produced commodities are produced through household production processes, with inputs of the time of household members and goods and services purchased in the market. The relative proportions of the inputs may vary, of course, as well as the amount and kind of home processing performed to make the good or service available for use. For example, a home-cooked meal takes a substantial amount of time to bring the product to the point of being ready to consume, since we need to consider time required for shopping and cleanup, as well as food preparation and service. A restaurant meal, on the other hand, takes only the amount of time needed for traveling to and from the restaurant, plus any additional time that might be required for special dressing and grooming to prepare for eating out. In some cases, the amount of household member time might be at or near zero. Carry-out food eaten from a disposable container requires little more than transportation time.

An advantage of the Beutler-Owen concept of household production is that all commodities can be regarded as belonging to the same group; the differences are in the kinds and amounts of inputs. This eliminates the difficulty of classifying commodities, such as a meal in which some of the foods were purchased in a form ready to eat and others were prepared from raw ingredients, into the arbitrary categories of home produced or market produced.

The household production model has been used in whole or in part in many empirical studies of household consumption. For example, Weagley and Norum (1989), applying this approach to the study of demand for market-purchased versus home-produced commodities, found evidence that households do take value of household time into consideration.

Assessment of Approach

Many consumption problems involve time as a critical variable in decisions. It is not surprising, therefore, that household production theory, like characteristics theory, has been frequently used in recent studies of consumption choices. The application that has perhaps received the most attention is the work versus leisure decision, but the acquisition of time-saving goods and services—the substitution of purchased commodities for household production time—is another area to which household production theory is relevant. There have also been attempts to estimate household production functions.

The most serious limitation of the theory is probably the problems encountered in obtaining reasonable measures of the concepts. As an input into household production, time can be measured (though time-use data are scarce and expensive to obtain), but number of minutes spent on a task is a rather poor measure of the input into household production, since the amount and quality of the output produced in a given amount of time varies considerably from one person to another and even from one work episode to another. Similarly, the output of household production is likely to be variable depending on the kinds and amounts of actual processing of materials done by household members.

THE INSTITUTIONAL APPROACH

Concepts

The main idea of an institutional approach to the study of the consumption process is the interdependency of consumption with the economic and cultural systems of society. In this approach, individual needs and preferences are not assumed to be constant but to be influenced by the social and cultural value system.

Veblen explained the process of consumption pattern formulation of the lower strata as a process of expressing their desired social status. He defined emulation as "the stimulus of an invidious comparison which prompts us to outdo those with whom we are in the habit of classing ourselves" (1953, p. 81). He believed that emulation makes the members of lower-income strata tend to acquire the consumption patterns of the leisure class (higher-income strata). This leads to conspicuous consumption. This process is not always achieved with a conscious effort; rather it is a conventional process:

For the great body of people in any modern community, the proximate ground of expenditure in excess of what is required for physical comfort is not a conscious effort to excel in the expensiveness of their visible consumption, so much as it is a desire to live up to the conventional standard of decency in the amount and grade of goods consumed. (p. 80)

Kyrk (1923) proposed a theory of consumption from the institutional viewpoint. She saw the problem of consumption as one of choice and valuation because values lie behind and influence consumers' choices. The valuation process is an aspect of a "tentative organic process," which results from the reaction of a human organism and the influence of social organizations. Kyrk believed that "values are organized, unified and harmonized into systems in which the whole is greater than the sum of its parts" (pp. 168–169).

Kyrk developed this into the concept of standard of consumption, pointing out that "the process of consumption is organized according to certain standards of the appropriate and the necessary" (p. 171). These standards are not individual but group or mass phenomena, which are social products:

They [standards] reflect the entire personality of the individual, and the "cultural content" of his group and time. . . .

Certainly it is not difficult to show that many of our consumption values are socially determined and sanctioned, and are a part of the social environment into which the individual is born and in which he lives. . . .

To explain our standards of living we must go back to a social process. (pp. 189, 191, 193)

Kyrk assumed that such consumption elements as physiological requirements, conventional necessities, and other elements (e.g., education and recreation) are incorporated into standards because of their survival, prestige, or aesthetic value, respectively. The actual content of consumption of some groups (e.g., classes or countries) varies either by differences in economic power, by which she meant "command over resources, effective desire as expressed in goods available and in income" (p. 207), and in culture, "all those common interests and common attitudes which will mean a different organization of life even with the same resources'' (p. 209).

Hawtrey included custom, tradition, and marketing influences in his model of consumer choice:

The greater part of his [the consumer's] expenditure is directed to meeting continuing needs for food, clothing, shelter, heating, lighting and cleaning. The methods of meeting these needs are dictated by custom and tradition. . . . His household expenditure is a matter of routine. . . . Consequently in the last resort changes have to be effected by means of advertisement. (1925, p. 204)

It is not the consumer's individual preference but ethical or social value that actually determines consumer choice. This view is similar to Kyrk's with respect to regarding standards of consumption as a group phenomenon. Hawtrey regards each consumer as being content to meet his or her needs in the same manner as others meet theirs. Hawtrey called this phenomenon "rationality of conservatism" (p. 204). Yet he assumed the existence of class differences in consumer choice behavior. For example, for the poor, defensive products assume a special importance, and for the rich, conformity to the system (standards of culture prevailing around them) is more important.

Parsons and Smelser (1956) viewed consumption in relation to cultural symbolism. For them, the household sector is primarily a pattern maintenance subsystem of society:

In the first place the institutionalization of the family system . . . implies a certain minimum of possessions in order for the family to meet the cultural definitions . . . of a family. This list of goods of course varies in accordance with value changes. But it certainly includes a minimum level of nutrition necessary for "cultural survival," which implies far more than mere biological survival; shelter of a certain quality; some minimum symbolic differentiation of intrafamilial sex and generation roles. . . . Its acquisition is the culturally defined goal of the family as a consuming unit. (p. 222)

In this respect, consumption of goods for cultural survival is also important.

Levy's work (1981) is an example of studies focused on the symbolic meaning of consumption. By conducting a qualitative analysis, he showed that food preparation, service, manners, and consumption are all used in symbolic ways. For example, food at home has such meanings as maternal, comfortable, familiar, dependent, and routine, while food eaten at a restaurant carries various other meanings. Age, sex, and social class are associated with demand for different food attributes, he concluded. For example, high social status is associated with consumption of foods symbolizing strength, maturity, and food professionalism, while low social status is associated with consumption of foods symbolizing softness, greasiness, and sweetness.

McCracken (1988) investigated symbolic meanings of clothing from an anthropological perspective. He concluded that there is an intimate relationship between culture and consumption pattern:

The consumer goods on which the consumer lavishes time, attention, and income are charged with cultural meaning. Consumers use this meaning to entirely cultural purposes. They use the meaning of consumer goods to express cultural categories and principles, cultivate ideals, create and sustain life-styles, construct notions of the self, and create (and survive) social change. (p. xi)

McCracken noted that clothing is an expression of material culture. It expresses the categorical scheme established by culture, reveals cultural principles such as themes and formal relationships, and represents social distance. Advertising and the fashion system play an important role as instruments of meaning transfer from "world-to-good." In the medium of a magazine or newspaper, new styles of clothing or other goods, which display new cultural meanings, can be introduced (p. 77).

Some authors have concluded that consumption plays a role as a method of achieving or expressing social status. According to Riesman and Rosebourough (1960), there is "the standard package" of consumption at different levels of a man's career, for example, a working-class standard package or an upper-middle-class standard package. Similarly, Parsons and Smelser suggested that consumption is a function of income class rather than of income. In other words, the level of consumption remains the same within particular income ranges and rises only when men cross an income threshold into the next higher stratum.

Assessment of Approach

The institutional approach provides a holistic view of the concept of consumption pattern. It considers source of value or needs and wants in the context of a social and cultural value system and thereby gives a framework to explain group consumption values and, in turn, group consumption patterns according to different income classes, occupation, race, or education. Since the approach views consumption as a symbolic expression of values and needs, it deals with quality as well as quantity aspects of consumption pattern. Because the institutional approach emphasizes the importance of culture, it provides a broad concept of necessity, which includes goods and services for cultural survival, as well as physical survival.

The institutional approach assumes the importance of culture and economic power in consumption pattern formulation, which implies that there exist observable differences between the consumption patterns of people living in different cultures or in different economic situations. An implication of the approach is that standard of consumption is likely to become more and more uniform in U.S. society due to the effects of mass media and marketing strategies.

LIFE-STYLE AND LIFE-QUALITY APPROACHES

According to Kyrk (1933, pp. 377–379), a complete description of standard of living should include not only the kinds and quantities of goods and services consumed but also how they are used—activities in which they are used, order, arrangement, rituals—and the values that the household seeks to realize through its consumption of goods and services. The theories already described have focused on only kinds and quantities of goods and services and their cost. The narrow focus has advantages, but it omits information that could shed light on why households consume what they do and improve the accuracy of predictions and forecasting of trends. An approach consistent with Kyrk's recommendation is the identification of life-styles.

The use of the life-style concept in the social sciences dates from Veblen, Weber, and Adler (Wells & Cosmas, 1977, pp. 299–300). Veblen regarded life-style as a fashion represented in consumption and leisure of households. Weber used life-style in a collective sense, regarding it as a subculture originated and perpetuated in status groups. Adler stressed the uniqueness of each individual with respect to life-style.

Definitions and Examples

The life-style concept has been used in connection with individuals, groups, and classes or categories. Meanings of the concept have varied, but recent studies of consumer behavior have generally defined life-style to encompass both characteristic patterns of behavior and cognitive style, including values, attitudes, interests, and opinions (Anderson & Golden, 1984, p. 406).

Life-style characterizations are part of common speech. In the early 1980s, the term *yuppie* ("young, urban professional") was used to characterize high-spending, young middle managers who travel, buy high-fashion merchandise, and have values that differ from earlier generations (Huntley, Bronson & Walsh, 1984, p. 39). The "voluntary simplicity" life-style is associated with such behaviors as meatless meals, making gifts, and recycling (Leonard-Barton & Rogers, 1980, pp. 246–247).

Suranyi-Unger (1977) believed that the majority of Americans adhere, to a greater or lesser extent, to some institutionalized common life-style. He argued that such life-style groups or "standard classes" could be identified either with respect to the similarity of their behavioral patterns (e.g., spending patterns) or with respect to their demographic characteristics. He stated:

The existence of standard classes in any society implies that any given lifestyle . . . imposes certain *minimum requirements* on its adherents in the acquisition and maintenance of certain commodities or amenities, such as dwelling, clothing, or transportation. These socially . . . mandated minimum requirements . . . constitute the bundle of *nondiscretionary* expenditures for a standard class. Expenditures for all commodities above the nondiscretionary floor may be said to reflect *discretionary* consumer demand within the standard class. (pp. 1–2)

Suranyi-Unger investigated standardized consumer behavior empirically using 1960–1961 data. He concluded that life-style groups existed and could be identified with respect to their expenditure behavior as well as demographic characteristics. He found that occupation was the characteristic most strongly related to differences among expenditure patterns and identified two standard classes: the professional class and the blue-collar class.

Mitchell (1983) proposed a comprehensive classification of life-style types. His typology was based in part on developmental psychology, drawing on Maslow's hierarchy of needs. The typology consists of four comprehensive groups subdivided into nine life-styles: need-driven groups (survivors, sustainers), outer-directed groups (belongers, emulators, achievers), inner-directed groups (I-am-me, experiential, societally conscious), and an integrated group similar to Maslow's self-actualizing level. Each of the types has a unique way of life described in terms of demographics, attitudes, financial status, frequency of involvement in selected activities, and use or ownership of selected consumer goods (pp. 3–31).

Firat (1987) argued that under the restriction of socially available goods and services, current consumption patterns in the United States are becoming individualized, private, alienated, and passive. He tested his hypothesis with data from households in a small southeastern town and concluded that this is indeed a dominant consumption pattern.

Life-style types represent not degrees of well-being but merely differences in manner of living. This is a critical difference between life-style measures and measures of quality of life, another composite measure that may include some or all of the variables used to identify life-style. Quality of life, according to McCall (1975), is the degree to which an individual or group has obtained the conditions for happiness and is thus a measure of well-being.

Quality of life, as defined by the Environmental Protection Agency, "refers to the well-being of people individually or in groups and to the well-being of the environment in which these people live" (cited by Hawkes, Hanson & Smith, 1980, p. 5). Quality-of-life measures frequently take the form of an index or set of indexes based on an array of variables. The measures are generally interdisciplinary and include environmental, economic, and social components (Hawkes et al., 1980). Social indicator variables are often included.

A number of different models have been proposed as a basis for selecting quality-of-life variables and interpreting empirical results. Some models emphasize social indicators, measures that are "descriptive of the normative aspects of . . . society" and "are relevant in the formulation, implementation, and evaluation of social policy" (p. 11). Implicit in quality-of-life models based on social indicators is an interest in the degree to which social goals are met. In contrast, Maslow, and later Flannagan, emphasized fulfillment of individual needs and goals (Hawkes et al., pp. 21–22). Gerson suggested a "negotiated approach," a "balance . . . between the good of the individual and the good of the society" (Hawkes et al., p. 21).

Assessment of Approach

A major strength of life-style and quality-of-life approaches is their breadth. Measures are composite, designed to represent the large numbers of factors that express or influence patterns of consumption behavior, including time use and subjective variables, such as values, beliefs, and attitudes. The approaches are flexible in that the factors used in identifying (for example) life-style can be selected to reflect the purpose and interests of the user.

A major limitation is the lack of consensus regarding choice of model or underlying theory. Although many variables may be taken into account in representing life-style or quality, they are nonetheless only a fraction of the thousands of variables that could be used. Selection of variable and method of forming indexes vary from one study to another. Since this is the case, there is little consistency among the life-style typologies or life-quality assessments.

APPRAISAL OF THEORIES

It is clear from this brief review of approaches that there is no single, logically coherent theory adequate for the analysis of all aspects of household consumption behavior. Instead we have several theories and conceptual constructs, some of them more or less closely linked to each other. Research models often combine concepts from two or more approaches.

Some of the concepts and theories are rooted in economic theory; others originate in sociology, psychology, anthropology, or other social sciences. Many of the concepts seem to have been formulated in applied research and education programs in home economics or in government statistical programs. Much of the published information about household consumption is not explicitly based on any theory.

The lack of a single, comprehensive theory has both good and bad results. A disadvantage is that we cannot always see clear relationships between statistical results from different sources. In some cases, such results may actually be incompatible with each other. Lacking a comprehensive theory, we may be unable to reconcile differences or decide which results are valid. Concepts may be defined and interpreted differently by different authors, thus leading to error and confusion.

But existence of a single dominant theory can also constrain a field of study. The lack of a single theory of household consumption behavior has allowed scholars to draw freely on concepts, theories, and methods used in many fields of study, thus developing a richer knowledge base than might otherwise have been possible.

For readers and users of information on household consumption, the principal benefit from a knowledge of approaches used in generating such information may be the loose conceptual framework that it provides. For example, our understanding of a newspaper item reporting a change in the consumer price level is greater if we understand that prices are one of the fundamental factors influencing demand; that without a corresponding increase in income, we can expect demand to decline; and that the decline is likely to affect spending on different commodities differently, depending on the relationship of the commodity to current life-styles, income distribution, and many other factors. In the chapters that follow, we show how the empirical information reported fits within this framework.

3

Methods of Studying Household Consumption

Why is it of value to people in general, who are not involved or expecting to be involved in conducting research, to understand something about how household consumption data are collected and analyzed? Two reasons can be advanced: it enables us to make a better assessment of the accuracy of published information and improves our understanding of how the actions of institutions that use such data—government, business, and private organizations—affect our lives.

Before considering the topic in detail, it will be useful to consider some specific reasons for collecting and analyzing household consumption data:

1. To plan investment and other business activity. Firms obtain data on demand as a basis for their planning. For some purposes they may want data on a specific product or product category, but they may also use data on more general patterns and trends in household spending and consumption behavior.

2. To identify and evaluate the probable impact of government policy options. Before new legislation or regulations are enacted—for example, changes in tax laws, new product safety regulations, or measures to protect the environment—governing bodies need information on whether the action is likely to achieve the desired result and whether it may have other impacts, good or bad, on some constituencies. Effectiveness of government action often depends in part on the behavior of individual citizens or business firms. For example, if a sales tax increase is enacted to raise revenues, will consumers continue their previous level of purchasing, or may they cut back to the point where total tax revenues do not increase? And may the added taxes create an unfair burden on some consumers or business firms or change their behavior in unexpected and undesirable ways? Household consumption is interrelated with many other aspects of society and therefore affects and is affected in some degree by most government policy.

3. To evaluate the well-being of a population or population group. Assessments of well-being are used by governments and educational or service organizations to identify the need for new programs and assess the effectiveness of existing ones. Well-being

assessments are also of interest to concerned citizens and to those who are simply curious to know "how well we are doing." Well-being is often assessed on the basis of consumption (e.g., of food) or command of resources needed for consumption. In either case, data on household consumption are needed to establish standards of consumption or resources and to find out how consumption behavior or resource ownership in the population of interest compares with accepted standards of adequacy. An example is the National Nutrition Monitoring System, a federal program for periodic assessments of the nutritional and dietary status of the U.S. population and the nutritional quality and healthfulness of the national food supply (Peterkin & Rizek, 1984, pp. 15–19).

4. To obtain knowledge of determinants of consumption behavior. In addition to its value as general knowledge, an understanding of the determinants of consumption behavior has practical applications. Suppose that the U.S. government were to revitalize the effort begun in the 1970s to reduce the nation's consumption of its nonrenewable energy resources. A large share of total energy consumption—about three-fourths in 1967 (Herendeen & Tanaka, 1976, p. 165)—is controlled by consumers, either directly (through household expenditures for gasoline, electricity, and so forth—one-third of the total) or indirectly (through purchase of goods and services that consumed energy in their manufacture and distribution). Hannon (1975) found that household consumption of energy is related to income almost linearly and argued that an energy tax would be an effective way to reduce energy consumption.

Probably all statistical information about household consumption and related factors contains some error or bias. This may occur in data collection, in the selection and definition of variables, or in selection of analytic methods. Thus, it is probable that empirical conclusions about household consumption behavior are at best only approximately correct. Knowing this, how much credence should we give a particular piece of information as a basis for our own actions? Should we seek other information and, if so, what? We can make a better judgment about these matters by understanding the nature of the methods used and alternative methods available.

OBTAINING CONSUMPTION DATA: SOURCES AND MODES OF COLLECTION

Logically, there are three possible ways of collecting data on individual and household consumption of goods and services: (1) observing the consumption activities of households or their inventory of goods, (2) obtaining information from the consumers themselves through questionnaires or interviews, and (3) obtaining and analyzing reports from producers or distributors of consumer products. In fact, all three methods are used. Each has advantages and disadvantages.

Data obtained from producers and distributors are likely to be more accurate than data collected by other methods since business firms must keep records of their activities and may be subject to penalties for false reporting. Among the statistical activities of the federal government to provide data from these sources are the national income accounts, aggregate data that describe income and expenditures for the nation as a whole, and monthly and annual retail trade and service industry statistics collected by the U.S. Bureau of the Census. A drawback of such data is that it is rarely possible to link this information with household characteristics.

For most of the purposes for which consumption data are collected, it is necessary or at least desirable to analyze the data in relation to household income and demographic characteristics. To do this, we need data obtained directly from consuming units, either by observation or by interview or questionnaire.

Data from households may be obtained through collections at a single point in time (cross-sectional surveys) or through continuous or periodic collections of data from the same households over a period of time (diaries or longitudinal surveys). Each method has advantages and limitations. Cross-sectional surveys are usually less expensive to conduct than longitudinal surveys and therefore make it possible to obtain data from a larger and more representative sample. However, they do not provide direct evidence of how households change their behavior in response to changes in their characteristics (e.g., age or income) or external environment. Moreover, the survey constitutes a time sample as well as a population sample. If the data are collected at a time of stability, when most households are at equilibrium, then the data can be regarded as representative of a longer period of time. The reverse will be true if by chance the data collection coincides with a period of instability or change, as happened with the Consumer Expenditure Survey of 1973, a period in which energy prices began to rise rapidly. Longitudinal surveys, if they extend over a lengthy period of time, are expensive, require an extended time commitment on the part of the data collector and respondents, and usually have a high dropout rate of households from the sample. On the other hand, they give direct evidence of variation and change in the behavior of individual households and provide a more extended time sample.

A major source of inaccuracy in household data is reporting error. As a basis for assessing the possibilities of error and bias in data obtained from consuming units, let us first summarize some of the characteristics of consumption behavior and then identify the sources of inaccurate reporting.

Characteristics of Consumption Behavior

Purchasing patterns vary not only by household and commodity but by other factors as well. In order to estimate the relationship between household expenditures and, for example, income, we need to be sure that variation due to other factors has been appropriately dealt with.

Variations in Timing of Consumption. Total expenditures of households vary by season. According to a study by Norum (1989), expenditures for clothing by a household were the highest in winter and the lowest in spring. Purchases of types of products vary also. Amount of specific kinds of foods consumed varies by season (U.S. Department of Agriculture [USDA], 1983).

Consumption and consumption expenditures also vary by time of week. Weekdays are likely to be dominated by job and school expenses, and weekends may be occasions for major shopping trips, for entertainment and recreation, and for wearing different clothes and eating different foods from the rest of the week. Holidays and special events also are occasions for variations in consumption.

The frequency and timing of purchases vary by type of commodity. Some items, such as food, are purchased by most people every week. Some expenditures, such as automobile license fees or insurance premiums, may occur regularly but only once or twice a year. Other expenditures, such as clothing, may be purchased several times a year but at irregular intervals. Still other items, such as household appliances, may be purchased only a few times in a lifetime. Refrigerators and sewing machines, for example, are sometimes kept in service for 40 years or longer.

In addition, consumption is affected by events in the external environment of the household, such as floods and other natural disasters or political or economic crises. An example of the latter is the oil crisis of 1973, which resulted in panic buying of gasoline and gasoline shortages in parts of the United States.

The implication of timing variation for consumption data is that the time when data are collected needs to be considered, both in planning a consumption survey and in evaluating the results. Averages based on data covering a short period are generally poor estimates of longer-term averages. Either the sampling design or the reporting period for households needs to be such that a normal or average pattern can be identified. Usually this means obtaining data covering at least a year from a sample large enough to ensure that rare purchases, such as refrigerators, are adequately represented. Even then, events such as the 1973 oil crisis may affect the results.

Other Variations in Purchasing Pattern. The accuracy with which a consumer can remember and report the cost of items is affected by many factors. The prices of individual items vary widely, from a few cents to thousands of dollars. Price may remain constant over an extended time period or vary from one purchase to the next. Several low-cost items are often purchased in a single shopping occasion, making it less likely that the consumer will accurately remember the individual items. Several different items are sometimes purchased as a package. Examples are bonus items given "free" with other purchases, appliances that include installation and a period of free maintenance in the purchase price, and tours that include transportation, food, lodging, and some other expenses. The cost of separate items in a package may not be possible to determine.

Method of payment varies also. For items purchased on credit, the true total cost of the item includes interest and finance charges. For items purchased by installment contract, the finance charges can be calculated, but if an item was charged on a revolving account with a balance outstanding, the interest charges for the separate item are impossible to determine.

Consumers also purchase from different types of vendors: large department stores or supermarkets, discount stores, second-hand stores, specialty shops, roadside stands, friends and acquaintances. This adds to both the difficulty of respondent recall and variability in price.

Some overall implications of these variations are that special arrangements may be needed to improve the accuracy of respondent recall, careful definitions are needed of what is included in price, and sampling design and/or questionnaire needs to take into account possible variations in vendors.

Product Variability. Most products are highly variable in quality, form, and special features. This creates problems in deciding on what items should be grouped together, in the lack of homogeneity in product categories, and in lack of product comparability in different time periods. (This problem was mentioned in Chapter 2 in the discussion of characteristics theory.) Differentiation of product price into a set of hedonic prices could be used to make comparisons more exact, but in most cases we simply have to be alert to the variability within product categories and the need for accurate information about the composition of categories.

Variations in Social Acceptability of Products and Desire for Privacy. Consumers are more willing to provide some kinds of information than others and be more honest in their responses. To take an extreme example, heroine and other recreational drugs are consumed by many individuals and represent substantial outlays of money but are not included in general surveys of household consumption. The strong assurances of privacy needed to obtain this information would not usually be feasible (and perhaps not ethical) to provide.

Ownership or consumption of highly regarded items, such as smoke detectors, is likely to be overstated by respondents, while consumption of less acceptable items, such as candy, alcohol, or pornographic literature, is likely to be underreported. Data on income and assets are likely to be underreported also.

Distribution of Consumption and Buying Responsibility within the Household. Some consumption items, such as apparel, are purchased for and used by a particular individual; other items are consumed by all household members although not necessarily in equal amounts. This creates difficulties for the development of estimates of the average consumption of individuals.

Some consumption takes place in the home; other consumption occurs in other locations. If total consumption needs to be taken into account, then consumption in all locations needs to be reported. This is a particularly severe limitation on data collected by observation, since it is difficult, and often impossible, to obtain a complete observational record on a household at more than one location.

Responsibility for purchasing items is also likely to be dispersed. Items consumed solely by a given member (such as lunches eaten at school or work) are likely to be purchased by the individual, who may be the only person in the household with accurate knowledge of the purchase. Responsibility for purchasing items for the household may be divided up. As a result, no single person in the household may have accurate information about all household expenditures.

Types of Error and Ways of Handling Them

Several types of error or bias that result from the nature of household consumption can be identified. They include limitations that result from sampling, reporting errors, and nontypical household behavior during the reporting period.

Sampling Limitations. Limitations due to sampling arise from the time periods (timing and duration) to which the data pertain, population sampled, and the design used to select consuming units from the population. Definitions of consuming unit are not always consistent from one study to another. For some purposes, the consuming unit is the individual; in other cases, it may be the household or the family. Some types of consumption behavior (e.g., purchase of a freezer) may be so rare that good estimates are not possible unless the sample of consuming units is very large or the sample has been designed to obtain adequate numbers. A similar problem is encountered with small population groups, such as farm households or Spanish-speaking or Asian households. Regression methods tend to obscure the effect of small sample size but do not eliminate the problem.

Reporting Error. Because of the cost of observations and the limited range of time and location data that can generally be obtained in that way, most data on household consumption are obtained from responses of a single household member. The knowledgeability of the respondent, errors of recall, and willingness to provide accurate responses all affect the accuracy of data.

To illustrate the problem, consider the 1960–1961 Survey of Consumer Expenditures (U.S. Bureau of Labor Statistics [BLS], 1964). In this and some earlier nationwide surveys of expenditures, a respondent for the household was asked to provide detailed data on household purchases during the entire 12 months prior to the interview. The interview lasted about 8 hours on the average. Respondents were encouraged to refer to household records if any had been kept. The amount of reporting error was unknown but was probably substantial.

Continuing panel surveys of consumer expenditures, begun by the Bureau of Labor Statistics in 1980, involve five interviews at three-month intervals so that the recall period is limited to three months. Because respondents often have difficulty in remembering the dates of purchases and have a tendency to include purchases made before the beginning of the reporting period, the first interview is used only for bounding purposes. Data on low-cost, frequently purchased items, such as food and gasoline, are obtained from a separate sample of households, who are asked to keep a diary for three weeks.

Nontypical Behavior. One of the difficulties with some data collection methods is that participation in the data collection procedure may trigger changes in the household's consumption behavior. This problem is particularly severe with observation and diary keeping by respondents. It is almost impossible to avoid some change from the normal pattern of behavior. If the subject is aware that he or she is being observed, there is a tendency for the subject to avoid embarrassing behavior, do things in a way he or she deems socially acceptable, or simplify behavior in order to ease the observer's task or shorten the observation. Similar tendencies affect diary entries.

In summary, no completely accurate or most desirable method of collecting consumption data exists; however, accuracy can be improved by a number of techniques. Before accepting and acting on the results of studies, we need to consider whether the data have been collected by a reputable organization using professional methods.

WELL-BEING

Measures

The conceptual framework used in this book is a process framework in which various inputs are converted by households into an output: well-being. The input we are most concerned with is the consumption goods and services acquired by the household through expenditures of its income and use of other resources. The amount of input owned or available to the household is often used as a measure of well-being. If we assume that goods and services have a regular functional relationship with well-being, then quantity (or value) of goods and services is an indirect measure of well-being. If we assume further that quantity of goods and services acquired is primarily a function of the household's income, then income also can be used as a measure of well-being. Income, expenditures, and various related variables, such as wealth and net worth, are in fact frequently used as measures of well-being. Fuchs, for example, in a comparison of men and women with respect to their incomes and responsibilities to dependents, described his analysis as a comparison of economic well-being (1986).

Sometimes, however, a direct measure of well-being is used, that is, a measure of the output produced through the household's use of inputs. For example, global measures of the quality of life focus on well-being. However, quality-of-life indexes frequently include measures of inputs used to produce well-being, such as income, quality of housing, ownership of household durables, availability of services, and quality of the residential or work environment, as well as measures of health status or other aspects that are an integral part of well-being.

The following examples illustrate some of the measures of well-being that are used (Juster, Courant & Dow, 1981). They include some that are associated with consumption of specific commodities, such as health care, and some that are more global in nature:

- Objective indexes of well-being, which might include indexes reflecting quality of personal economic situation, health, employment, and the physical and social environment.
- Social indicators, for example, life expectancy, disability-free life expectancy, infant mortality rates, and average days sick or with limited activity per capita per year.
- Subjective measures of satisfaction with personal economic situation, health, housing, neighborhood, work, marital situation, and other areas of living.
- Process benefits, which would include the satisfaction derived from performing the activities in which inputs are used to produce well-being. These might include satisfaction received from taking care of children, care of the home, preparation of meals, or personal care.
- Social welfare indexes, which measure achievement of the ultimate goals of the consumption, such as level of living in relation to standard, security, pleasure, and accomplishment of personal goals.

Correlations between input measures and measures that reflect output more directly are generally far from perfect. The low correlations may be due to limitations of the assumptions (for example, that wealth brings happiness) or may simply be the result of problems inherent in the measures themselves. If we had a true measure of well-being, we could compare other measures with the true measure and discover which ones measured well-being best. In the absence of such a measure, choice of measure becomes a matter of judgment regarding the appropriateness, reliability, and availability of alternative measures.

Standards

Standards of well-being may be incorporated into the question form. Andrews and Withey noted that measures of well-being may be classified with respect to whether the perspective taken is absolute, relative, or concerned with change (1976, pp. 65–74). To assess well-being from an absolute perspective, one might ask the respondent, "How do you feel about your life as a whole?" (p. 66). If a relative perspective were to be taken, one might ask, "Compared with [specify a group of other people], do you feel your life is better, worse, or about the same?" To get a change-oriented perspective, one might rephrase the question as: "Compared with five years ago, do you feel your life is better, worse, or about the same?"

Each of these perspectives implies a standard. In the first case, each respondent must formulate his or her own standard. A disadvantage of this perspective is that we do not know what that standard is. The relative perspective is somewhat better in that respect, provided that all respondents are asked to compare themselves with the same group of people and that they are able to make an informed comparison. The difficulty is identifying a comparison group with whom all respondents are sufficiently familiar as to enable them to make an accurate comparison. The change-oriented perspective enables each respondent to make the comparison with a person with whom he or she is very familiar—himself or herself—but has the disadvantage that the referents of the comparisons are all different and likely to be at different levels of well-being.

HOUSEHOLD CONSUMPTION

Measures

Consumption as a concept refers to the process of acquiring and using goods and services and disposing of any consumption residues. A distinction should be made among three types of variables that are used as measures of household consumption of goods and services: acquisition, purchase, and use. Also, each type of variable may be measured in terms of quantities of goods and services or in terms of their monetary value.

Data on these three types of variables will not yield the same results. Acquisition and purchase refer to obtaining goods and services by the household. Purchase, however, means only commodities obtained (usually from market sources) in exchange for money, while acquisition includes, in addition, goods and services acquired by household production, gift, or barter and also services and goods provided by the community or government or as employee benefits.

Acquisition is clearly the more inclusive term. Data that pertain to goods and services acquired only through purchase may seriously underreport what is actually acquired. Moreover, the underreporting is not uniform among households. Some population groups (e.g., rural households or older households) do much household production; others do little. Some live in communities with many free facilities and services; others do not. Statistics on total acquisitions would not merely show a higher average than statistics on purchased goods and services; they would indicate a different distribution of consumption among population groups.

Use, in turn, differs from acquisition. Although the household can consume only goods and services it has first acquired, a measure of use during a given time period will not coincide with a measure of acquisition. One type of discrepancy has to do with the timing of use in relation to acquisition. Some nondurable goods (for example, canned or frozen foods) may have been carried over from the preceding period, while some items may be acquired but not consumed during the survey period. This problem of timing can appropriately be neglected in the case of nondurables because beginning and ending carryovers are likely to balance each other out. A more serious problem stems from the household's inventory of durable goods, both those acquired in previous periods but used in the current period and those acquired but only partially used in the current period. Some groups, such as the elderly, have low expenditures but are receiving services from owned housing and other durables. Data based only on their expenditures or current acquisitions give too low an estimate of their current consumption.

Another type of discrepancy between acquisition and use stems from the fact that not all goods and services acquired by a household are used by members of the household. Examples are pet foods, which are purchased with the household's food supply but are not part of the food intake of household members, and gifts and hospitality provided by the household to nonmembers. Waste and loss are another source of discrepancy. Substantial amounts of food, for example, are wasted by households. Other examples of waste and loss are exercise equipment purchased but not used, clothing spoiled by laundering and discarded after one wearing, and losses due to theft.

Of the three variables, use is conceptually the most accurate; however, it is the most difficult and costly to measure. Moreover, data on use are subject to some measurement problems in addition to those related to data on purchase or acquisition. All three variables are found in studies of household consumption.

Acquisition. When a measure of total acquisition is desired, the most common practice is to obtain data on purchases and supplement them with information on other acquisitions. If the data are in the form of quantities of goods and services, then the amounts from market and nonmarket sources may be added together, although care must be taken to ensure that quantity measures are the same and quality differences are taken into account. When goods and services acquired from nonmarket sources are to be added to expenditures, an estimate of the money value of such commodities is needed. The value of goods and services received without payment should be added to both consumption and income in order to provide a complete picture of the household's economic status.

Goods and services acquired by means other than purchase include gifts, noncash income such as employee benefits, other subsidies, home-produced commodities, and services provided by the community. Gifts are perhaps the easiest on which to obtain data, since most gifts were originally purchased and thus have a market price. The respondent may be asked to report the type of gift and estimate its cost.

The simplest way of estimating the value of a commodity received as noncash income, called the market value approach, is to equate its value with the price that the household would have to pay to purchase the commodity from normal market sources. The value of home-produced food can be estimated by multiplying the quantity produced of each type of food times the average retail price for such foods. The value of subsidized housing can be estimated as the average rent paid for a nonsubsidized unit with similar characteristics. In cases where a market equivalent cannot be identified—for example, free or subsidized health care services paid for by Medicare or Medicaid—the value may be estimated as the cost of the program divided among enrollees or beneficiaries.

The market value approach is simple in concept but tends to overestimate the value of the noncash commodities to the household. Bear in mind that the household does not pay the market price but pays either no money for the commodity or a price less than the market value. Thus, the fact that the household acquires the commodity is not evidence that the commodity is worth its market price to that household. If the household were given an equivalent amount of money, it might purchase the commodity but alternatively might spend all or part of the money on something else.

Two other methods have been developed for estimating the value of noncash income: the cash-equivalent approach and the poverty budget share approach. McNeil described the cash-equivalent approach as "the amount at which the recipient would be indifferent as to whether he or she received cash or the [commodity]" (1985, p. 17). Since direct questions to recipients of such commodities (e.g., "How much is the commodity worth to you?") may elicit responses that are unrealistically high or unrealistically low, the usual method is to equate the value of the free or subsidized commodity to the average expenditure for the commodity by a household that has similar income, size, and age-sex composition but does not produce the commodity at home or receive it free or subsidized. For purposes of this comparison, income is calculated to include the market value of home-produced, free, or subsidized commodities. For example, suppose family A, with a cash income of $10,000, spent $800 on food from market sources and consumed additional home-produced food valued at $400 by the market value approach. Comparison family B, with no home-produced food and cash income of $14,000, spent $1,000 on food. We conclude, using the cash-equivalent approach, that family A's home-produced food had a value to them of $200, the amount by which they would have increased their food expenditures had they had an additional $400 in cash. The result of using the cash-equivalent approach is usually to reduce the estimated value of noncash income. In a number of studies by the U.S. Department of Agriculture, the value of home-produced food to the household was estimated as half of its market-equivalent value.

A still lower estimate results from using the poverty budget share approach. This method is similar to the cash-equivalent approach except that the comparison is to the average expenditure of similar households with income at the poverty level.

Community services are also part of the total consumption of the household received from nonmarket sources. They include police and fire protection, parks and recreational facilities, social services, postal service, streets and highways, and garbage pickup. They are, of course, not free but are supported by tax revenues, private contributions, and volunteer help. Use of the services is not linked to and may differ widely from amount contributed by the household.

Acquisition and use of community services is generally ignored in studies of household consumption because of the difficulties in estimating their value to any given household. Information on amount or frequency of use, with no money value, is sometimes obtained; however, much of the value of such services may stem from their availability rather than their use. The value of police protection, for example, is related not to how often we have to call the police but to how often we do not have to call them. For such services, their value to the household lies in their availability in case of need. On the other hand, information on the availability of such facilities as parks and limited-access highways may overestimate their value to households that make little use of them.

Purchase. Measures of consumption goods and services acquired by purchase from market sources provide a less comprehensive measure of consumption than measures of total acquisition but are easier to obtain and more frequently used. Data are sometimes obtained on quantities purchased or frequency of purchase of a given item; however, data on household expenditures for consumer commodities, perhaps expanded to include value of home-produced, free, or subsidized commodities, are the most common measure of household consumption. Expenditure data are convenient to use because they summarize information in a single statistic rather than requiring an array of data, as is generally the case with data on quantities of goods and services. Expenditure data are generally regarded as being more accurate than data on the value of other acquisitions or of commodity use.

Operational definitions of expenditure variables are likely to vary slightly from one survey to another. There may be differences in the categories into which commodities are grouped. There may also be differences in the way expenditures are defined and calculated.

The most common difference among consumer expenditure surveys is probably in the way expenditure categories are defined. Given the thousands of different types and variations in products and services, some grouping is necessary simply to ensure a sufficient number of cases on which to base an estimate. Categories vary from specific (e.g., refrigerators—or even two-door refrigerators with frozen-food storage and more than 10 cubic feet capacity) to broad (e.g., household appliances and furnishings), depending on the purpose and convenience of the researcher. The Bureau of Labor Statistics, which collects expenditure data on a continuing basis and is thus a major source of such data, collects information on expenditures in more than 500 specific categories, which are then summarized in broader categories. One must often read descriptions of the data carefully to find out where some expenditures have been categorized. Are expenditures for television sets, for example, included under house furnishings or under entertainment? (In its ongoing panel survey of consumer expenditures begun in 1980, the Bureau of Labor Statistics included expenditures for televisions in entertainment.)

The value of a commodity may be reported in several forms, which we will term *price-tag price*, *full price*, and *cash outlay*. Price-tag price is the amount on the ticket or sticker. Full price is price-tag price; plus sales tax, cost of delivery and installation (if applicable), and any charges (interest or other) incurred in connection with purchasing on credit; minus discounts or rebates. Cash outlay is that part of the full price that is actually paid during the period covered by the survey.

The amount of an expenditure might vary considerably depending on which operational definition was used. The Bureau of Labor Statistics generally defines expenditure as full price. Total expenditure in a given period, defined as the sum of the full price of each commodity purchased during the period, does not give an accurate picture of cash outflow since most purchases of automobiles and other costly items are financed. On the other hand, cash outlay for items purchased on revolving charge accounts would often be impossible to determine.

Use. Still another way of measuring consumption is to obtain information on commodities used by the household. In the case of services and nondurable goods, use can be equated with acquisition without serious distortion and is therefore generally measured by expenditures. Use of major durables, however, cannot be measured accurately by acquisition and needs to be measured separately.

The use received from durable goods is sometimes measured by ownership. A household may be asked to list its inventory of appliances and other durables in usable condition. Use is inferred from ownership. However, amount and value of use cannot be estimated accurately from ownership. Additional data are needed on frequency of use or value of services received from the durable.

Two methods are available for estimating the value of flow of services from owned durables: the rental-equivalent approach and the cost-of-services approach. The rental-equivalent approach may be used for durables that may be either owned or rented. An important example is dwellings. Many households rent rather than own their homes. Furniture and many items of equipment can also be rented. The cost of renting an equivalent item can be used as an estimate of the value to the household of services obtained from the item.

In cases in which rental-equivalent costs are not easy or feasible to obtain, the cost-of-services approach may be used. The cost of services provided by an owned durable is the total cost to the household of owning and operating the item, allocated over its service life. Cost of services per year is total lifetime cost of owning and using the item divided by total number of years the item is used by the household. Cost per occasion of use would be lifetime cost divided by number of times used.

Social indicators are a source of some consumption data. These are provided as averages for a nation or population group and so are not easy to relate to other characteristics of the household but can be used for some comparisons. Some of the social indicator variables that indicate use of consumption commodities are food consumption measures, such as per capita food consumption (expressed, for example, in cereal-equivalent quantities or in calorie equivalents) or calorie or protein consumption per day; numbers of automobiles, telephones, or other durable goods owned per 1,000 population; measures of housing consumption, such as average square feet per dwelling or per person, or percentage of dwellings with electricity, piped water, or other services; and measures of consumption of educational services, such as percentage who have completed high school or college. Social indicators based on consumption expenditures (based on national income accounts) include per capita expenditures for personal consumption and percentage of consumption expenditure spent on food, housing, or other consumption categories (Andorka & Harcsa, 1990).

When measures of the use of goods and services are to be obtained, it is especially important to take into account services provided free or at minimal cost by government and other public sources. Examples are police and fire protection and the use of public parks. If all households benefit by these services equally, then it may not be necessary to obtain data on them. One can simply specify that in addition to the consumption that is actually measured, there is a residue of unmeasured consumption that affects the total consumption of households but not their level of well-being relative to other households. Assume, in other words, that if the additional consumption were included, all households would move up the scale by the same amount. Even when households do not use public services in the same degree (for example, one household visits the park daily while another never does), they can be said to be on the same footing if they have equal access to the services.

An example of a study in which actual use of public services was the focus is *Rural Household Use of Services: A Study of Miryalguda Taluka* (Wanmali, 1985). The study, conducted in India, focused on services believed to be important inputs in rural development, such as banking, bus service, health services, postal services, and primary schools. Wanmali was concerned with two aspects: distance from household to the service provider (i.e., degree of access to the service) and frequency of use of the service. In rural India, he found, access to services was not equal, which partially accounted for differences in frequency of use. Differential access to services may also be found in the United States, especially in rural areas.

Standards

From the beginning of the study of household consumption, the need was felt for standards with which actual consumption behavior could be compared. There are many needs for scientifically based, empirical information that can be applied normatively. It is all very well to talk about social science as value free, but in the area of consumption economics, at least, many research users want to be able to say that the level of consumption of one household or group of households is better or worse, acceptable or unacceptable, adequate or inadequate. To do this, a standard of comparison is needed. Such standards may be informal and comparison specific, for example, "John Brown's family lives better than James Jones's family," or "I am better off today than a couple of years ago." Standards are far more useful, however, if they are generally understood and accepted, which means that they need to be stated formally and precisely.

Consumption standards are measures of the adequacy of consumption. A consumption standard is a level of consumption associated with a given level of well-being. A standard might specify level of consumption for a single commodity, or it might pertain to the level, pattern, or balance among all goods and services consumed by the household. It might be specified in terms of quantities or expenditures. Consumption standards are used to (1) measure the level of well-being of an individual, household, population, or population group; (2) make comparisons between or among individuals, households, or populations with respect to their relative well-being; (3) guide the consumption (or consumption-related) choices of individuals or households; and (4) help society to achieve those societal goals that either pertain to consumption-dependent well-being of its members or depend on quality of human resources as influenced by consumption of goods and services.

Consumption standards are based on assumptions. These may include assumptions about the goals of society (e.g., that no one should go hungry), about the nature of well-being (e.g., the belief that the well-being of an individual depends on his or her level relative to that of others), about the nature of the consumption process (e.g., that a given level of income will generally result in a given level of consumption), or about the goals of other individuals.

Scientifically Based Standards. In principle, it should be possible to identify objectively levels of well-being and discover through scientific research the kinds and amounts of commodities needed to achieve and maintain each level. Perhaps the best example of scientifically based standards are the recommendations for intake of food energy and nutrients in order to ensure nutritional health. The nutrient-intake standards used in the United States, called Recommended Dietary Allowances (RDAs), were developed and are periodically updated by panels established by the National Academy of Sciences/National Research Council (National Research Council, 1989). They are defined as "the levels of intake of essential nutrients that, on the basis of scientific knowledge, are judged by the Food and Nutrition Board to be adequate to meet the known nutrient needs of practically all healthy persons" (p. 1). The RDA for energy represents the mean population requirements, while the RDAs for nutrients "provide a safety factor appropriate to each nutrient and exceed the actual requirements of most individuals" (p. 2). Recommendations are also published about other diet components that have been linked to chronic diseases, including fat, cholesterol, carbohydrates, sodium, and alcohol (Behlen & Cronin, 1985).

Behlen and Cronin (1985) summarized the dietary recommendations prepared since 1977 by 10 government agencies, professional associations, and health organizations. Recommended intakes of food energy and nutrients are also published by the United Nations and other institutions.

Dietary recommendations are used for assessing the adequacy of the food supply available to a population and the adequacy of diets consumed by individuals or population groups. They are also used for developing dietary guidance materials and for defining poverty. Since the recommendations are designed to reflect the needs of specific populations, selection of which dietary recommendation should be used is an issue, and the choice will affect the results. When the RDAs are used, the standard of adequacy is sometimes set at a percentage of the RDA, since the RDAs are higher than needed by the average person. RDAs have been used in a number of ways, including the following:

- Tippett, Mickle, and Roidt (1990) used the RDAs as a standard to evaluate the adequacy of food and nutrient intakes of low-income women and children.
- The seventh edition of the RDAs (published in 1968) was used as the basis for establishing guidelines for the nutritional labeling of foods (National Research Council, 1989, p. 8).
- The RDAs were used to define lower limits for food energy and nutrients in the USDA Family Food Plans, which became the basis for defining poverty (Cleveland & Peterkin, 1983).

Although dietary standards are the best known of the scientifically based consumption standards, and perhaps the only ones used by consumers themselves, standards for other types of consumption are in use. For example, the Environmental Protection Agency set standards for ambient air quality in the United States that are designed to "protect human health with a reasonable margin of safety" (Council on Environmental Quality, 1979, p. 54), which specify levels of particulate matter, sulfur oxides, carbon monoxide, nitrogen dioxide, ozone, and hydrocarbons. There are also standards for emission of hazardous air pollutants, such as asbestos, beryllium, and mercury (p. 61). Standards for safe drinking water have also been promulgated, as well as standards for the purity, safety, and labeling of many products.

Relative Standards. Another type of standard is based on assumptions that wants are formed by experience or knowledge of the consumption patterns of others, and wants are insatiable (therefore, more is better). The assumption of insatiability enables us to say that one level of consumption (that which uses larger quantities or higher qualities of commodities or greater expenditures) is higher than another. The assumption regarding the origin of wants, the basis for the relative income hypothesis, provides a rationale for various commonly used comparisons.

The consumption level (quantity or value) of a given population group—say, the elderly or Hispanics—may be compared with the mean of another group or the mean for the entire population. Comparisons may be made between two populations (for example, in different countries). Comparisons may also be made of consumption levels of the same household at two different points in time, with the implication that if the amount consumed has increased, the household's well-being has increased. Note that the assumption that more is better is not consistent with dietary standards or some philosophies of life.

Standard budgets may be included in this category. A standard budget is a description of a level of consumption, expressed in quantities of goods and services to be consumed by a household at that level or the cost of those goods and services. The implication is that all households consuming goods and services in the recommended quantities or spending at the specified level may be regarded as being at the same level of consumption. The USDA Family Food Plans are examples of standard budgets, in this case, for food only (Kerr et al., 1984). Four food plans were produced. Three of the plans were based on average food consumption patterns of households with per person food spending at the second, third, and fourth quartiles, respectively. The lowest-cost food plan is at the level of households eligible for the food stamp program. To develop the food plans, scientists adjusted usual food consumption patterns at the given cost level to meet dietary standards for food energy and nutrients. The food plans have been published in the form of lists of foods (kinds and quantity) that an individual of a given age, sex, and condition should consume at that consumption level. Cost of the diet at current price levels is also published. These recommended amounts for individuals may be aggregated to obtain household budgets.

Another example of a consumption standard is the Prevailing Family Standard (Table 3.1), a level of total expenditures designed to reflect the level of living of the typical family. The Bureau of Labor Statistics defined this as the median level of total expenditures of a two-parent family with two children. Other levels were derived from the Prevailing Family Standard: the Social Minimum Standard (half of the Prevailing Family Standard), the Lower Living Standard (two-thirds of the Prevailing Family Standard), and the Social Abundance Standard (50 percent higher than the Prevailing Family Standard) (Hefferan, 1987).

Budget-Share Standards. The average or recommended budget share allocated to a given expenditure category can also be used as a standard. In consumption, goods and services are interrelated. Limitations on resources mean that in most households, not all desired commodities can be purchased; an increase in one expenditure is associated with a decrease in another. Commodities may also be complementary in their use—for example, automobiles and gasoline. Many commodities have substitutes that may be used to satisfy the same want. Thus, we can conclude that consumption of any one commodity affects the consumption of all others in some degree.

Many scholars believe that there is a hierarchy of needs that is similar for all people, at least in broad terms. An example is Maslow's hierarchy of needs. Another example is the basic needs approach, used by some economic development planners (Sharif, 1986, pp. 559–560). Although there is not complete agreement on what should be regarded as basic needs or on the exact ranking of needs in a hierarchy, there is a consensus that food is a basic need—probably the most basic need of all. Food is also a major expenditure. Satisfaction of other consumption needs is limited by the proportion of resources that must be devoted to satisfying the need for food. Based on this rationale, proportion of income spent on food has become a generally accepted indicator of consumption level. It is used in international comparisons and is sometimes used to identify the poor.

Proportion of income spent on shelter also has some uses, with the same rationale: that shelter is a basic need and limits the amount of income available for other consumption. Budget guidelines for consumers sometimes suggest a

Table 3.1
Adult Equivalent Scale and Family Budgets at Four Levels

Number of persons	Equi-valence scale	Social Minimum Standard	Lower Living Standard	Prevailing Family Standard	Social Abundance Standard
1, aged	.50	$7,905	$10,545	$15,809	$23,715
1, nonaged	.54	8,537	11,388	17,074	25,612
2, aged	.61	9,644	12,865	19,288	28,932
2, nonaged	.67	10,592	14,130	21,185	31,777
3	.80	12,648	16,872	25,295	37,943
4	1.00	15,809	21,090	31,619	47,428
5	1.20	18,971	25,308	37,943	56,914
6	1.39	21,975	29,314	43,950	65,925
7	1.57	24,821	33,111	49,642	74,463
8	1.74	27,508	36,696	55,017	82,524
9	1.90	30,038	40,071	60,076	90,114
10	2.05	32,410	43,235	64,819	97,229
11	2.19	34,622	46,186	69,245	103,867
12	2.32	36,678	48,928	73,355	110,033
Each additional person ...	+.12	1,897	2,531	3,794	5,692

Source: Heffernan (1987, pp. 1–9). Budgets were calculated from expenditure levels reported in the 1984 Consumer Expenditure Survey, U.S. Department of Labor, Bureau of Labor Statistics. The budget figures are updated to 1988 price level here.

maximum percentage of income that should be spent on housing—generally a maximum of 25 to 35 percent of income. Lenders or insurers of home mortgages use this proportion as a basis for deciding if the household can afford to buy a particular house. The U.S. Department of Housing and Urban Development regards housing as affordable to the poor if it takes no more than 30 percent of their adjusted income (Leonard, Dolbeare & Lazere, 1989, p. 1).

Social Consensus Standards. Social indicators, based on what might be termed societal goals, are also used for comparing the well-being of groups. They might be regarded as social consensus standards. Social indicators are not usually thought of as consumption standards, but they often include many consumption indicators, such as availability of running water, number of bathrooms in the dwelling, and number of rooms or of persons per square foot. One example, the Physical Quality of Life Index (Brodshy & Rodrik, 1981), was designed for international comparisons. Such indicators are based on social judgments regarding what is needed rather than on scientific evidence.

Scales

A central question, and a classic one, is how to measure equivalence in consumption levels. Equal consumption does not necessarily mean equal well-being. Equal well-being means that needs or wants are satisfied to an equal degree. But needs and wants vary with age, sex, cultural expectations, status in society, and many other factors. The identification of consumption equivalence between households in terms of equal well-being must, at a minimum, take into account the number of persons consuming from the household store and their needs, as reflected in age and sex and perhaps other characteristics, such as health conditions or pregnancy.

The fact that needs vary is generally recognized in consumption standards. For example, the USDA Family Food Plans indicate amounts for age-sex groups, with separate recommendations for pregnant and lactating women. To construct the costs for a household, the amounts recommended for members are summed and adjusted by a factor representing economies and diseconomies of scale.

A convenient way of summarizing the impact of household size and member characteristics is the equivalence scale. An equivalence scale for individuals is an index in which the consumption quantity or expenditure deemed appropriate for an individual with given characteristics is expressed as a ratio or percentage of that of a base person. The earliest example of such a scale was developed by Ernst Engel in 1883 (Monroe, 1974, p. 54). His scale was expressed in units of expenditure he called "quets." The base person in his scale was an infant, whose level of consumption was assumed to be 100 quets. He estimated that expenses would increase by 10 quets each year until the age of 20 to 25. More recent estimates of consumption equivalent scales have been computed using large data sets and more sophisticated analytic methods.

Equivalence measures are based on standards of some sort. Often the standard is simply the mean or median level of consumption of a given segment of the population. For example, Salathe and Buse (1978) developed adult equivalent scales for six food groups. They calculated the average cost of food consumed by individual household members, grouped by age and sex, making separate cost estimates (and adult equivalent scales) for fruits, vegetables, grain products, beef and pork, dairy products, and total food. The mean cost of food consumed by an adult male aged 20 to 55 was used as the base. Mean costs for individuals in other age-sex groups were expressed as a fraction of the base. The Salathe-Buse scale was consistent with that of Engel in that they found that mean costs increased from infancy to age 20, but they found declining costs for food after age 55 in all food groups except fruits. Total food costs for males at all ages were higher than those for females.

Equivalence scales may also be developed with the household as the unit to be equated. Seneca and Taussig (1971) estimated equivalence scales for households of different sizes using data from the 1960 Survey of Consumer Expenditures. They divided the sample of households into 16 income groups, each subdivided according to size of household. For each income-size group, they computed an Engel function: expenditure in a given category as a function of income. The estimated expenditures were then converted into a set of equivalence scales, one scale for each income group, by expressing the estimate for each household size as a percentage of the estimate for a four-person household. A similar method was used by Gaag and Smolensky (1982), who developed equivalence scales using data from the 1972–1973 Survey of Consumer Expenditures.

The Prevailing Family Standard, proposed by the Bureau of Labor Statistics, embodies the concept of equivalence among households. (See Table 3.1.) Although based on median expenditures of a four-person household, an equivalence scale for adjusting the standard to other household sizes is suggested (Hefferan, 1987).

All of the equivalence scales examined used the actual behavior of households as a standard. It is also possible to use a scientifically based standard. An example is the equivalent nutrition scale. A simple form of this kind of scale is used in describing or comparing the nutritional quality of foods, for example, on nutrition labels. Suppose, for example, that the nutritional content of a food were presented in the form of milligrams of calcium or grams of protein per package. Few consumers are sufficiently familiar with the RDAs to be able to evaluate the nutritional impact of adding so many milligrams of calcium to their diets. The information is likely to be more useful if the amount provided of each nutrient is expressed as a percentage of the RDA. But the RDAs differ according to age and sex of the consumer, so what RDA should be used? A common practice is to use the RDA for an adult male as the base and express the amount provided of each nutrient as a percentage of the RDA for an adult male. The percentages are not appropriate to the needs of most individuals but do enable buyers to compare the relative nutrient content of foods. For more precise comparisons, the needs of individuals in other age-sex groups may be expressed as a percentage or fraction of those of an adult male. The latter type of scale was used, for example, by Morgan, Peterkin, Johnson, and Goungetas (1985) to compare the nutrients per dollar expenditure of food by households differing in size and composition.

COST MEASUREMENT

Just as consumption can be measured in terms of acquisition, purchase, or use, so can the cost of consumption be measured in different ways. One way is to look at the purchase price (usually including sales tax) of an item or group of items. This may not, however, reflect the true cost of consumption or even of acquisition.

The Consumer Price Index

When prices increase, the cost of living increases. This relationship, and the need to take price changes into account in setting fair wages, has long been recognized (BLS, 1977). During World War I, this became a practical problem for the U.S. government. As in most other wars, consumer prices were rising rapidly and labor was in short supply. The Shipbuilding Labor Adjustment Board decided that wages in shipbuilding yards should be increased when the cost of living increased. The Bureau of Labor Statistics, asked to investigate price increases and provide the information needed to make cost-of-living increases, obtained data on expenditures of wage-earning families in 92 cities and price records from retail firms in 32 cities. These data were published in the form of "cost-of-living" indexes. In 1921, the Bureau of Labor Statistics began regular publication of the Consumer Price Index (CPI).

The CPI has undergone several major revisions, although the basic method was established in 1921. Until 1977, only one version of the CPI was available, the Consumer Price Index for Urban Wage Earners and Clerical Workers (CPI-W). After that date, a second index was published, the Consumer Price Index for All Urban Consumers (CPI-U). The CPI-U is the more comprehensive index, covering about 80 percent of the total noninstitutional population. Excluded from coverage under the CPI-U are the military (about 2 percent), rural families living outside Standard Metropolitan Statistical Areas (about 18 percent), and others living in institutions. In addition to the all-items CPI, there is an array of CPI subindexes and special indexes. (See Table 3.2.) The subindexes for commodity groupings and for specific cities can be used to achieve greater precision in particular applications.

Uses of the CPI. The CPI has several uses (BLS, 1977):

1. To monitor the impact of government economic policies on the economy.
2. To deflate other economic series, such as data on retail sales, earnings, and personal consumption expenditures, so that the adjusted data will be inflation free.

Table 3.2
Consumer Price Index, 1946–1988

Year	All items	Food & beverages	Housing	Apparel & upkeep	Trans-por.	Medical care	Enter-tainment
1946	19.5	–	–	34.4	16.7	12.5	–
1947	22.3	–	–	39.9	18.5	13.5	–
1948	24.1	–	–	42.5	20.6	14.4	–
1949	23.8	–	–	40.8	22.1	14.8	–
1950	24.1	–	–	40.3	22.7	15.1	–
1951	26.0	–	–	43.9	24.1	15.9	–
1952	26.5	–	–	43.5	25.7	16.7	–
1953	26.7	–	–	43.1	26.5	17.3	–
1954	26.9	–	–	43.1	26.1	17.8	–
1955	26.8	–	–	42.9	25.8	18.2	–
1956	27.2	–	–	43.7	26.2	18.9	–
1957	28.1	–	–	44.5	27.7	19.7	–
1958	28.9	–	–	44.6	28.6	20.6	–
1959	29.1	–	–	45.0	29.8	21.5	–
1960	29.6	–	–	45.7	29.8	22.3	–
1961	29.9	–	–	46.1	30.1	22.9	–
1962	30.2	–	–	46.3	30.8	23.5	–
1963	30.6	–	–	46.9	30.9	24.1	–
1964	31.0	–	–	47.3	31.4	24.6	–
1965	31.5	–	–	47.8	31.9	25.2	–
1966	32.4	–	–	49.0	32.3	26.3	–
1967	33.4	35.0	30.8	51.0	33.3	28.2	40.7
1968	34.8	36.2	32.0	53.7	34.3	29.9	43.0
1969	36.7	38.1	34.0	56.8	35.7	31.9	45.2

Year							
1970	38.8	40.1	36.4	59.2	37.5	34.0	47.5
1971	40.5	41.4	38.0	61.1	39.5	36.1	50.0
1972	41.8	43.1	39.4	62.3	39.9	37.3	51.5
1973	44.4	48.8	41.2	64.6	41.2	38.8	52.9
1974	49.3	55.5	45.8	69.4	45.8	42.4	56.9
1975	53.8	60.2	50.7	72.5	50.1	47.5	62.0
1976	56.9	62.1	53.8	75.2	55.1	52.0	65.1
1977	60.6	65.8	57.4	78.6	59.0	57.0	68.3
1978	65.2	72.2	62.4	81.4	61.7	61.8	71.9
1979	72.6	79.9	70.1	84.9	70.5	67.5	76.7
1980	82.4	86.7	81.1	90.9	83.1	74.9	83.6
1981	90.9	93.5	90.4	95.3	93.2	82.9	90.1
1982	96.5	97.3	96.9	97.8	97.0	92.5	96.0
1983	99.6	99.5	99.5	100.2	99.3	100.6	100.1
1984	103.9	103.2	103.6	102.1	103.7	106.8	103.8
1985	107.6	105.6	107.7	105.0	106.4	113.5	107.9
1986	109.6	109.1	110.9	105.9	102.3	122.0	111.6
1987	113.6	113.5	114.2	110.6	105.4	130.1	115.3
1988	118.3	118.2	118.5	115.4	108.7	138.6	120.3

Source: U.S. House of Representatives (1990, p. 359).

3. To escalate income payments to reflect changes in the cost of living. In 1977, the Bureau of Labor Statistics estimated that such adjustments were made, for example, to the social security payments received by 38 million beneficiaries, food stamp allotments to 20 million recipients, pension payments to 3.5 million federal retirees, and the wages of 8.5 million workers covered by collective bargaining contracts that link wage increases to CPI increases. The poverty thresholds used by the Bureau of Census in counting the poor are adjusted by the CPI.

4. To adjust expenditure estimates for price changes. For example, estimates of child-rearing costs by the U.S. Department of Agriculture, based on data from the 1960–1961 Survey of Consumer Expenditures, were regularly updated to current price levels using the CPI until they were replaced by estimates based on 1987 data (Lino, 1990a, p. 2). Such updated estimates reflect changes in prices, not changes in purchasing patterns.

The requirements of these diverse uses are not identical. The first two require an accurate price index, showing changes in the prices of a fixed market basket of goods and services purchased in fixed quantities at a fixed level of quality. The last two need a cost-of-living index in which all major expenses are included and adjustments are made periodically to reflect changes in income allocation and in concepts of what is necessary for living.

The CPI is primarily a price index. Although sometimes used as a cost-of-living index, it has several deficiencies for such applications. It does not include income and social security taxes, nor does it take into account goods and services acquired by means other than purchase. It is not immediately adjusted to include new products, drop products that have declined in popularity, or reflect changes in purchasing patterns due to changes in relative prices, income changes, or changes in tastes and preferences. It does not accurately reflect changes in prices paid by particular population groups, such as the poor or the elderly, whose expenditure patterns differ from that of the majority.

Construction of the CPI. The CPI shows changes in price level for a fixed market basket of goods and services, which means that prices must be aggregated. One possible way of aggregating would be simply to add the prices of all items to form an unweighted index. The result, however, would not accurately reflect the impact of price changes on consumers, since a price change in an item taking a large share of the consumer's budget will have more impact on the consumer's level of consumption than one taking a small share. A more accurate measure of impact is provided by weighting the items by average quantities purchased by consumers in time period i, i.e., $\Sigma p_i q_i$. By obtaining the weighted sum in two different time periods, using current prices but holding the quantities constant, the percentage change can be calculated.

Two types of indexes are available: the Laspeyres price index, in which quantities from the initial time period are used, and the Paasche price index, in which quantities from the current time period are used. The CPI is a modified Laspeyres index (Pearce, 1986). The formula is

$$I_i = I_{i-1} \left[\left(\Sigma(p_{i-1}q_a) \, (p_i/p_{i-1}) \right) / \left(\Sigma(p_{i-1}p_a) \right) / \Sigma(p_{i-1}q_a) \right].$$

The indexes are published monthly. The unadjusted index shows the price level in the current month as a percentage of the price level in the base period. Percentage changes from the previous month and from the previous year are also reported. Because some prices vary seasonally, change from preceding periods is also reported in a seasonally adjusted form.

Several questions need to be decided when constructing or using a price index:

1. Base period. Beginning in 1986, the period 1982 to 1984 was used as a base for CPI indexes, replacing the 1967 base that had been used for many years. However, the series can be converted to any selected base year by dividing the CPI index value for each year by the value for the selected base year (and multiplying by 100 to convert to a percentage).

2. Population covered. To provide accurate results, a price index needs to reflect the spending patterns of the population of interest. The first indexes (CPI-W) were based on spending patterns of urban wage earners and clerical workers. This focus was continued with some expansions of definition until 1978, when the CPI-U, reflecting expenditure patterns of all urban consumers, was initiated, together with separate indexes for 28 cities.

3. Market basket. The selection of items for the fixed market basket is based on consumer expenditure surveys, which were conducted about every 10 years prior to 1980 but annually beginning in 1980. Personal insurance and income and personal property taxes are not included in the CPI, but the market basket does include real estate taxes and sales and excise taxes. The market basket and expenditure weights are revised periodically to reflect changes in purchasing patterns. Changes in product quality present a difficult problem. In order to reflect pure price change, the market basket should be fixed in terms of item quality as well as quantity, but this is not feasible for two reasons: the quality of products offered on the market changes as new features and designs replace older models, and quality selections of consumers change. Where possible, the Bureau of Labor Statistics obtains measures of quality change in order to separate these from price changes. The measure used is the additional cost associated with producing the change in quality. Where the cost of quality change cannot be measured, it is ignored.

4. Price surveys. Prices are obtained on a regular schedule for items in the market basket; however, prices vary widely among retail outlets, and therefore all types of stores must be surveyed. Prices are weighted to reflect average allocation of consumer purchases among different types of retail outlets, as shown in household expenditure surveys.

5. Home ownership. Homes are durable goods and are purchased infrequently by individual households. Moreover, houses often appreciate in value as market prices rise so that purchase of a home is partly an investment. There are two methods of calculating the price of a durable good: the asset approach, in which the item is treated as if all its value were consumed in the year of purchase, and the flow of services approach, in which the annual cost of the services from the durable is used to represent the price (BLS, 1983). Prior to the 1978 revision of the CPI, the asset approach was used to

obtain the price of all durables, including houses. Problems in using the asset approach for valuing housing included quality changes, unrepresentativeness of sample from which data were obtained, and the failure to take into account equity costs and capital gains. After some experimentation, the Bureau of Labor Statistics adopted the flow of services approach. Two possibilities also exist for estimating the value of flow of services. A user-cost function may be calculated, which would include mortgage and equity financing costs, maintenance costs, taxes, and other expenses. User-cost functions have some of the same measurement problems as the asset approach. The rental equivalence method, which was adopted by the Bureau of Labor Statistics, involves obtaining an estimate from home owners of the "implicit rent" associated with their house (the amount of rent they could obtain if they were to rent the house instead of occupying it themselves) and then calculating weights for the sample of rental units in such a way that price changes in the rental units also represent changes in the implicit rent of owner-occupied housing. The flow of services approach has some measurement problems—especially the problem of comparability of owner-occupied and rental housing—but the Bureau of Labor Statistics believes that if provides a more accurate measure of the true costs of home ownership than does the alternatives.

Cost of Consumption

There are several types of situations in which purchase price is not an adequate measure of the cost of consumption.

Cost of Credit and Other Charges. When an item is purchased on credit, the cost of the credit must be added to the purchase price in order to arrive at the true cost of the item. Credit costs include finance and interest charges and other costs, such as insurance required by the lender.

In the case of fixed-rate mortgages or installment credit (loans in which the payments and term of the loan are fixed), credit costs are relatively easy to calculate. Variable-rate mortgages are more complex than fixed-rate ones since the rate of interest and monthly payments change in response to changes in the interest rate; however, although variable-rate mortgages are somewhat more complicated to calculate, the amount of interest charges is known. A substantial part of consumer debt, however, is in the form of revolving credit, in which new credit purchases are added to the unpaid balance, interest is charged on the unpaid balance, and the consumer is required to pay only a percentage of the unpaid balance each month. Total amount of interest paid on revolving credit in a given period can be ascertained, as well as fees for credit card privileges, but it is generally impossible to allocate those charges among individual purchases.

There are other charges also that might accompany purchase of an item, such as cost of delivery and installation. Often these are included in the purchase price but must sometimes be ascertained separately.

Full Cost. For some purposes it is desirable to include the cost of household production time and use of owned durables associated with the consumption of an item. Suppose we wanted to compare the cost of convenience foods with foods prepared at home from ingredients. Preparation from ingredients requires more household production time to make the food ready to eat; thus, unless time is regarded as having no value, a true comparison of costs must take into account the difference in preparation time and the cost of time.

A cost associated with the use of durables is the cost of maintenance and repair. If other commodities, such as utilities, are required in order to use the durable, their costs must be included. In estimating the cost of doing laundry at home, for example, Mork (1975) included the cost of gas, electricity, water, detergent, and other supplies as part of the cost of doing a load of laundry. She also included a fraction of the cost of the equipment used. She did not include the cost of the time required for doing a load of laundry, although in a comparison of home laundry costs with the cost of using commercial facilities, the cost of time ought to be considered.

The laundry example illustrates the situation in which cost of a durable item needs to be calculated. In order to estimate the total lifetime cost of the durable, the total cost of owning and using the item over its entire service life is needed. Total lifetime cost includes the original cost of the item plus maintenance and repair expenses in each year of its service life minus any part of its cost recouped by selling the item at the end of its service life (or plus any charges incurred in disposing of the item).

The exact number of years a household will keep an item is rarely known, but estimates of service life expectancy are available for a few equipment items (Tippett & Ruffin, 1975). If the household is at equilibrium (neither building up its stock of a given durable nor allowing the stock to decline), the service life will be equal to the ratio of inventory to acquisitions.

Mork used an estimate of 11 years as the service life of a washing machine and assumed that neither the service life nor the cost of repair and maintenance would vary with amount of use. Using those assumptions, she was able to estimate the cost per load of doing laundry for different numbers of loads per week. The cost per load declined with the higher number of loads because the cost of the equipment was allocated over the larger use.

To summarize, we can define annual cost (c_a) of consuming a durable as

$$c_a = (p + rs - d_c)/sl + m,$$

where p represents the full purchase price, including credit charges and installation fees, if applicable, rs represents the amount received from the sale of the item when it is disposed of by the household, d_c represents cost of disposing of the item if it is not sold (note that either rs or d_c might be zero), sl represents the number of years the durable is kept in service, and m represents annual cost of maintenance and repairs. If cost per use is wanted, then c_a should be divided by the number of times the item is used in a year.

The role played by service life and frequency of use in calculating the cost of durables deserves special attention. In comparing the cost of alternative products, for example, the expected service life as well as original price must be taken into account in order to determine which is actually cheaper. Cost per use of an item that is used infrequently may be very high.

Net Cost over Service Life. Some purchases result in savings in future expenditures. For example, a durable item with a high purchase price but low maintenance costs may have a lower net cost over its service life than one that has a lower initial cost but frequently needs repairs. An important example of expenditures that save money is expenditures to retrofit a house to make it more energy efficient. The expenditure for retrofitting can be regarded as an investment that will yield future savings in the form of lower utility bills. Evaluation of the true cost of such investments requires us to take into account both the amount of expected savings (which may pay, or more than pay, for the initial investment) and the opportunity cost of the investment—the interest or other benefits forgone when the money was put into retrofitting (for example) rather than used in some other way.

Hanna (1978, pp. 65–67) described methods of calculating the value of such investments. Two are the most frequently used:

1. Apparent payback method. This is the ratio of the marginal cost of the item (its initial price or, if two items are being compared, the price difference) to the value of the benefits in the first year. It is, in effect, the number of years needed to recover the cost of the investment, disregarding opportunity costs. An item that will "pay for itself" long before its service life expires is considered to be a good investment because after that point, net savings are experienced.

2. Present value method. This method takes into account the number of years (t) during which the investment can be expected to yield savings, the expected amount of the savings in each year (S), and an interest rate (r), which should be equal to the after-tax rate of return that would have been received had the amount invested in the item been invested elsewhere. The present value of the investment, then, would equal $S_t/(1+r)^t$.

One might also want to take into account variations in the amount of future benefits over the life cycle of a durable good and the cost of credit, if the item were purchased on credit.

INCOME

Income, like time, is a flow concept and must be measured in amount per unit of time. Unlike time, it is comprised of receipts. Economists speak of two types of income: money income, which is the money or purchasing power received by the household per unit of time, and real income, which is the flow of commodities acquired by or available to the household per unit of time.

Money Income

The money income of a household encompasses dollar amounts received by household members from all sources, including earnings, returns on savings and investment, pensions, social security benefits, welfare benefits and other monetary subsidies, gifts, insurance claims, and inheritance. Many households receive income from several sources.

The diversity and irregularity of income sources and respondent concerns about privacy add to the difficulty of obtaining accurate reports of income. Income is probably underreported by many respondents in surveys.

Several alternative forms of the money-income variable are used in statistical analyses.

Before-Tax versus After-Tax Income. Before-tax income is gross income. After-tax income is gross income minus income taxes. If the analysis is concerned with the effect of income size on household expenditures, then after-tax income (if known) is probably the more appropriate measure of money income, since it shows how much income is actually available for consumption. Because of the nature of income tax laws (e.g., progressive tax rates, deductions, and exclusions from taxable income), the distribution of after-tax income is somewhat different from the distribution of before-tax income.

Money Receipts versus Money Plus In-Kind Income. In-kind income is the monetary value (over and above whatever portion of the expense is paid by the household) of home-produced commodities, employee benefits, and government subsidies to households, such as free commodities and subsidized housing or health care. Money plus in-kind income is a more comprehensive measure than money receipts and thus a better indicator of household well-being. Inclusion of noncash income changes the shape of the income distribution somewhat. For example, in 1979, 11 percent of the U.S. population was officially classified as poor; their money income was below the poverty threshold. If the value of in-kind subsidies had been included in income, the poverty rate would have been 6.4 percent (using the market value approach to valuing noncash income) or 8.9 percent (using the poverty budget share approach) (Smeeding, 1982).

Constant Dollar Income. The level of consumer prices changes over time. For many purposes, it is useful to have a measure of household income in which the dollars represent equal purchasing power. To obtain such a measure, we choose a base year and inflate or deflate the incomes in other years to the price level of the base year by dividing current dollar income by the appropriate price index (i.e., the index formed by expressing price level in each other year as a percentage of price level in the base year) and multiplying by 100. Since CPI values for any given period may be regarded as representing the price level for that period, constant dollar income may be computed for any base year.

Discretionary Income. A large share of household expenditures consists of purchases or payments over which the household has little control, at least in the short run. These include rent or mortgage payments and other basic expenditures. The part of income spent on such expenditures is called nondiscretionary and the remainder discretionary income. Discretionary income is of particular interest to marketers.

Estimates of discretionary income and its distribution have been developed by the Conference Board in cooperation with the U.S. Bureau of the Census (Linden, Green & Coder, 1989). To estimate discretionary income, they first grouped households by size, age, and place of residence, factors they regarded as the most important determinants of the household's level of consumption. After-tax income in excess of 130 percent of average expenditures for the household's group was considered to be discretionary. They estimated that 30 percent of all households had discretionary income in 1987. Households with the most discretionary income were likely to have one or more of the following characteristics: be in the 35 to 60 age range, have two or more earners, have some college education, work in a professional or managerial occupation, be members of the white race, live in the suburbs, own their own home, or live on the East or West Coast.

Per Capita or Equivalent Income. Needs of the household vary with household size; therefore, household income is sometimes divided by number in the household to obtain per capita income. While per capita income is a more precise indicator of income adequacy than total household income, it ignores differences in needs associated with age and sex. A better measure could be obtained by dividing total income by the number of members expressed in adult equivalent units. Adult equivalent scales based on food needs (for example, as estimated by the USDA Family Food Plans) are sometimes used for this purpose; however, the validity of using scales based only on food is doubtful, since there is evidence to indicate that other needs are not related to age and sex in the same way as food.

The difference between the distribution of total household income and per capita income can be seen by examining average incomes by size of household. Average after-tax income of one-person households in 1987 was $13,121. The corresponding figure for households of six or more persons was $30,458, more than twice that of the one-person household. Per capita income, however, was only $4,531 for the household of six or more persons, just over a third of the per capita income of the one-person household (Linden, Green & Coder, 1989, p. 26).

Permanent Income. One theory of expenditure determinants is that consumers make decisions about how much of their income to spend on the basis of their permanent income—the income level they expect will continue over a period of years or their lifetime (Friedman, 1957, pp. 25–27). Several approaches to measuring permanent income have been used.

1. Total expenditures. Total expenditures are often used as a proxy for income. The permanent income hypothesis provides a rationale since the permanent level of consumption is hypothesized to be a constant proportion of permanent income. A limitation

is that total expenditures include some expenditures for durables not consumed entirely within the survey period. Therefore, expenditures for major durables are sometimes subtracted from total expenditures in order to construct a closer permanent income proxy (e.g., Britton, 1973).

2. Average expenditures for demographic group. This may be closer to the household's permanent income than current total expenditures, since the effect of durable goods purchases is averaged out. Average expenditure for durables could be taken as an estimate of their use value. (For an example of a study using this method, see Keeler, James & Abdel-Ghany, 1985.)

3. Three-year average income. The respondent may be asked to report the previous year's income and expected income for next year in addition to income for the current year. The average of the three provides an estimate of income over a longer time period than a year and may encompass the relevant time horizon for many families.

Real Income

Real income is the flow of goods and services acquired by the household within a given period of time. Expressed in monetary terms, it is the money value of consumption. Money value of consumption is difficult to measure accurately, and the necessary data are seldom available. Real income can be easily estimated, however, if we make two simplifying assumptions: that the value of consumption is equal to current expenditures and that all income is spent on current consumption. Given those two assumptions, real income is equal to money income. In order to compare real income in different time periods, money income must be expressed in constant dollars.

Poverty Thresholds

The concept of poverty, that is, the condition of having insufficient resources to obtain essential goods and services, is easily understood. But defining it in a way that enables us to agree on which households are in poverty and measure their degree of poverty is not simple. Although most poverty measures have a basis in consumption, many are expressed in terms of income thresholds that differentiate between the poor and nonpoor. Several alternatives are available.

First, should poverty be measured in absolute or relative terms? If, for example, money income is regarded as a measure of poverty, should we regard the lowest 25 percent (for example) of the income distribution as poor, or should we establish a specific income cutoff that is regarded as the minimum amount of income that would enable households to acquire those goods and services deemed essential in that society? The former measure is a relative measure. It has validity in the sense that we regard those with lower incomes as less well off, regardless of the absolute level of their income. Relative measures such as the one cited have a major defect, however: if we adopt a relative measure of poverty, the poor will be, literally, always with us. If we regard the lowest quartile of the population as being poor, we can never make progress in reducing the percentage of the population in poverty. Moreover, most people would not agree that "less well off" means the same as "poor."

Absolute measures are most frequently used to measure poverty, although even absolute measures are relative in the sense that thresholds are set at different levels in different societies, reflecting differing concepts of what constitutes true poverty in the prevailing conditions. Glewwe and Gaag (1988, pp. 5–9) listed several alternatives for measuring poverty, including total or per capita household income, total or per capita household consumption, per capita food consumption, proportion of household budget spent on food, calories consumed as a percentage of the amount recommended, medical indicators of health and nutritional status, and the extent to which the household's basic needs for consumption goods and services are met. Several advantages and limitations of these measures may be noted:

1. Income as a measure of poverty. Data on income are relatively easy to obtain, and the concept comes close to the popular notion of poverty. Moreover, programs designed to eliminate or alleviate poverty frequently use strategies that involve income supplements or helping households earn more income. Income as a poverty measure has several limitations, however. Needs for income vary, depending on the number of persons to be supported and their age, sex, and other characteristics. Using per capita income makes an adjustment for household size but not for other differences. Since the truly poor may differ from the rest of the population on one or more important characteristics, per capita income may be an inaccurate measure of poverty. Equivalence scales, based on the relative consumption needs of individuals of given characteristics, are needed to make an accurate adjustment. There are, however, no generally accepted equivalence scales that take into account all consumption needs. Money income has the further limitation that it does not take into account the value of household production, services provided by owned durables, and other noncash income, and therefore it may misrepresent the poverty status of many households. Variations in prices at which necessary goods and services are available also need to be taken into account.

2. Total consumption as a measure of poverty. Consumption is closely linked to well-being, and use of data on actual consumption to measure poverty eliminates the need to be concerned about prices and how income is actually used by poor households. On the other hand, equivalence scales are needed. Also, data on complete consumption (as opposed to expenditures) are difficult and costly to obtain and usually have substantial error.

3. Food consumption as a measure of poverty. If one accepts the concept of a needs hierarchy and that food is the most basic need, then measures based on food consumption may be interpreted as indicating the degree to which all consumption needs are met, at least for households near the bottom of the income distribution. One can argue that if caloric needs are not fully met or if food absorbs a high proportion of the budget, then most other needs will be largely unmet. Moreover, generally accepted standards of food adequacy that reflect individual food needs are available. Food

deficiencies show up very quickly in young children, which makes their status a good indicator of consumption needs in the entire household. Accurate data on food consumption, either in relation to food needs or as a proportion of the budget, are difficult and expensive to obtain, however. Also, environmental conditions and individual health problems that affect food needs ought to be taken into account in recommendations for food consumption. Finally, a food-deprivation standard of poverty may be too low in affluent countries such as the United States. Some (e.g., Leonard, Dolbeare & Lazere, 1989) have recommended that housing cost burden be used instead of food.

4. Medical data as indicators of poverty. These include height and weight of young children in comparison with norms for their age and sex and various medical tests of nutritional status. Medical data have the major advantage that they come very close to being direct measures of well-being. While the use of income as a measure of well-being requires assumptions or information about prices, commodity availability, household use of income, and many other factors that affect the amount of well-being derived from consumption, medical measures apply to conditions that directly affect well-being. Health is, however, only one aspect of well-being.

5. Basic needs indicators as measures of poverty. The concept of food consumption as a measure of poverty may be broadened to include measures of the adequacy of consumption of other necessities, such as housing, health care, water, sanitation, clothing, and education. Basic needs can be interpreted as forming a hierarchy, for example, minimum needed for survival, minimum needed to maintain health and productivity, and level at which all basic needs are satisfied. Measures of basic needs are likely to take the form of sets of indicators rather than a single measure, which complicates their use. There is little agreement regarding the types of consumption that should be regarded as basic needs and the levels that should be regarded as minimally adequate (Sharif, 1986).

In the United States, income thresholds are used to classify families as poor and nonpoor. The basis used is the cost of the lowest-cost USDA Family Food Plan, multiplied by three. This concept has been used since 1964, with some modifications. Use of the food plan provides some assurance of adequacy, since the plans provide nutritionally adequate diets using commonly eaten foods. The multiplier of three was consistent with a 1955 survey of food consumption, which indicated that families of three or more persons spent about one-third of their income on food. (This proportion has since declined to about one-sixth.) Table 3.3 shows the 1988 poverty thresholds. Separate thresholds are provided for different family sizes and types. The thresholds are increased each year by the same percentage as the annual average CPI.

One of the primary uses of poverty thresholds is to estimate the poverty rate, or the percentage of the population who are poor. It is also used to compute the aggregate and the average income deficit, that is, the amount of additional income that would be required, in total or on the average per poverty-level household, to bring all households up to the poverty threshold—in other words, to eliminate poverty. The ratio of the average income deficit to the poverty threshold income is called the poverty income gap. Measures of the distribution of income among

Table 3.3
Federal Poverty Thresholds, 1988

Size of family unit	Average thresholds
One person (unrelated individual)	$5,478
15 to 64 years	5,597
65 years and over	5,160
Two persons	7,006
Householder 15 to 64 years	7,236
Householder 65 years and over	6,509
Three persons	8,580
Four persons	10,997
Five persons	13,009
Six persons	14,686
Seven persons	16,595
Eight persons	18,442
Nine persons or more	21,947

Source: U.S. Bureau of the Census (1989, p. 127).

the poor are also used as measures of the degree of poverty in the population. An example is the Sen index (Sharif, 1986, p. 559).

The thresholds can be used to compute a variable that can serve as an alternative to income: the welfare index, defined as the ratio of the household's income to the poverty threshold corresponding to its size and type. The welfare index has the advantage that it reflects consumption needs of the household more accurately than total income or even per capita income since it is adjusted for differences in household size and composition. (See, for example, Hurd, 1990, p. 557.)

WEALTH

The economic wealth of households is their possessions—anything they possess that could be sold for money or used to acquire commodities: real property, durable goods, financial assets, and human capital. Households accumulate and maintain wealth for several purposes. Financial assets and physical property are used to maintain the consumption stream over time, especially after retirement. Wealth may be acquired for the purpose of increasing total lifetime consumption, to provide reserve funds for emergencies, or to leave an estate to one's heirs. Since wealth is a stock concept, it is measured at a point in time (unlike income, which is measured over a period of time). We are concerned either with amount of wealth on a given date or in change in wealth (the difference between wealth at two different dates).

Assets and Liabilities of Households

Assets. Assets may be used in different ways by households, depending on their type, especially on their liquidity and whether they are earmarked by the household for some specific purpose. Thus, it is meaningful to examine assets by type.

Households accumulate assets in two ways: by saving out of current income and by increases in the value of owned assets. The household savings rate, calculated as total personal saving divided by disposable personal income, ranged from 8.0 to 4.2 in the period from 1970 to 1988 (U.S. Bureau of the Census [Census], 1990g). Since housing is such an important asset to households (64 percent reported some home equity in 1979), changes in property values are an important source of asset accumulation. For example, from 1972 to 1981, a period in which housing prices increased rapidly, home equity increased from 15.8 percent of total household assets to 19.9 percent.

Debt. Wealth must take into account both the value of property and financial assets owned by the household and household debts. In addition to dollar amounts of debt outstanding, several measures of debt load are used, including the ratio of total consumer debt to disposable income and the ratio of debt to total assets.

Human Capital

The value of human capital is usually measured as educational attainment, although other variables, such as age, experience, and health status, might also be relevant. The value of a college education can be seen in the differences in lifetime earnings between high school and college graduates. College graduates can expect lifetime earnings about 60 percent higher than those of high school graduates. Lifetime earnings are higher even when the cost of the education, including earnings forgone during college, is taken into account (Bryan & Linke, 1988. pp. 3–7).

TIME

Measures of amount of time spent in paid employment are frequently obtained in household surveys, either as number of hours per week or whether employed full or part time. Occasionally information on time spent traveling to and from the job is also obtained. Paid employment time is valued at the amount of pay received per hour on the job.

Although information on hours spent in paid employment is relatively easy to obtain from respondents, the responses may frequently fail to provide accurate information about patterns of time use. Some persons are employed irregularly and may have difficulty describing a normal pattern. If the question is framed in terms of work hours in the previous week, the response may be accurate, but the week may not have been typical. In some types of employment, overtime work (paid or unpaid) is frequent and may be quite variable. Commuting to and from work may also be time-consuming. Lapsed time, that is, amount of time from leaving for work until returning home, is seldom asked for but might be meaningful in some analyses. If lapsed time were used to measure time spent in paid employment, the hourly rate of pay would be substantially lower for some workers than the hourly rate for time actually on the job.

Information on time spent on household activities is more complex to obtain. It may be obtained by asking household members to respond to checklists of activities, keep a log on occasions and amount of time spent on a given activity (such as television viewing), or keep a diary in which they record all activities during a specific time period (Harvey, 1990). If a log or diary is used, the form may be open, allowing the respondent to specify types and grouping of activities, or closed, requiring the respondent to record activities in predetermined categories. The respondent may be asked to record the exact amount of time for each activity or, alternatively, the activity performed in each time segment (e.g., 15 minutes).

Results of a survey of time use will vary with method of data collection used. For that reason, results from different surveys may not be comparable. Type of information about time use varies also. The respondent may be asked to record the amount of time spent on different activities during the day. This amount can then be summed. For example, according to one survey, average number of minutes spent per person per day on free-time activities in Jackson, Michigan, ranged from 221 minutes for an unmarried employed man with a child to 420 minutes for an unemployed man with no child. Time use data can also be collected in the form of number of episodes of each activity. For example, a multinational study showed that the activity for which episodes are most frequent is personal hygiene. Other frequent activities (in order of frequency) are eating, sleeping, preparing food, traveling to and from job, working at a regular job, cleaning house, watching television, marketing, child care, and doing laundry (Harvey, 1990, pp. 315–316).

The form of data most useful for economic analysis is probably total amount of time spent on given activities in a day or week. But consider the nature of the actual situation in households. Household members frequently conduct two or more activities simultaneously (e.g., washing dishes, monitoring children, and listening to the radio). Some activities are performed intermittently (e.g., 10 minutes spent sorting laundry and loading the machine; later, 2 minutes spent putting clothes in dryer; and still later, 15 minutes spent folding and putting away clothes). Uniformity in categorization of activities is difficult to attain. Consider, for example, a simple division of household time into household work time and leisure. Whether an activity should be regarded as work or leisure depends on how burdensome it is, but the burden (what might be termed the psychic cost) of performing a given household activity is affected by time of day performed, where performed, sequence of activities, and the entire social and physical environment of the activity. These aspects of household time use not only affect the accuracy of data but also the validity of measures of cost applied to household time.

The value ascribed to time spent in productive activities in the household is generally arrived at by one of two methods: the market value approach or the opportunity cost approach. If the market value approach is used, household work time is valued at the cost of obtaining an equivalent service from market sources; for example, time spent on food preparation would be valued at the average wage rate for cooks, time spent on child care at the average wage rate for child care providers, and so on. If the opportunity cost approach is used, the hourly rate earned by the individual in paid employment is used as the value of his or her time spent on household work. Both methods yield values that are probably too high in most cases. The opportunity cost approach is based on the implicit assumption that the individual could choose to have more or fewer hours of paid employment, and thus, if he or she chooses to spend an hour on household work, it is because that hour of household work is worth at least as much as what the individual would earn by extending his or her hours of employment. This assumption is seldom true to life. Thus, in most cases, time spent on household work is time in which the individual could not earn money at his or her regular wage rate. The market value approach also appears to overvalue household time. Data on household expenditures provide little evidence that employed wives are more likely to purchase household services that they could themselves provide than are nonemployed wives (Yang & Magrabi, 1989).

INFORMATION

Information is a resource used by consumers. The amount and quality of pertinent information affects the quality of consumer choices. In order to choose the items that will maximize their satisfaction, consumers need information about what products and services are available on the market and their characteristics with respect to use, care, and durability. They also need information about the prices at which a given product is offered and which stores offer the item at the lowest price.

In one sense, information might be thought of as a commodity obtained and used by consumers. The acquisition of information requires inputs of time and (sometimes) market goods and services. The consumer may acquire informational materials and study them at home before shopping. He or she may spend time and money on comparison shopping.

The utility derived from information about products and prices is the increase in utility from making a better choice. If the consumer, through the information he or she obtains, is able to find and purchase an item that has characteristics that yield greater utility than any item he or she might have purchased without the additional information, total utility is increased. If he or she is able to find the desired item at a lower price because of the additional information, then the information has provided utility equal to the value of the money saved. But information is not cost free; the net change in utility after subtracting the cost of information seeking may not be positive.

How much information should the consumer obtain? This question can be analyzed as a problem of estimating consumer demand for information or as decision making under conditions of uncertainty. Consumers wish to maximize satisfaction, subject to constraints on time and money. They must therefore compare the expected amount of additional utility that would be provided per additional units, respectively, of time and money spent in information seeking with the utility of other uses of the marginal units of time and money. Utility will be maximized at the point where the marginal utility per unit cost of additional information seeking exactly equals the marginal utility of using the resources in some other way.

A complication in maximizing the utility from information search is that we usually do not know how much utility we will obtain from additional information. Suppose we want to purchase a washing machine. We go to a department store, look at the models available in that store, and choose one that seems to suit our purpose. Should we purchase it or spend the time and gasoline needed to go to another store to find out whether it offers the same model at a lower price or perhaps a better-quality model at the same price? If another store offers a better buy, it may be worth the expenditure of time and gasoline to find it, but until we search, we do not know whether that better buy exists, or, if it exists, whether the savings are worth the cost of searching. The problem of deciding how much information to obtain is thus an instance of decision making under uncertainty. The best we can do is estimate the expected value (and perhaps the expected cost) of additional information.

NEEDS AND PREFERENCES

We have reviewed the variables, prices and resources, that constrain consumption choices. We now turn to variables that measure the motives for choices, that is, that measure or indicate needs and preferences of the household for consumer goods and services—the variables, in other words, that determine the utility functions of individuals in the household.

Direct Measures

Needs and preferences may be measured directly. We could ask respondents to evaluate alternative commodities and tell which they have a greater need for or which they prefer. Erickson and Johansson (1985), for example, asked respondents to rate a set of products on several attributes in a study to investigate role of price in product evaluations. Barwise and Ehrenberg (1987) asked respondents how much they liked television programs and compared the respondents' answers to their viewing habits. We could ask questions about attitudes in order to obtain more general information about preferences or predict consumption choices (Katona, 1975, pp. 72–77).

Studies of consumer preferences are frequently conducted, especially when the purpose is to assess demand for specific products or product characteristics. Preference studies are of less value when the purpose is to study general patterns of expenditure or consumption. It makes little sense to ask, for example, "Which do you prefer to have, shelter or food?" Attitudes and values of consumers undoubtedly have a substantial effect on their specific purchases, as well as on their allocation of income among shelter, food, and other consumption categories. Attitude surveys, such as surveys of consumer confidence or economic expectations, have exhibited some predictive power with respect to consumer behavior.

Proxy Measures

The most commonly used indicators of the needs and preferences of a household are its demographic characteristics. These are not direct measures but characteristics that have been shown empirically to be correlated with consumption patterns. Although a rationale can usually be given, explaining why such characteristics are associated with differences in consumption pattern, their strongest justification is the empirical evidence.

Household Size. Amounts consumed of many commodities can be expected to increase with household size, although usually not proportionately because greater efficiencies can be realized in larger consumer units than in smaller ones. Larger units are likely also to have greater pressure on their resources because of the need to share them with more members.

Household Composition. Composition refers to the age and sex of each household member and their relationship to each other. Both needs and preferences are likely to vary with these factors. Food needs, for example, change with age. And cultural expectations, which entail certain kinds of consumption behavior, are associated with sex, age, and role in the household.

Stage in Family Life Cycle. Although family life cycle is usually defined in terms of household (or family) composition, it carries the additional implication that families in a given stage have passed through certain other states previously. Since previous acquisitions or experience may influence current choices, family life-cycle stage is a more powerful concept than composition. Stampfl (1978) proposed the concept of consumer life cycle, pointing out that consumption in later stages of the life cycle depends in part on the amount and kind of durables accumulated in earlier stages.

In the United States, many different sequences of family life-cycle stages occur because of the frequency of divorce, remarriage, unmarried parenting, and living together without marriage. For that reason, the interpretation of family types in terms of life cycle must be done with caution.

Education. Consumption behavior is learned. Some of the learning takes place as part of the formal educational experience and much of it, perhaps, through contact with other people.

Racial, Religious, or Ethnic Background. Cultural and religious groups have values and beliefs that influence the consumption practices of their members. Membership in the group may entail participation in rites or festivities that require special foods, clothing, or other commodities.

Employment Status and Occupation of Household Members. This indicator may affect consumption because of requirements for special clothing or other job-related expenses, because it brings the worker into contact with a particular reference group that has expectations about appropriate consumption behavior, and because it may limit the time available for productive activities in the home.

Urbanization. Activities, needs, and the availability of specific products are likely to vary with population density. Automobiles, for example, are a near-necessity for the rural resident but may be an expensive luxury for the consumer living in the inner city of a major metropolitan area. Prices may vary because of differences in distribution and retailing costs.

Geographic Area of Residence. Some consumer needs (for example, for air-conditioning) and the availability of some consumption opportunities (for example, skiing) vary with geographic area. Climate, as a proxy for consumption need, is sometimes measured directly as degree days (the number of days per year the temperature is above or below a given level). Prices of some commodities may vary because of differences in distance to source of supply. Geographic area may also reflect other environmental factors in the natural or the man-made environment that may affect consumption, such as air or water pollution, which may cause health problems requiring medical treatment or use of special products such as air purifiers.

The United States is usually divided into the four regions defined by the Bureau of the Census: West, Midwest, South, and Northeast. An alternative is the U.S. Climate Zone Map (U.S. Department of Energy [DOE], 1989, p. 261), which divides the country into five climate zones based on number of heating degree days and cooling degree days.[1] The coldest zone contains the mountainous parts of Washington, Oregon, Idaho, Nevada, Utah, and Colorado; all of Montana, North Dakota, Minnesota, Wisconsin, Maine, New Hampshire, and Vermont; most of South Dakota, Michigan, and New York; and parts of Iowa, Pennsylvania, and Massachusetts. The hottest zone contains Florida and Mississippi; most of Texas, Oklahoma, Alabama, and Georgia; and parts of California, Nevada, Arkansas, Alabama, and South Carolina.

Housing Tenure and Type of Dwellings. While not a demographic characteristic of households, housing arrangement does have an impact on consumption choices. Size and style of dwelling and whether owned or rented influence needs and preferences for furnishings and services, as well as the activities of household members (which, in turn, also influence their consumption choices). Shelter expenses of home owners are directly affected by whether the home is mortgaged.

ANALYTIC APPROACHES

Description of Consumption Patterns

Consumption pattern refers to the elements or components of consumption (the goods and services consumed) and how they are arranged with respect to each other—that is, the amounts consumed and the time relationship among consumption episodes.

Consumption Categories. Since there are many ways of grouping specific goods and services, part of the description of a consumption pattern consists of specifying categories of goods and services. The commonest way is to group them into categories of commodities that have characteristics in common or serve the same purpose—perhaps into "natural" groups, as described by Lancaster (1971). Such categories generally include food, housing, apparel, transportation, health care, and other specific categories such as education, entertainment, insurance, and personal care. The groupings may be broad (e.g., food) or relatively specific (e.g., fruits, vegetables, or red meats). The number of categories and how items are grouped varies depending on the purpose of the analysis and data constraints.

Another way of grouping items is by degree of need. Consumption items may be categorized as necessities or luxuries. The concept of basic needs is also used to designate a category of goods and services for which need is high.

Since there is so much variation in groupings, readers of reports on consumption pattern need to pay attention to how consumption categories are defined. The interpretation of the results may be affected by the way items are grouped.

Identification of Relationships. The commonest way of displaying relationships among consumption categories is to express amounts consumed in each category (usually measured by expenditure) as a percentage of total expenditures or of income. Income, and hence total expenditures (a function of income), is regarded as a constraint. To the extent that this is true, an increase in consumption in one area must be offset by a decrease in one or more other consumption areas. Sometimes the percentage of income spent on a single category, food, is used to represent the entire consumption pattern, based on the assumption that food is the most basic need. Households that spend a high proportion of their income on food have little left over for other kinds of consumption.

Other statistical methods used to identify consumption pattern include factor analysis and cluster analysis. Both are data reduction methods; they are ways of representing the effect of a large number of variables in a smaller number of constructed variables. Factor analysis is a multivariate technique concerned with the identification of dimensional structure within a set of observed variables, based on the correlations between variables. When data on the consumption behavior of households are used to identify the factors, consumption pattern may be defined in terms of the scores on the factor scales (Kim & Mueller, 1978, pp. 11, 60–73). For example, Uusitalo (1980) used factor analysis to analyze data on goods and services consumed and time use of households in Finland. She identified three dimensions of consumption, which she labeled modernity, mobility, and variosity (the last meaning high spending on recreation, education and culture, a varied diet, and household furniture).

Cluster analysis is a method of grouping observations (in this case, households) into groups, based on their similarity with respect to an array of variables (in this case, consumption variables). Once the households are grouped, cluster membership can be used to indicate pattern of consumption, described as mean values of the variables used as the basis for clustering. Consumption patterns of United States households, as identified through an application of cluster analysis, are described in Chapter 5.

Determinants of Consumption

Many uses of consumption data require the identification of factors that influence the consumption behavior of the household. This is done by measuring the degree of relationship between consumption elements (e.g., expenditure for food or housing) and other variables hypothesized to be determinants of consumption. The relationship measured is one of association rather than cause and effect, which can only be inferred.

A complicating aspect of consumption analysis is that consumption behavior is affected by a number of factors. For this reason, if the purpose is to identify determinants of consumption and not simply to describe the average consumption of different groups, all relevant factors need to be taken into account. To take a simple example, suppose our interest was in discovering whether household food expenditures increase or decrease with the age of the householder. One approach is to classify households into several groups by age and calculate mean expenditures for each. If we did so using data from the 1986 expenditure survey of the Bureau of Labor Statistics, we would find that food expenditures increased from $2,145 for householders under age 25 to $4,675 for ages 45 to 54 and then declined to $1,929 in the 75 and over group. However, average number in the household changes also (1.8, 2.9, and 1.6, respectively). Maybe the change in food expenditures is simply due to changes in the number of people to feed. And income changes also, averaging $12,444, $33,413, and $12,461, respectively, for these three age groups. To discover whether age is associated with expenditures, we need a multivariate analysis in which all three possible explanatory variables are included. The commonest type of analysis is some form of multivariate regression, in which we calculate the coefficients in an equation such as,

$$E = a + b_1X_1 + b_2X_2 + \ldots$$

Degree of relationship between income and expenditures is often measured by the income elasticity of the expenditure. By elasticity, we mean the ratio of percentage change in one variable to percentage change in another. Income elasticity is the ratio of percentage change in expenditure to percentage change in income. We can also measure the price elasticity of expenditure with respect to changes in its own price (own-price elasticity) or to changes in the price of another commodity (cross-price elasticity). The elasticity of expenditure with respect to household size or education is also sometimes measured.

Several methods are used for computing elasticity. A simple method is to calculate arc elasticity, where change in expenditure is calculated as the difference between two expenditure levels ($E_1 - E_2$) expressed as a percentage of the mean expenditure (($E_1 + E_2)/2$) and change in income is calculated in the same way:

$$e = [(E_1 - E_2)/(E_1 + E_2)]/[(Y_1 - Y_2)/(Y_1 + Y_2)].$$

Arc elasticity can also be calculated from regression results. The b coefficient represents the slope of the regression line (($E_1 - E_2)/(Y_1 - Y_2)$) and the actual means of E and Y may be used ($E^\sim$ and $Y^\sim$); thus, the arc elasticity would be

$$e = b(Y^\sim/E^\sim).$$

Arc elasticity shows elasticity within a given range in which the relationship is assumed to be a straight line. More often, the relationship between expenditures and other variables cannot be accurately represented by a straight line. Constant elasticity, the *b* coefficient when both income and expenditures are expressed in logarithmic form, is a way of dealing with that problem.

Elasticities are generally described as unit elastic (elasticity equal to one, meaning that a 1 percent change in one factor is accompanied by a 1 percent change in the other), relatively inelastic (an elasticity of between zero and one in absolute value), and relatively elastic (an elasticity greater than one in absolute value).

Commodities are sometimes categorized on the basis of their income elasticity. A commodity with an income elasticity greater than zero is normal; one with a negative elasticity is inferior. Necessities are sometimes defined as commodities with an income elasticity less than one, while luxuries have elasticity greater than one.

Price elasticities may be positive or negative. Own-price elasticities are generally negative; cross-price elasticities may be either positive or negative. Sun (1982), for example, estimated that the own-price elasticity of beef frankfurters was -2.3, while the cross-price elasticity of demand for beef frankfurters with respect to the price of poultry frankfurters was 4.3.

Estimating Response to Change and Future Trends

The simplest form of consumption prediction is to assume that existing patterns or previous trends will continue. That assumption is justified, however, only if the factors that influence consumption do not change. If real income rises, previous experience indicates that households will increase their consumption and probably change the pattern somewhat. Changes in other factors are likely also to result in changes from the previous pattern or deviations from a straight-line projection from previous trends. A solution is to estimate consumption using a multivariate model in which coefficients are estimated from previous periods, assumptions are made about the direction and rate of change in explanatory variables, and equations in the model are solved for future points in time. In effect, one first develops projections for each of the explanatory variables and then uses those projections to estimate the consumption variable.

Such predictions are often useful but may have limited accuracy for several reasons. Some pertinent explanatory variables may be omitted because they had not been identified as factors influencing consumption, because data were lacking, or because reliable estimates of the relationship were lacking. The assumptions about explanatory variables may not be realized.

A limitation that deserves special note is what is sometimes called the cohort effect, which can result in misleading results when predictions are made on the basis of cross-sectional rather than longitudinal data. For example, if we want to estimate the impact of a rise in income on expenditures, we might use income elasticity; however, if the elasticity was calculated from cross-sectional data (as is almost always the case), then we are comparing two different groups of consumers. We do not have data on how a given group of consumers would change their expenditures if their income changed.

The cohort effect is the effect of their previous history on the behavior of members of a given cohort. For example, 1988 expenditure data show that elderly households spend less, on the average, on shelter than do younger households, largely because a larger percentage of them are living in owned, mortgage-free homes. Should we then expect that today's consumers will have low housing expenses when they are elderly? The elderly households of 1988 purchased their homes in a period of relatively low housing prices and low-interest mortgages. Today's consumers may lack that opportunity and hence not enjoy low-cost housing during retirement.

NOTE

1. A heating degree day is "a measure of how cold a location was over a period of time, relative to a base temperature" and is calculated by subtracting average daily temperature (the mean of the maximum and minimum temperature in a 24-hour period) from 65 degrees in each day when the average daily temperature fell below that level and summing over the year. Cooling-degree days is a measure of how hot a location was and is calculated similarly, in terms of days in which the average daily temperature was above 65 degrees (DOE, 1989, pp. 277–278, 281).

Part II

Patterns and Trends in
Household Consumption

4

Household Consumption of Commodities in the United States

This chapter examines commodity groups in some detail, identifying consumption trends, patterns, and determinants. It provides a basis of information for Chapter 5, in which we look at selected population groups.

The framework used is the one presented in Chapter 1. Each commodity section is divided into two main subsections. In the first subsection, we present information on amounts consumed, sources from which the commodity is obtained, expenditures, prices, and, in some cases, government assistance programs. We also describe some of the variation that exists in consumption patterns among population groups. In the second subsection, we discuss the well-being of American households as it is affected by consumption of the commodity.

The consumption process includes not only acquisition and use but also the disposal of consumption residues. The final section of the chapter therefore is concerned with the disposal of household waste, mainly solid waste.

This attempt to provide a comprehensive picture of commodity consumption in the United States is an ambitious one. In pursuing it, we have relied to the extent possible on national data collected by agencies of the federal government and on analyses of these data, usually drawn from published sources but in some cases from our own analyses. Thus, the data, except where noted, are representative of the United States as a whole. Unless otherwise noted, all data are from public use tapes of the 1988 Survey of Consumer Expenditures, the most recent source of data available at the time this book is written.

There are many gaps and thin places in our coverage, especially of acquisition and use, as distinguished from expenditure, and of impacts on well-being. This partly reflects lack of published data. One useful result of our summary may be to make these gaps apparent. Our focus, however, was on providing as complete a picture as possible.

FOOD

Consumption Patterns and Trends

Acquisition, Selection, and Use. Food is a frequent purchase for most house-holds. A 1980–1981 study showed that 92 percent of all households purchased some food during a one-week period. Most likely to be purchased were cereals, bakery products, and dairy products. Seventy-eight percent of the households purchased items in one or more of those categories during the week; 75 percent purchased meat, poultry, fish, or eggs, 67 percent purchased fruits, 64 percent purchased vegetables, 61 percent purchased nonalcoholic beverages, and 40 percent purchased alcoholic beverages (Dunham, 1987, p. 27).

Children in the United States eat with other household members on most of their eating occasions. A 1977–1978 survey showed that 71 percent of the eating occasions for children aged 6 to 8 were shared with other household members, and on only 11 percent of the occasions did the children eat alone. Adults, on the other hand, shared only about half of their eating occasions with other household members and were alone in nearly one-third of those occasions (Evans & Cronin, 1986).

Eating out is frequent, especially among school-aged children (who eat lunches at school), single persons living alone, and households with an employed female head; however, frequency of eating out declines with age (Morgan, 1988). About 75 percent of children and teenagers reported eating some meals and snacks away from home. Where food was eaten away from home varied with age and sex. Among adults, nearly two-thirds of the eating-out occasions were at work or in a restaurant; among children aged 6 to 8, eating out was mostly at school (58 percent) or in someone else's home (19 percent); among teenagers, although school was still the most frequent place of eating out, fast food establishments accounted for more occasions than eating in someone else's home (Evans & Cronin, 1986).

Sixty-four percent of all individuals reported eating three meals a day. Of those who ate only two meals, 46 percent skipped breakfast and 28 percent skipped lunch. Skipping breakfast was not common among children but increased during the teenage years, especially among girls. About 30 percent of teenage girls reported skipping breakfast at least once during a three-day period (Evans & Cronin, 1986). A 1985 survey showed that slightly over half of all adults eat breakfast daily. About one-fourth rarely eat breakfast. Frequency of eating break-fast increases with age (National Center for Health Statistics [NCHS], 1988, p. 31).

Snacking was common at all ages. About 75 percent of all individuals reported snacking in the 1977–1978 study. Snacks provided significant amounts of the total calories consumed by the individual (16 percent for adults, 21 percent for teenagers, 18 percent for younger school-age children). Popular snacks for teen-agers, in decreasing order of importance, were soft drinks, bakery products, milk or milk desserts, salty snacks, fruits, meat, candy, and bread, but frequencies varied with age and sex. About three-fourths of the boys and girls aged 15 to 18 consumed soft drinks at least once during a three-day period. The percentage was slightly lower for children (65 percent of those aged 6 to 8) and adults (53 percent of males and 57 percent of females) (Evans & Cronin, 1986).

Changes have occurred during the past couple of decades in the kinds and amounts of foods consumed by Americans. Among the reasons for the changes are changes in relative prices, which, for example, accounted for much of the shift from beef and veal to pork from 1976 to 1988, and health concerns, illustrated in the shift from whole to low-fat milk (Putnam, 1989).

The greatest change in per capita consumption of food at home has been increases in the consumption of poultry, fish, and shellfish and a decline in per capita consumption of beef (which by 1988 had declined to 24 percent of the consumption high point in 1976). Other trends included a shift from processed to fresh noncitrus fruits, increased consumption of frozen and dried fruit, increases in consumption of fresh or frozen vegetables and a decline in canned vegetables (although 84 percent of all processed vegetables in 1984 were canned), and increased consumption of flour and cereal products (especially pasta, cornmeal, rice, and breakfast cereals) (Putnam, 1989).

Consumption of nonalcoholic beverages remained relatively stable during the 1970s and 1980s, although the composition of consumption changed as soft drinks were substituted for milk and coffee. Per capita consumption of fruit juices, especially noncitrus juices, increased, as did the consumption of bottled water. Consumption of low calorie beverages, such as diet soft drinks and light beers, increased (Bunch & Kurland, 1984).

The most frequently consumed items, eaten by more than half of the respondents in the 1977–1978 Nationwide Survey of Household Food Consumption in a three-day period, were meat, bread, milk, eggs, potatoes, lettuce, coffee, and soft drinks. The consumption of many foods was concentrated in a relatively small part of the population. These include dietary soft drinks, turkey, candy, hamburgers and cheeseburgers, pasta, peanut butter, and rice (Gallo, 1983).

Use of prepared and convenience foods increased. Data from the 1977–1978 survey indicate that approximately 45 percent of spending for food at home was for convenience foods—those for which "preparation time, culinary skills, or energy inputs have been transferred from the home kitchen to the food processor and distributor" (Havlicek, Axelson, Capps, Pearson & Richardson: 1982). The most frequently used items classified in the USDA survey as convenience foods were bread, instant coffee, frozen orange juice concentrate, cheddar or American cheese, soft margarine, mayonnaise, peanut butter, cola-type soft drinks, ice cream, canned green beans or peas, frankfurters, bologna, corn flakes, catsup, and jelly. The most frequently used nonconvenience foods were milk, sugar, eggs, fresh vegetables (white potatoes, lettuce, tomatoes, onions, carrots, celery, cabbage, cucumbers), fresh fruits (apples, bananas, oranges), meats (bacon, chicken, ground beef), tea, coffee, flour, cottage cheese, butter, fats and oils, macaroni, and rice (Richardson, Pearson & Capps, 1985). The household with high expenditures for prepared foods is likely to have one or more of the following characteristics: high income, employed wife, older wife, older children, white, living in the Northeast region of the country, or living in an urban area (Redman, 1980).

Purchase of take-out food has risen rapidly—by 62 percent from 1983 to 1986. According to the Food Marketing Institute, about 80 percent of all households purchased some take-out food during a four-week period in 1987. Most of the expenditures were made in restaurants, especially pizza parlors and fast food or ethnic restaurants, but about one third of take-out food expenditures were in food stores (Price, 1988).

The proportion of households engaging in home food production has declined (from about three-fourths in 1964 to two-thirds in 1976) but is still a common activity among households that eat half or more of their meals at home. The most commonly produced foods were tomatoes, potatoes, and other vegetables and fruits. About one-fourth of the households caught fish for home consumption and 7 percent produced eggs, milk, or meat. The proportion producing food for home use increased with income. It was most frequent in the North Central region and least frequent in the Northeast (Hatfield, 1981). The profile of those most likely to produce food at home is: older, larger household, higher education, own their own homes, and live in the country rather than in an urban area (Volker & Winter, 1989). Households that produced food at home spent less on food (Volker, Winter & Beutler, 1983).

The majority of households (according to the 1977–1978 food consumption survey) do some food preservation. About 55 percent reported freezing food; about 35 percent did some canning. Home freezing or canning was somewhat more frequent in the North Central and southern regions and in higher-income groups (Hatfield, 1981).

Quantity of food consumed by Americans increased slightly during the 1970s and early 1980s. Gallo and Connor (1982) attributed increases in average consumption and changes in the composition of food consumption to changes in household income, including increases in food stamps and other welfare subsidies that redistribute income to the poor; family size and age distribution; prices of foods relative to all other consumer budget items; advertising of food relative to all other consumer budget items; race or ethnic composition of the population; nutrition attitudes; and amount of food waste.

Expenditure Patterns. Like other commodities, the price of food has tended to rise. In 1988, the CPI for food stood at 118.2, 18 percent higher than in the 1982–1984 base period (U.S. House of Representatives, 1990, Table C-59). The price index for food away was higher (121.8) than the index for food at home (116.6).

Annual increases in the price index for food at home have generally been lower than increases in the all-items index, except for the 1972–1980 period, when the price index for food at home was higher than the all-items index. The

Figure 4.1
Budget Share Spent for Food, 1901–1987

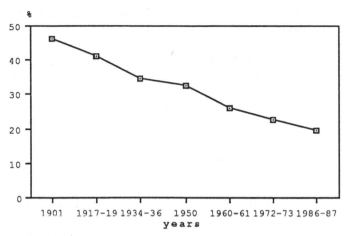

Source: Jacobs & Shipp (1990, p. 22).

price index for food eaten away from home has generally been higher than the index for food at home or the all-items index (U.S. House of Representatives, 1990, Table C-58).

Households vary in the prices they pay for food and the amount of nutrients they obtain per dollar expenditure. When average prices paid for 425 foods were compared, the cost of food per person was found to decrease with household number. One-person households, on the average, paid prices that were 9 percent higher per person than did households with six or more persons. The greatest difference was found in prices paid for potatoes and bakery products (Ritzmann, 1982).

In 1988, food accounted for 11.8 percent of after-tax income (Blaylock, Elitzak & Manchester, 1989). Food has steadily declined as a percentage of income. In 1950, food comprised 22.2 percent of personal disposable income (PDI); in 1985 it was 15.0 percent. All of this decline came in food at home, which in 1950 was 17.6 percent of PDI and by 1985 had declined to 10.4 percent. Spending for food away from home remained relatively stable at values ranging from 3.9 to 4.8 percent of PDI (Dunham, 1986).

Similar trends are evident in data from expenditure surveys of urban wage earner and clerical consumer units (Figure 4.1). In 1901, food and alcoholic beverages comprised 46 percent of the current consumption expenditures of the consumer units surveyed. By 1986–1987, the percentage had declined to 19 percent.

In comparison with other countries, U.S. households spend the smallest share of their income (11 percent in 1984) on food. Comparable figures for other countries in 1984 ranged from 61.6 percent in Niger to 13.4 percent in Canada (Korb, 1987).

The trend toward eating out can be seen in the distribution of food expenditures between food away and food at home. In 1965, spending for food eaten away from home was 30 percent of total food spending; in 1988 it was 45 percent (Blaylock et al., 1989). Much of the increase came in the patronage of fast food restaurants, which accounted for 5 percent of food-away-from-home sales in 1958 and 32 percent in 1985 (*National Food Review*, 1987). In terms of quantity of food consumed, change was not so dramatic. In 1965, food eaten away from home constituted 24 percent of the total quantity purchased; in 1988 it was 43 percent (Blaylock et al., 1989).

Food expenditures vary with income and other household characteristics. Table 4.1 shows mean expenditures for food in 1988 and the distribution of the food budget among food groups according to income quintile. Families in the highest income quintile spent a much larger share of their food budget (49 percent) on food away from home than did households in the lowest quintile (32 percent). Higher-income households allocated a larger share of their food-at-home budget to bakery products, beef, fish and seafood, dairy products other than fresh milk and cream, and sugar and other sweets and a lower proportion to cereals and cereal products, pork, eggs, fresh milk and cream, fresh and processed vegetables, processed fruits, and fats and oils. Food budget share for cereals and bakery products and fruits and vegetables tended to increase with age, while share for dairy products tended to decline (Dunham, 1987).

The allocation of the food budget among food groups varies by characteristics of the household. Households in the western region of the United States have tended to allocate a higher proportion of their food budget to fruits than those in other regions. Compared with white households, black households allocated lower proportions to vegetables, fruits, and bread; households of Spanish origin allocated higher proportions to lower-cost meats, eggs, beans, nuts, cereals, rice, and pasta and lower proportions to vegetables and mixtures, condiments, and bakery products. Households with higher per capita income spent a higher proportion on beverages and a lower proportion on all other food groups except lower-cost meats. Consumption of cereals, rice, pasta, milk, and cheese increases with household size, while consumption of vegetables, fruits, higher-cost meats, eggs, beans, nuts, fats and oils, and beverages decreases (Morgan, 1988).

A regression analysis of 1986 and 1987 expenditure data indicated that food expenditures are related to several other characteristics of the household:

Total household expenditures. When other factors were held constant, expenditures for food, both at home and away, increased as the total expenditures of the household increased. However, as total expenditures increased, food at home declined as a proportion of total expenditures, but the budget share for food away increased. Total expenditures is often used as a proxy for permanent income; thus, the above relationships with total expenditures can be interpreted as a reflection of the relationship between

Table 4.1
Food Expenditures, 1988

	All Consumer Units	Income quintile				
		Lowest 20%	2nd 20%	3rd 20%	4th 20%	Highest 20%
Food (total)	3,748	1,950	2,815	3,545	4,633	6,071
Food at home	2,136	1,322	1,831	2,074	2,570	3,084
Cereals and bakery products	312	194	269	303	371	447
Cereals & cereal products	109	73	103	107	131	142
Bakery products	203	121	167	196	240	305
Meats, poultry, fish, & eggs	551	347	499	521	636	795
Beef	182	96	169	180	217	256
Pork	110	82	104	107	123	155
Other meats	82	52	72	77	97	120
Poultry	84	55	71	80	91	130
Fish and seafood	65	40	55	50	77	104
Eggs	28	23	28	28	30	30

Table 4.1 (continued)

	All Consumer Units	Income quintile				
		Lowest 20%	2nd 20%	3rd 20%	4th 20%	Highest 20%
Dairy products	274	164	234	272	337	381
Fresh milk and cream	134	91	124	133	156	168
Other dairy products	141	73	110	139	181	214
Fruits and vegetables	373	247	323	352	442	517
Fresh fruits	121	76	102	112	145	170
Fresh vegetables	110	78	99	104	121	151
Processed fruits	85	56	74	79	104	121
Processed vegetables	57	38	48	57	72	75
Other food at home	625	370	505	625	784	942
Sugar & other sweets	78	45	67	75	100	116
Fats and oils	55	37	48	58	68	72
Miscellaneous foods	264	153	210	270	334	397
Nonalcoholic beverages	199	125	167	202	239	288
Food prepared on trips	30	10	13	21	42	69
Food away from home	1,612	628	984	1,471	2,063	2,987

Source: U.S. Bureau of Labor Statistics (1990).

income and food. Income elasticity is about 0.48 (Abdel-Ghany & Foster, 1982); thus, we can conclude that food at home is a necessity. Food away is more income elastic than food at home, although the elasticity of food away is not high enough to put it clearly in the luxury category. As income rises, households spend more on food away—perhaps because they eat out more frequently or perhaps because they purchase higher-cost meals when they eat out. But households at all income levels do some eating out. The income elasticity of food varies by life-cycle stage. Blanciforti (1981) found an income elasticity per adult equivalent expenditure on food of .05. Elasticities ranged from − .009 for single consumers and other unmarried households to .101 in households with children whose average age was 12 to 17 years. Blanciforti also calculated separate income elasticities for foods that are relatively more nutritious and those relatively less nutritious.[1] Expenditures in the relatively more nutritious food group were most income elastic among families with no children present and wife over 40 years old.

- Age. Food-at-home expenditures were relatively low among young and old households and were the highest among households with householder aged 45 to 54, when other factors were held constant. Share of the total budget spent for food at home generally increased with age of householder. However, there was no relationship between age and amount spent on food away when the effect of income, household size, and other factors was controlled.

- Household size. Both dollar expenditures and budget share for food at home rose with increases in household size, but the reverse was true for food away. The size elasticity for food at home was substantially less than one, suggesting significant economies of scale.

- Education. The level of education of the householder was not related to dollar expenditures for food, either for food at home or food away; however, the budget share for food at home was negatively and the share for food away was positively related to education.

- Race. Black households had lower expenditures for food, both at home and away, than other households, but the budget share for food at home was higher and that for food away was lower.

- Employment and occupation. Other factors being equal, budget share for food at home was lower in households with an employed householder than in households in which the householder was unemployed or retired, while the share for food away tended to be higher.

Food away from home has a different expenditure pattern from food at home. Results from an analysis of data from the 1977–1978 Nationwide Food Consumption Survey (McCracken & Brandt, 1990) suggest the following profile for the household with high expenditures for food away from home: high income, high estimated value of time, white race, smaller household, and a household composition that includes an adult male and teenage children.

Convenience foods form a substantial share of total food consumption. About 45 percent of expenditures for food at home was spent on convenience foods in 1977–1978. Nearly one-fifth of expenditures for food at home was spent on complex convenience foods (multi-ingredient mixtures that save time, energy, and/or culinary expertise, such as cake mixes or frozen entrees) and an additional 7 percent on convenience foods, such as soft drinks and ready-to-eat breakfast cereals, that have no home-prepared counterpart. Nonconvenience foods—fresh or unprocessed foods, ingredients, and home-produced or home-preserved foods—comprised about 55 percent of food costs (Morgan, 1988).

Changes in the age distribution and growth in real income are expected to be reflected in per capita food spending. Population projections indicate that median age will increase from about 31 years in 1983 to about 36 years by the year 2000 and to nearly 41 years by 2030. The percentage of the population aged 65 and older is expected to increase from 12.3 in 1980 to 27.3 in 2050. According to a projection by Blaylock and Smallwood (1986), these changes in age distribution will result in an increase in per capita food spending of 1.2 percent by the year 2000, compared with spending in 1980. The composition of food spending will also change as age distribution changes. Spending for food away from home and alcoholic beverages is expected to decline. Increases are expected in spending for food at home, with the greatest increases in margarine, pork, poultry, fresh vegetables and fruits, and eggs.

Increases in real income will also result in higher food spending. Blaylock and Smallwood, assuming a 2 percent annual increase in real income, projected that per capita food spending in the year 2000 will be about 16 percent higher than in 1980, with most of the increase in food away (expected to increase by nearly 28 percent). Higher incomes will also change the distribution of spending for food at home, with the greatest increases in spending for alcoholic beverages (projected to increase by 29 percent), fish, butter, beef, processed fruits and vegetables, and dairy products other than milk, cream, and cheese. Spending on eggs will slightly decline, and only slight increases will be expected for milk and cream, margarine, and poultry.

Combining the effects of an aging population and increased income, increases in spending for food away and alcoholic beverages would be expected to exceed increases in food at home. The greatest increases in spending for food at home are expected in fish, butter, fresh vegetables and fruits, and cheese.

Food Assistance Programs. A number of programs have been established to assist needy persons to obtain an adequate diet.

- Food Stamp Program. This federal program provided assistance to an average of 18.7 million persons per month in 1988 (Matsumoto & Smith, 1989, p. 34). Families are eligible to receive food stamps if their income is less than 130 percent of the poverty threshold. Eligible families may receive food stamps equal to the cost of the USDA Thrifty Food Plan (Table 4.2). The stamps may be used to purchase foods in the grocery store (U.S. Department of Agriculture [USDA], 1988).

- Child nutrition programs. The National School Lunch Program helps pay the costs of serving school lunches. In 1988, about 24 million children participated in this program, and over 3.7 million participated in the School Breakfast Program. About 10 million children received free lunches in 1988. Assistance is also provided through the Child

Table 4.2
USDA Family Food Plans

Sex-age group	Cost for 1 week				Cost for 1 month			
	Thrifty plan	Low-cost plan	Moderate-cost plan	Liberal plan	Thrifty plan	Low-cost plan	Moderate-cost plan	Liberal plan
FAMILIES								
Families of 2:								
20-50 years	$41.20	$52.10	$64.60	$80.40	$178.60	$226.10	$279.90	$348.30
51 years and over	39.00	50.20	62.00	74.40	169.50	217.10	268.70	322.40
Family of 4:								
Couple, 20-50 years & children—								
1-2 and 3-5 years	60.00	74.90	91.80	113.00	259.80	324.90	398.10	489.90
6-8 and 9-11 years	68.80	88.20	110.70	133.60	298.10	382.00	479.40	578.60
INDIVIDUALS								
Child:								
1-2 years	10.80	13.10	15.30	18.50	46.80	57.00	66.40	80.40
3-5 years	11.70	14.40	17.80	21.40	50.60	62.40	77.20	92.90
6-8 years	14.30	19.10	24.00	28.00	62.00	82.60	103.80	121.30
9-11 years	17.00	21.70	28.00	32.50	73.70	93.90	121.10	140.70
Male:								
12-14 years	17.70	24.60	30.80	36.20	76.80	106.60	133.50	156.70
15-19 years	18.40	25.50	31.60	36.80	79.80	110.30	137.10	159.30
20-50 years	19.70	25.20	31.70	38.40	85.40	109.30	137.40	166.40
51 years and over	17.90	24.00	29.60	35.60	77.80	104.00	128.40	154.30
Female:								
12-19 years	17.70	21.30	25.90	31.30	76.70	92.10	112.00	135.80
20-50 years	17.80	22.20	27.00	34.70	77.00	96.20	117.10	150.20
51 years and over	17.60	21.60	26.80	32.00	76.30	93.40	115.90	138.80

Source: Family Economics Review (1988, p. 22).

Care Food Program (serving about 1.3 million children per month in 1988) (Matsumoto & Smith, 1989, p. 35).

* Other food assistance. Food supplements to low-income women and children are provided through the Special Supplemental Food Program for Women, Infants, and Children (WIC), which provided high-nutrition food supplements to about 3.6 million participants per month in 1988, and the Commodity Supplemental Food Program, which serves the same clientele as WIC but was available in only 12 states and the District of Columbia and served 165,000 persons per month in 1988. The Nutrition Program for the Elderly served about 800,000 participants per month. Other programs, including the Food Distribution Program on Indian Reservations (140,000 per month in 1985) and the Elderly Feeding Pilot Project (USDA, 1988), served a few thousand participants each.

Only a fraction of those eligible for food assistance from government programs actually receive it, as we can see by comparing the participation rates just cited with the number in poverty: 32 million, about 20 percent of them children (U.S. Bureau of the Census [Census], 1990g, p. 460). Many families are deterred from applying for assistance by the embarrassment or difficulties in applying. The waiting period after application for food stamps reduces the percentage of those eligible who are receiving food stamps at any given time. Insufficient funding has also prevented some programs from serving all of those eligible.

Food assistance to the needy is also provided from many private sources. Such assistance is important as a means of tiding families over until more permanent help can be obtained, providing assistance to hungry persons not eligible for government programs, and feeding the homeless, who lack the means to receive and use food stamps or commodities. Raab, Holyoak, and Raff (1988) provided a profile of the users of emergency food assistance in Oregon in 1986. They found that users of emergency food assistance had lower education than average. Size of household was larger than average—3.3 persons, compared with 2.6 for the state as a whole. They also tended to be young. Forty-nine percent were aged 18 or younger, and only 3 percent were aged 60 or over, compared with 27 and 16 percent, respectively, in the state as a whole. Thirty-eight percent of the household members in emergency-food-user families were under the age of 13. Home ownership was lower than average but not zero. Ten percent of the emergency food users were home owners, compared with 60 percent in the general population of the state. Six percent were homeless. Many of the recipients lacked some facilities: a heat source (12 percent), indoor plumbing (11 percent), a refrigerator (7 percent), running water (6 percent), or a cook stove (5 percent).

Many of the emergency-food-user households included members in poor health (29 percent), a pregnant woman (9 percent), or a handicapped member (23 percent). Half of the households had no health insurance, and over half (64 percent) had unpaid bills for health care. Nearly three-fourths (71 percent) reported delaying needed health care.

Not all the emergency food users were without income. Nineteen percent of the households had a member employed full time, and 15 percent had a member employed part time. Nearly half of the households (48 percent) reported that they had a member looking for work; 21 percent said they could not work because they had no child care.

Impact on Well-being

Types of Impacts. Consuming food to satisfy hunger gives a feeling of comfort, and satisfying the palate gives positive pleasure. Aside from this, three important impacts can be identified: on health and safety, on the quality of human resources, and on the realization of social values.

Food safety has a serious impact on health. A common cause of death, especially in developing countries, is diarrhea. Diarrheal infections and parasites, in many cases associated with poor food sanitation, account for 17 percent of all deaths in developing countries and 1 percent of deaths in developed countries (Chandler, 1984, p. 6). Other concerns about food safety relate to the safety of food ingredients (such as artificial sweeteners), food additives (such as preservatives), and contaminants and residues (such as pesticide residues in fruits and vegetables and antibiotic and hormone residues in poultry and livestock products).

Nutrition affects the general health status of individuals. Some health conditions (e.g., goiter) are directly linked to nutrient deficiencies. Improper nutrition may make the individual more vulnerable to disease. Cardiovascular disease, cancer, and diabetes, for example, have been linked to quantities and kinds of foods eaten. Overconsumption of food as well as underconsumption causes problems (National Center for Health Statistics, 1990, p. 174).

Inadequate intake of food energy and poor health may result in loss of work time and reduced productivity on the job. This link between nutrition and productivity is recognized by the practice, in very poor households, of giving priority to the food needs of the breadwinner. Studies in developing countries have provided evidence of significant linkages between nutrition and the productivity and earnings of agricultural workers (Popkin, 1978; Behrman, Deolalikar, & Wolfe, 1988; Jolly, 1988).

No biological link has been found between poor nutrition and reduced fertility of women, but some authors (e.g., Behrman, Deolalikar & Wolfe) believe that there is an indirect link by changes in behavior accompanying better nutrition. There is substantial evidence linking the nutritional state of the mother to the physical status of the infant (Rhodes, 1979).

The nutritional status of infants and small children has been linked to their physical and mental development. Severe malnutrition is related to lower intelligence, behavioral changes (e.g., shorter attention span and lower motivation), and reduced learning ability (*Dairy Council Digest*, 1973, 1979; Selowsky & Taylor, 1973; Cravioto, 1979). Nutritional status is linked to educational attainment, which, in turn, is linked to earnings (Popkin & Lim-Ybanez, 1982; Behrman et al., 1988; Boissiere, Knight & Sabot, 1985).

Food plays an integral part in social life. We express social role and status through the foods we consume and the foods we avoid. The offering of food to guests and the kind of food offered are ways of offering hospitality and displaying social status. Specific rituals and cultural events often have specific foods associated with them—for example, the Thanksgiving turkey. The ability to obtain and consume foods appropriate to role, status, and occasion contributes significantly to well-being.

Standards. The Recommended Dietary Allowances (RDAs) are generally used as standards of nutritional adequacy of food. (See Chapter 3.) Median heights and weights and recommended energy intake are also provided (National Research Council, 1989, p. 33).

Percentage of income spent on food is used as an indicator of well-being, but the choice of percentage is arbitrary. Lipton, for example, commented that "even the poorest people seem to spend an irreducible minimum, about 20 percent, on nonfood. People who spend 80 percent or more on food, yet fulfill less than 80 percent of average calorie requirements for their age, sex and activity groups, are probably both hungry and undernourished [and may be termed] ultra-poor" (1988, p. 8).

Nutritional Adequacy and Safety of Food Consumption. Many Americans are concerned about food safety. A 1988 survey in four states indicated that about one-fourth of the respondents believed they had experienced some form of food poisoning. Over half said they had reduced their consumption of some foods because of safety concerns (Smallwood, 1989). Concerns about the safety and nutritional quality of food have led to the increasing popularity of natural foods, which "cannot contain synthetic or artificial ingredients and can only be minimally processed" (Price, 1985, p. 14).

The majority of Americans consume nutritious diets; however, about one-fourth are overweight (NCHS, 1989, p. 76). Pao and Mickle (1981) studied mean intakes of food energy, protein, four minerals (calcium, iron, magnesium, and phosphorus), and seven vitamins (vitamin A, thiamin, riboflavin, preformed niacin, and vitamins B6, B12, and C) using data from the 1977–1978 Nationwide Food Consumption Survey. They regarded intakes of less than 70 percent of the RDA as inadequate. Using this criterion, they identified four problem nutrients: calcium, iron, magnesium, and vitamin B6. Adequacy varied by age and sex. Average intake of calcium was low for females over age 12, especially those aged 15 to 18 and 35 to 64. Iron intakes were low among children aged 1 to 2 years and females aged 12 to 50. Magnesium intake was especially low among females aged 15 to 22. Vitamin B6 was especially low among females over age 14 and elderly males (age 75 and over).

Nutritional adequacy of diets varied by factors other than age and sex:

- Region. The South had a higher proportion of people consuming diets inadequate with respect to calcium, iron, magnesium, and vitamins A, B6, and C.
- Urbanization. Deficiencies in calcium and magnesium were most frequent in central

cities, deficiencies in iron were most frequent in suburban areas, and deficiencies in vitamins A, B6, and C were most frequent in metropolitan areas.

- Race. Deficiencies were more frequent among blacks than whites.
- Income. Low intakes of all nutrients but iron were more frequent in low-income than in high-income groups.
- Food Stamp Program participation. Nutritional adequacy of diets was higher among those receiving food stamps than among those eligible but not receiving food stamps (Allen & Gadson, 1984).
- Eating out. Nutrient intake averages are lower among those who eat meals away from home. This was especially true of those over age 60 (Bunch, 1984).

In summary, lower than recommended intakes of calcium and iron are typical of many women. Men, for whom the RDAs are lower for these nutrients, generally have diets close to or even exceeding the RDA for calcium and greatly exceeding the RDA for iron. Calcium intake tends to be higher for whites than blacks and for the employed than the unemployed; increase with income, education, and urbanization; and be the highest in the Midwest.

In addition to the RDAs, the Department of Health and Human Services has issued dietary guidelines related to the consumption of fat, sweeteners, and other food components. An analysis of data from the 1977–1978 Nationwide Survey of Household Food Consumption indicates that, on the average, American men and women get about 40 percent of their calories from fat. The average percentage of calories from fat was slightly higher for men than for women, was less than 40 percent for children, and increased slightly with age. About 17 percent of women aged 35 to 50 obtained less than 35 percent of their calories from fat but only about 13 percent of men (Evans & Cronin, 1986). The mean serum cholesterol level of adults aged 20 to 74 over 1976–1980 was 5.5 percent above the recommended level for men and 7 percent above for women (NCHS, 1989, p. 76).

Intake of sweeteners and sodium is also a matter of concern. According to Evans and Cronin (1986), added sweeteners (e.g., refined sugars) accounted for about 15 percent of the caloric intake of children and teenagers and about 10 percent of the caloric intake of adults. A substantial share of the added sweeteners consumed by children and teenagers comes from soft drinks. Teenage girls and boys obtain 35 to 40 percent of the added sweeteners they consume from soft drinks. According to the Department of Health and Human Services, average sodium intake for adults (not including salt added at the table) was within the Established Safe and Adequate Daily Dietary Intake range established by the National Academy of Sciences (NCHS, 1989, p. 76).

How well do Americans—especially the poor—perform when they shop for food? One measure of food-shopping ability is the amount of nutrients obtained per dollar expenditure on food. This question was investigated using data from the Nationwide Food Consumption Survey of 1977–1978 (Morgan, Peterkin, Johnson & Goungetas, 1985). Some findings from the study are:

- As size of household increased, amount of nutrients per dollar's worth of food increased for food energy, protein, calcium, iron, and magnesium and decreased for vitamin A.

- As income increased, amount of nutrients per dollar's worth of food decreased. Income was measured as a percentage of the poverty threshold in order to even out differences in household size and composition.

- Families who received food stamps obtained more nutrients per dollar expenditure, except for vitamin A, than did families who were eligible for but did not receive food stamps.

HOUSING

Population Trends

The type of housing needed depends in part on population characteristics. Housing consumption is affected by the formation and dissolution of households and by the distribution of households with respect to size and type. In the 1970s and 1980s, several trends were apparent:

- More single persons in the population. In 1970, 28 percent of all adults were not currently married; in 1988, 37 percent were unmarried. These included adults who delayed marriage, were divorced, or were widowed. Median age at first marriage increased by about three years from 1960 to 1988, and approximately half of all marriages occurring in that period were expected to end in divorce (Census, 1989f, p. 1). In 1988, 14 percent of men and 49 percent of women aged 65 or over were widowed (Census, 1989f, p. 4).

- An increasing tendency of young adults (aged 18 to 24) to live with their parents rather than in their own home. In 1988, 61 percent of young men and 48 percent of young women lived with their parents compared with 54 percent and 41 percent, respectively, in 1970 (Census, 1989f, p. 7).

- An increase in the number of unmarried-couple households (from less than 1 percent of the population in 1970 to nearly 3 percent in 1988).

- An increase in the elderly population, from 10 percent of the population in 1970 to 12 percent in 1987.

- An increase in single-parent households. In 1970, 13 percent of all family groups with children had only one parent present; in 1988 the percentage was 27 percent.

- A decline in the average size of household, from slightly over three persons in 1970 to slightly under three in 1988.

Mobility (frequency of moving) also affects housing needs and costs. About 23 percent of all households moved from one dwelling to another in 1987 (U.S. Bureau of the Census & U.S. Department of Housing and Urban Development [Census & HUD], 1989, p. 52).

Ownership and Use of Housing

Housing refers to all shelter, that is, the dwelling itself together with taxes, insurance, repairs, and maintenance; furnishings and equipment used in the home; housekeeping supplies; household operations; and utilities (fuel, water, telephone, and sewage and trash disposal).

Shelter. In 1987, the available housing stock in the United States consisted of 102.7 million housing units, including 6.7 million mobile homes. Of the available stock, 99.8 million were occupied, 64 percent of them by owners and the remaining 36 percent by renters. Mobile homes comprised about 6 percent and cooperatives and condominiums about 4 percent of the occupied dwellings (Census & HUD, 1989, p. 1).

The median age of occupied units, both owner occupied and rented, was 25 years, but age varied by location. Farm homes were the oldest, with a median age of 38 years. Median age of dwellings in the central cities was 32 years; in rural areas outside metropolitan areas, it was 30 years. The newest homes, on the average, were in the suburbs (median age 16 years). In comparison with other regions, the oldest homes were found in the northeastern region (median age 37) and the newest homes in the West and South (median ages 20 and 19, respectively) (Census & HUD, 1989, p. 1).

The majority (62 percent) were single-family detached houses. The typical dwelling unit (as reflected in the median) had 5.3 rooms, including 2.6 bedrooms, but owned housing was larger, with about two more rooms (one a bedroom) than rented housing units. Less than 1 percent lacked a complete bathroom, but these were more likely to be rented than owned units. The number of bedrooms tended to be smallest in central cities and largest on farms. Data on square feet per person showed somewhat different tendencies, however. Owned housing provided more space per person than rented housing, but median space per person was higher on farms and in central cities than in the suburbs (Census & HUD, 1989, pp. 38–39).

Home ownership is the preferred mode of acquiring housing for most American households. In 1987, 64 percent of all occupied units were occupied by the owner. This high rate of home ownership is a relatively recent phenomenon. Prior to 1940, less than half of all households were home owners. Following World War II, the home ownership rate rose rapidly, partly because of the low-interest, insured mortgages available to veterans. By 1960, about 60 percent of all households were living in owned housing; thereafter, the rate of increase slowed (Census & HUD, 1989, p. 34).

Data from the 1988 Consumer Expenditure Survey indicate that home ownership rates vary by

• Region. They were the highest in the Midwest and South (66 and 64 percent, respectively) and lowest in the West (55 percent).

• Urbanization. Over three-fourths (77 percent) of those living in rural areas were home owners, compared with 59 percent of urban households.

• Income. Rates increased with income, from 41 percent for households in the lowest income quintile to 87 percent in the highest quintile.

• Household size. Home ownership rates were the lowest for one-person households, of whom 60 percent were renters, and highest for four-person households (73 percent).

• Household type. Rates were higher for husband-wife households (78 percent) than for other consumer units and lowest for one-parent households (33 percent).

• Age of householder. Home ownership rates increased from about 10 percent among householders less than 25 years old to nearly 80 percent among those aged 55 to 75, and thereafter declined slightly. Seventy-three percent of the very elderly households surveyed (householder aged 75 and over) were home owners, suggesting a strong preference for continuing to live in their own home.

• Race. Sixty-four percent of white households and 41 percent of black households are home owners.

Furnishings and Equipment. Few units (less than of 1 percent of all occupied units) lacked some kind of heating equipment. The commonest form of heating was by warm-air furnace, with over half of the units (55 percent) using this as the main heating equipment. About 5 percent relied on stoves or fireplaces (Census & HUD, 1989, p. 40).

About two-thirds of all occupied units had some form of air-conditioning. Air-conditioning was somewhat commoner in owned than in rented units (69 compared with 59 percent) and in the suburbs (69 percent) than in central cities (65 percent) or on farms (59 percent). Air-conditioning was most frequent in the South (85 percent of all units) and least frequent in the West (44 percent) and Northeast (53 percent) (Census & HUD, 1989, p. 40).

About 99 percent of all occupied units had complete kitchen facilities: sink, refrigerator, and burners. About three-fourths had a washing machine, two-thirds had a clothes dryer, 46 percent had a dishwasher, and 38 percent had a disposal unit in the kitchen sink (Census & HUD, 1989, p. 40).

Data from an 11-state study (Lovingood & McCullough, 1986) showed major appliance ownership (in addition to range and refrigerator) in two-parent families with children in 1981. Nearly all the families (over 90 percent) owned a vacuum cleaner, automatic washer, and clothes dryer. Appliances owned by over three-fourths included a sewing machine, power yard and garden equipment, and automatic defrosting refrigerator. Dishwashers were owned by over half the families and food waste disposers by 43 percent. Automatic cleaning oven, microwave oven, and trash compactor were less frequently owned in 1981. Over 60 percent of the families owned at least seven of the above appliances.

Families in the United States also own many small appliances (Hassoun, 1984). Households surveyed in one city in 1976 owned an average of 26 small electrical appliances. Those most frequently owned were electric clock, toaster, steam iron, blender, drill, heating pad, hand mixer, electric can opener, electric frying pan, electric coffee maker, and electric saw. Ownership does not necessarily mean use, however. Some appliances are never used by their owners. Small electrical appliances with the highest average usage per year by those who owned them were baby food or bottle warmer, can opener, coffee maker, toaster, makeup mirror, and shaver. Seldom-used items included ice cream freezer, roaster, warming tray, and deep fat fryer.

Ownership of appliances is likely to vary by the characteristics of the household (Wolfe & Abdel-Ghany, 1981). A study of appliance ownership in one state (Alabama) indicated that:

- Higher-income households were likely to own more appliances.
- Ownership of appliances for food preparation and for maintenance (e.g., floor waxer, sewing machine) increased with education of husband.
- Larger households were likely to own more laundry, entertainment, and personal care appliances than small households.
- Families with a full-time homemaker owned as many appliances of all types as did families in which the wife was employed.

The service life of appliances—that is, the average length of time they are kept in use by consuming units—has been estimated for a few appliances (Tippett, Magrabi & Gray, 1978): electric range, 12.1 years; gas range, 13.5 years; refrigerator, 15.2 years; washing machine, 10.8 years; electric clothes dryer, 13.7 years; and dishwasher, 11.1 years. Service life for the same items acquired used was about half as long. Higher-income consumer units did not keep their appliances as long as lower-income units. A major factor stimulating the discarding and replacing of an appliance was moving to a different residence.

Household textiles—blankets and linens, curtains and draperies, and other miscellaneous textiles—are another kind of furnishings. Winakor and Thomas (1978) estimated standard budgets for household textiles using data from three midwestern states. The inventory for small urban families (2 to 2.5 persons) at the moderate income level contained 122 items, including 15 washcloths, 12 bath towels, and 12 dish towels. The inventory for large families (5.6 or more persons) contained 145 items, while that for small families at the low-income level was only 94 items.

The average number of household textile items acquired from all sources each year was also reported (Winakor & Thomas, 1978). From the ratio of inventory to acquisition, we can estimate the service life of each textile item. Estimated service life of items in the budget for small, moderate-income families ranged from about 3.3 years for ironing board covers and dish cloths to 33 years for down or feather pillows. Face and hand towels had an estimated service life of 20 years and pillow cases, blankets, and mattress pads about 17 years. Estimated service life of household textile items appeared to be about the same among low- and moderate-income families, but service lives in large families appeared to be somewhat shorter than in small families.

Winakor (1975) found that about 90 percent of all families purchased at least one new household textile item during the survey year, and about two-thirds acquired one or more items from sources other than purchased new (e.g., as gifts or purchased second-hand). About half received gifts of household textiles during the year, and about 17 percent made items at home. Some household textiles were acquired as premiums or with trading stamps, purchased used, or inherited. Higher-income families were more likely than low- or moderate-income families to acquire textiles through purchase of new items rather than from other sources. Gifts were most frequently received by young families. Moving and having an infant were associated with increased acquisition of items.

Utilities. Water is supplied to the majority of U.S. households (86 percent) by a public system or a private company (Census & HUD, 1989, p. 40). Residential use of water averaged about 112 gallons per person per day in 1980, according to one estimate (Postel, 1985, pp. 40–42). Lawn and yard watering accounts for a substantial share of residential water use—40 to 50 percent in some western cities. Flush toilets take about 3 to 5 gallons per use, showerheads 3 to 5 gallons per minute, clothes washers about 37 gallons per use, and faucets about 13 gallons per minute (Postel, 1985, p. 44).

About three-fourths of all households were connected with a public sewer in 1987; most of the remainder had a septic tank, cesspool, or chemical toilet (Census & HUD, 1989, p. 40).

Piped gas was the commonest fuel for heating. It was the main heating fuel in about half of the homes. Electricity was the next most common (23 percent). About 6 percent used wood as their main heating fuel. Less than half of 1 percent relied on solar energy (Census & HUD, 1989, p. 42).

Piped gas was also the fuel most commonly used for heating water in houses. Over half of the houses with hot piped water used piped gas, and about one-third used electricity. Electricity was the commonest fuel for cooking (57 percent), central air-conditioning (92 percent), and clothes dryers (76 percent).

Over half of all energy consumed in the home (54 percent) was used for space heating in 1987. Water heating accounted for an additional 18 percent, air-conditioning 5 percent, and the remaining 23 percent was used by appliances (U.S. Department of Energy [DOE], 1989, p. 5).

Consumption of energy by U.S. households has declined. In 1987, average consumption of all fuels per household was equal to 100.8 million Btu, compared with 137.9 in 1978 (DOE, 1989, p. 3). Electricity consumption, which had been declining prior to 1984, rose by about 6 percent from 1984 to 1987, partly due to an increase in the number of homes with air-conditioning, increased use of air-conditioning by households that had it, and increased use of energy-intensive electric appliances. These factors were partially offset by two energy-conserving trends: an increase in the percentage of households using microwave ovens (from 34 percent in 1984 to 61 percent in 1987) and an increase (from 4 percent in

1984 to 5 percent in 1987) of households using heat pumps as the main type of heating equipment (DOE, 1989, p. 4).

Almost all energy-using appliances are powered by electricity. The major electricity user is the refrigerator, accounting for one-fifth of all household use of electricity. Three other major users (space heating, water heating, and air-conditioning, listed in order of magnitude) are actually more energy intensive than refrigerators, but their average energy consumption per household is lower because fewer households have them. A second group of appliances consumes an average of 1 to 6 percent of total electricity each: clothes dryers, color televisions, freezers, ranges and ovens, and waterbed heaters (DOE, 1989, p. 8).

Expenditure Patterns and Trends

Costs. The cost of shelter can be calculated in several ways. The Bureau of Labor Statistics publishes subindexes of the CPI for shelter for both home owners and renters. The costs of home ownership can be calculated with or without taking into account tax advantages and investment aspects.

In 1988 the CPI for housing stood at 118.5. Shelter stood at 127.1 (home owners 131.1 and renters 133.6), fuel and utilities 104.4, and household furnishings and operation 109.4. During the 1970s, the CPI for shelter more than doubled. The rate of increase was more moderate in the 1980s (U.S. House of Representatives, 1990, p. 359, Table C-59).

The estimated median price for houses purchased by young, first-time buyers increased from $19,244 in 1970 to $50,530 in 1980, an average annual increase of about 16 percent, and to $66,886 in 1987, an annual increase of about 5 percent.[2] Mortgage payments depend on the price of the house, amount of down payment, and rate of interest paid on the mortgage. Between 1970 and 1987, contract mortgage rates of the Federal Home Loan Bank Board ranged from a low of 7.38 percent in 1972 to a high of 14.78 percent in 1982. By 1987 the rate had dropped to 8.93 percent. The impact of changes in house prices and interest rates can be seen in estimated monthly mortgage payments, which increased from $122 in 1970 to $445 in 1980, and to $451 in 1987, reaching a peak of $508 in 1984 (Apgar & Brown, 1988, p. 20).[3]

Over half of all home owners and 17 percent of elderly home owners had a mortgage in 1987. Median amount outstanding was $32,563 ($15,087 for the elderly) (Census & HUD, 1989, pp. 116–119).

Additional costs of home ownership are property taxes, insurance, fuel and utilities, and maintenance. These rose steadily from $925 per year in 1970 to $2,736 in 1987 (Apgar & Brown, 1988, p. 20).

Federal income tax provisions allow home owners to deduct mortgage interest payments and thus provide substantial tax savings. When this deduction was taken into account, the estimated monthly cost (mortgage payment plus other

Figure 4.2
Budget Share Spent for Housing, 1901–1987

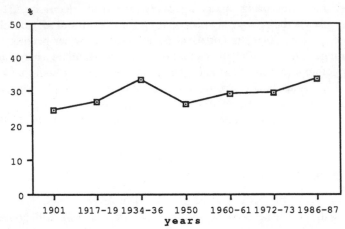

Source: Jacobs & Shipp (1990, p. 22).

costs minus tax savings) was $183 in 1970, $697 in 1982, and $643 in 1987 (Apgar & Brown, 1988, p. 20).

In addition to tax savings, investment aspects of home ownership must be considered. These include the fees and closing costs associated with the purchase, the opportunity cost of the down payment, since funds tied up in the purchase of the house cannot be drawing interest elsewhere, and the buildup of equity in the house as the mortgage is paid off. After taking these factors into account, the estimated monthly cost for 1970, 1982, and 1987 was $134, $574, and $519, respectively (Apgar & Brown, 1988, p. 20).

During the 1970s and 1980s, costs of renting increased at a consistent but moderate rate.[4] During most of the 1970s, total costs of home ownership (with tax advantages taken into account) were lower than the costs of renting. Since 1980, costs of renting have been lower than the costs of home ownership (Apgar & Brown, 1988, p. 20).

Expenditures. Trends in housing expenditures of households, as shown in nationwide consumer expenditure surveys, are shown in Figure 4.2. Housing comprised about 33 percent of total expenditures in 1986–1987, being the largest expenditure for most households. Except for the depression years of 1934–1936, when budget share for housing equaled the 1986–1987 figure, housing has ranged from about 26 to 29 percent of expenditures during most of the century. Since 1950, budget shares for shelter and utilities have increased, while shares for household operations and for household furnishings and equipment have declined.

According to the 1987 American Housing Survey for the United States (Census & HUD, 1989, pp. 60–61), median monthly cost for shelter and utilities was

$388. Costs varied with characteristics of the dwelling. Median costs were the lowest for households living in mobile homes or trailers, with the median ($269) being 70 percent that of households in one-family detached houses. Median costs declined as age of structure increased and increased with size of dwelling. Median monthly costs for renters was higher ($399) than costs for owners ($375). Amounts varied by other factors as well. The median for housing units with severe physical problems was lower ($241) and the median for those built within the past four years was higher ($588) than the overall median. The highest median costs were found in the suburbs of major cities and the lowest in rural areas. Costs also varied by region, with the highest in the West and the lowest in the South.

Consumer units spent about $8,000 per year on housing (Table 4.3). Renters averaged about $2,800 per year less than home owners. The mean expenditure for shelter was $4,493—about 56 percent of total housing expenditure. After shelter, utilities were the next largest item of housing expenditure. Average expenditures for housing increased with income, with those in the highest-income quintile spending more than three times as much as those in the lowest quintile. The income elasticity of shelter, according to Abdel-Ghany and Foster (1982), is 0.47, indicating that shelter is a necessity.

To sort out factors associated with shelter expenditures, a multivariate regression analysis of 1986–1987 data was conducted. The results indicated that expenditures on shelter are associated with age of householder, other factors being equal. Mean expenditures were relatively low for young householders, increased to a peak at about ages 35 to 44, and thereafter declined. The analysis indicated that expenditures decline with household size and vary with household type, being the lowest for households whose oldest child was older than 17. Home owners without a mortgage averaged lower shelter expenditures than home owners with a mortgage or renters.

In addition to mortgage and tax payments, home owners incur several other home maintenance expenses. The average expenditure for maintenance, repairs, insurance, and other shelter expenses, according to the 1988 expenditure survey, was $496, about 11 percent of the total cost of shelter. The most frequently incurred expenses for repairs, improvements, and alterations, according to the American Housing Survey (Census & HUD, p. 120), is for roof repair. About 16 percent of the home owners surveyed in 1987 reported replacing all or part of their roof. About 14 percent bought and installed storm doors and windows. Other expenses frequently incurred were for remodeling the bathroom or kitchen, replacing major pieces of equipment, adding insulation, replacing or adding siding, and building an addition to the structure.

Property insurance is an expense for both owners and renters. Almost all (94 percent) home owners carried some form of property insurance, according to the American Housing Survey. About one-fourth of the renters carried property insurance (Census & HUD, 1989, p. 60).

Expenditures for furnishings and equipment comprised about 13 percent of

Table 4.3
Housing Expenditures, 1988

	All Consumer Units	Income quintile				
		Lowest 20%	2nd 20%	3rd 20%	4th 20%	Highest 20%
Housing (total)	8,079	3,957	5,510	7,051	9,370	14,434
Shelter	4,493	2,209	2,982	3,850	5,171	8,126
Owned dwellings	2,569	708	1,013	1,708	3,157	6,172
Mortgage interest	1,569	285	380	859	2,059	4,211
Property taxes	504	189	308	380	585	1,016
Other expenses	496	233	325	469	513	945
Rented dwellings	1,468	1,372	1,710	1,830	1,504	933
Other lodging	456	129	260	312	509	1,021
Utilities, fuels & public services	1,747	1,121	1,432	1,675	1,928	2,473

Natural gas	234	152	207	216	243	342
Electricity	709	442	578	676	803	1,000
Fuel oil & other fuels	98	71	86	91	96	126
Telephone	537	352	441	538	585	727
Water & other public services	170	103	120	154	200	278
Household operations	394	143	209	284	446	853
Personal services	171	46	94	156	255	330
Other household expenses	223	97	115	128	191	522
Housekeeping supplies	361	173	302	354	464	620
Laundry and cleaning supplies	101	58	83	105	130	155
Other household products	147	61	113	132	192	289
Postage and stationery	113	53	106	118	141	176
Household furnishings & equipment	1,083	312	584	887	1,361	2,363
Household textiles	94	35	58	95	105	193
Furniture	326	73	147	241	374	761
Floor coverings	65	9	23	60	114	145
Major appliances	169	76	101	163	221	303
Small appliances, misc. housewares	60	23	39	41	65	134
Misc. household equipment	369	96	218	286	483	827

Source: U.S. Bureau of Labor Statistics (1990).

total housing costs in 1988. Expenditures increased with income but did not appear to vary consistently with other household characteristics, other factors being held constant. The income elasticity of furnishings and equipment, according to Abdel-Ghaney and Foster (1982), is 1.29.

Wagner (1986) studied expenditures for household textiles to identify the factors associated with expenditures in this area of furnishings. She divided household textiles into two groups: linens (such items as sheets, blankets, towels, and table linens) and textile furnishings (including rugs, curtains, slipcovers, and upholstery). Compared with households with low expenditures for textile furnishings, high-spending households were likely to be younger, home owning, live in a suburb, and have moved during the same year.

Household utility expenditures declined in real terms between 1973 and 1983 (Scoon, 1989). Electricity accounted for the largest share (37 percent) of utility expenditures in 1983, followed by telephone services (23 percent), natural gas (21 percent), fuel oil and other fuels (9 percent), and water, sewerage, maintenance, water softening, septic tank cleaning, and community antenna or cable television (10 percent).

After shelter, utilities was the largest component of housing expenditures, accounting for nearly one-fourth of the total in 1988. Their income elasticity is 0.75 (Abdel-Ghany and Foster, 1982).

When other factors are held constant, utility expenditures increase with income and household size. The relationship with age of householder is nonlinear, with expenditures reaching a peak at ages 35 to 44. Expenditures are higher for blacks than whites and lower for renters than home owners (probably because many renters have some utilities provided as part of the rental agreement).

The Department of Energy's 1987 survey of household energy consumption and expenditures provides data on expenditures for energy (electricity, gas, fuel oil, kerosene, and other fuels). Average energy prices vary by energy type. In 1987, U.S. households paid $10.71 per million Btu for all fuels. Electricity was the most expensive, averaging $22.34 per million Btu, followed by liquified petroleum gas ($8.91). Fuel oil or kerosene and natural gas were the cheapest, averaging $5.89 and $5.41, respectively (U.S. Department of Energy [DOE], 1989, p. 81).

Fuel expenditures vary by climate. In the coldest climate zone (over 7,000 heating degree days and fewer than 2,000 cooling degree days), median monthly cost for electricity was $48, much less than the $76 in the warmest zone. The reverse was true for piped gas, the commonest fuel used for heating. Median monthly cost was $54 in the coldest zone and $35 in the warmest zone (Census & HUD, 1989, p. 80).

Energy expenditures per household averaged the highest in the Northeast, next highest in the Midwest, and lowest in the West (DOE, p. 44). They also varied by number of dwelling units in the structure, with households in multiunit buildings paying less than those in single-family detached structures. Energy expenditures of households in mobile homes also averaged less than those in single-family detached structures. Expenditures increased with number of rooms and with income (DOE, 1989, p. 65).

Housing Assistance Programs. Assistance includes emergency shelters for the homeless, programs to encourage home ownership and the building of low-cost housing, and rent and fuel subsidies. Most assistance is provided through state or local governments or private nonprofit organizations. Federal government programs are administered by the Department of Housing and Urban Development and the Farmers Home Administration. Federal subsidies have encouraged new construction or rehabilitation of housing.

Federal housing programs encompass the following:

- Low-income housing programs, which provide subsidies to housing for low-income households.

- Public housing, built and administered by the government. This includes loans to finance nonprofit organizations to build housing for the elderly or the handicapped.

- Rent supplements, which help pay the cost to low-income families of renting units in the regular rental market.

- Rural housing programs, administered by the Farmers Home Administration of the U.S. Department of Agriculture, which provide loans for housing in rural areas.

Only a fraction of those in need receive housing assistance. In 1987, when about 13 percent of all dwellings were occupied by households with incomes below the poverty threshold (Census & HUD, p. 58), about 5 percent of all occupied housing units were owned by a public housing authority or subsidized by federal, state, or local government. Less than 40 percent of households below the poverty threshold received some kind of rent reduction (Census & HUD, 1989, p. 34). About 5 percent of all households received assistance for heating in winter (DOE, 1989, p. 46).

Impact on Well-being

Types of Impacts. Housing characteristics are usually included in quality-of-life measures. Housing plays a facilitating role in the life-style of the household, making it easy or difficult, pleasant or unpleasant, safe or unsafe, for household members to carry on their chosen productive, leisure, and personal care activities. It does this through the location of the dwelling as it affects access to employment, retail stores, schools, and other sites; the character of the neighborhood, in terms of both safety and access to congenial associates and in terms of the safety and quality of the physical environment; and the design and physical character of the structure and its furnishings, which affect the health and safety of household members, the amount of labor needed to maintain the home and carry on household activities, their aesthetic enjoyment, and their social status. Housing also affects well-being indirectly through its impact on the economic resources of the household:

• Budget share. For most American households, housing is the largest category of expenditure. Amount spent on housing limits the amount available for other needs. A high budget share for housing also puts the home owner in greater risk of being unable to keep up payments, and hence of foreclosure.

• Value of assets. Houses and their furnishings are durables that are a source of low-cost consumption for many, especially retired persons with paid-up mortgages. They can also be resold, sometimes at a profit, and the monetary value used for other purposes.

Standards. The physical characteristics of housing are generally assessed using a social indicators approach. Condition of the structure (cracks in walls, signs of rats, etc.) and amount of space per occupant are among the indicators used to assess housing quality. Neighborhood quality is also assessed. The comparison is either with an absolute standard (e.g., the existence of any dilapidated housing is bad) or with the mean at another time or in other populations. Specific standards have been promulgated for quality of air and water, for example, by the World Health Organization (French, 1990, pp. 10–11).

Various standards have been used with respect to percentage of income for housing. In subsidized housing programs of the Department of Housing and Urban Development, 30 percent of income is used as the maximum that families should normally pay for housing.

Assessment of Housing Adequacy. Shelter was adequate, on the average, for American households. Housing units provided an average of 648 square feet per person, a median of about five rooms (Census & HUD, 1989, p. 38). About three-fourths had a porch, deck, balcony, or patio, 31 percent had two or more living rooms or recreation rooms, 39 percent had a separate dining room, and over half had a garage or carport (Census & HUD, 1989, pp. 46–47).

Homes were generally in good repair and well equipped, but about 7 percent of occupied housing in the United States had moderate to severe physical problems, according to the American Housing Survey (Census & HUD, 1989, p. 36). Interior problems included open cracks or holes (6 percent), broken plaster or peeling paint (5 percent), signs of rats (5 percent), holes in floors (1 percent), and lack of or exposed electrical wiring (2 percent). Water leakage was reported by a few, from outside the structure (2 percent) or inside (1 percent). Problems were more frequent in central cities or rural areas than in the suburbs (Census & HUD, 1989, p. 46).

Less than 1 percent lacked a complete bathroom, and about 1 percent lacked complete kitchen facilities (Census & HUD, 1989, p. 38). Less than 1 percent lacked hot and cold piped water. Over a third had a waste disposer in the kitchen sink. Ninety-three percent had a telephone (Census & HUD, 1989, pp. 38–46).

Problems did exist in the function of services and equipment and were about equally common in the central city, suburbs, and rural areas. Some households (about 5 percent) reported a water stoppage during the past three months. Other problems, in order of frequency, were: blown fuse (15 percent), uncomfortably cold for 24 hours or more last winter (6 percent), a flush-toilet breakdown (5 percent), and a sewage disposal breakdown (about 1 percent) (Census & HUD, 1989, pp. 44–45).

While neighborhoods were generally good, over one-third of the households reported some problems (Census & HUD, 1989, p. 48). Problems most frequently reported were other people, noise, traffic, crime, and litter or housing deterioration. Households living in multiunit structures reported trash, litter, or junk (34 percent), streets in need of repair (28 percent), bars on windows of nearby buildings (2 percent), and nearby buildings vandalized or with the interior partially exposed (6 percent). Neighborhood problems were most frequent in central cities and least frequent in rural areas.

Although appliance ownership was high, studies have not provided evidence that appliance ownership reduces work time. Some researchers have hypothesized that households in which the wife was employed (and hence could be assumed to have less time for household work) would own more labor-saving appliances than households with nonemployed wives. They found, however, that when income and other factors were taken into account, there was no difference between the two types of households in ownership of time-saving durables (Strober, 1977; Strober & Weinberg, 1977, 1980; Weinberg & Winter, 1983; Nickols & Fox, 1983).

Using data from an 11-state survey of time use, Lovingood and McCullough (1986) conducted a direct test of the hypothesis that appliance ownership reduces household work time. They found that households that owned dishwashers and food waste disposers averaged slightly less time per day on the related tasks, but the difference was less than 5 minutes per appliance. Owners of power yard or garden equipment, sewing machines, or vacuum cleaners averaged 3 to 20 minutes more time per day on the related tasks.

Housing costs were not a serious economic burden for most households. Only 29 percent paid over 30 percent of their income for housing (Census, 1989f, p. 60). On the other hand, 12 percent used over half of their income for housing, and 7 percent used over 70 percent.

Housing costs were a problem for some groups. Half of poor households paid at least half and over one-third used 70 percent or more of their income for housing. Blacks and Hispanics were also somewhat more likely than the general population to be paying a high percentage of their income for housing. A larger percentage of renters than home owners (with or without a mortgage) spent more than half of their income for housing.

The proportion of poor households spending a high proportion of their income for housing has increased. In 1978, 44 percent of poor renter households and 31 percent of poor home owner households paid 60 percent or more of their income for housing. By 1985, the percentages had increased to 55 and 38 percent, respectively (Leonard, Dolbeare & Lazere, 1989, pp. xii–xiii).

One measure of the value of the home as an asset is the value-income ratio— the ratio of the value of the house (the home owner's estimate of the house's selling price if put on the market) to the total household income (before taxes).

The median for home owners with a mortgage was 2.1; that is, the value of the home was more than two times their annual income (Census & HUD, 1989, p. 126). The median for home owners without a mortgage was higher—nearly three times their annual income. Some home owners (11 percent of those with and 26 percent of those without a mortgage) owned homes worth at least five times their annual income. The median for all households with respect to total loan outstanding as a percentage of the value of the dwelling was 50 percent (Census & HUD, 1989, p. 118).

The extreme case of housing inadequacy is homelessness—the lack of any shelter at all, other than emergency shelters. Homelessness was a persistent and increasing problem in the 1980s. A 1984 study by the Department of Housing and Urban Development estimated the number of homeless at 250,000 to 350,000 persons. Estimates by private organizations have been higher. The Urban Institute estimated the total at 600,000; the National Coalition for the Homeless estimated that there are 3 million homeless (Rich, 1988). According to one study, in addition to those currently on the streets or in emergency shelters, there are 4 million to 14 million families on the brink of homelessness (Rich, 1989). The Neighborhood Reinvestment Corporation estimated that by the year 2003, there will be over 18 million homeless or near homeless in the United States (Jordan, 1987).

Who are the homeless? A study in Chicago in 1985–1986 indicated a disproportionate likelihood that the homeless individual would be male and black, with a high school education, and neither very young nor very old (mean age 40). The homeless group also included young black women (about 14 percent), many of whom had young children, and older white males who had been homeless for long periods of time. Although about one-fifth had received no income in the past month, 29 percent had received money from work, 21 percent from pensions or disability benefits, and 30 percent from welfare. Forty-three percent had worked within the previous month, and a few (4 percent) had steady jobs. About one-fourth had physical health problems, about one-fourth had a previous stay in a mental hospital, and about two-fifths had been in jail. Social isolation is a problem for the homeless. Although many had spouses or relatives, one-third of the homeless said they were not in contact with relatives; nearly one-fourth were not in contact with either family or friends (Rossi, Wright, Fisher & Willis, 1987).

APPAREL

Acquisition and Use

Apparel encompasses a variety of specific commodities, such as coats, sweaters, trousers and slacks, shorts, shirts and blouses, dresses, underwear, nightwear, hosiery, uniforms, hats, gloves, and other accessories, such as scarves.

Small children may also have snowsuits, diapers, and crawlers. Footwear refers to shoes, slippers, and boots and may also include special shoes for sports, such as running shoes or golf shoes. Other items are furs, watches, jewelry, material for making clothes, and apparel services, such as shoe repair, laundry, and dry cleaning.

Use of fibers is a comprehensive measure of consumption of apparel (excluding shoes) and household textiles. In 1988, per capita consumption of fibers in the United States was 52.2 pounds. Nearly three-fourths (72 percent) of the total was manufactured fibers, such as rayon or nylon. Slight over one-fourth (27 percent) was cotton; wool and other natural fibers (silk, linen, etc.) comprised less than 1 percent of the total (Courtless, 1990).

Total per capita consumption of fibers generally increased from 1960 to 1973— from about 37 pounds per capita in 1960 to 56 in 1973. In the period from 1973 to 1989, per capita consumption remained close to the 1973 level, ranging from about 48 to about 56 pounds. The composition of total fiber use changed dramatically, however. In 1960, cotton comprised nearly two-thirds of the total usage; by 1979 it had declined to 27 percent. Since then cotton has varied from about 27 to about 30 percent of the total. Wool consumption declined from about 8 percent in 1960 to slightly over 1 percent in 1974, and then it increased to over 2 percent in 1981–1984. Changes in synthetic fiber consumption have mirrored changes in cotton. Synthetics comprised about 28 percent of the total in 1960, increased to a high of 71 percent in 1979, and decreased during the 1980s (Courtless, 1990).

Although cotton comprised only 27 percent of total fiber consumption in 1988, it comprised 48 percent of the apparel market, an increase from 43 percent in 1986. Usage of cotton in apparel varies by age and sex. Only 40 percent of women's apparel is of cotton, compared with 58 percent of men's and about 50 percent of children's apparel. Cotton accounts for about half of the fiber used in home furnishings (excluding carpets) (Courtless, 1990).

Information is not available about wardrobe inventories and types of garments usually worn in different settings and occasions. Factors influencing clothing selection have been researched, however. Flame retardancy is a high priority in sleepwear and underwear for children and the elderly, according to a survey in the South Central region, an area where use of fireplaces and space heaters increases the risk of clothing burns (Kelley, Gray & Blouin, 1980). More than half of those surveyed indicated that they would be willing to trade aesthetic qualities (durable bright colors, ornamentation, and design lines) in order to have flame-retardant finishes on such garments. Fewer of the respondents were willing to give up performance characteristics (long wearing; odorless; soft, comfortable feeling; ease of care; permanent press; and shrink or stretch control). Aesthetic characteristics appeared to be most important in outer wear (dressy or casual) for all ages. Morganosky (1984) obtained similar results in a study of the relative preference of female shoppers for clothing and accessories in a North Central city. The shoppers in her sample indicated that they would be willing to pay more for high aesthetic qualities in outerwear (sweaters, shoes, aprons, gloves, and hats) than for a high degree of usefulness.

Fashion is an important determinant of clothing choice. A garment may be classified into temporal categories on the basis of the popularity of its style: newly introduced, current, outdated, and classic (always in style). Studies of male and female university students suggest that current and classic styles are the most preferred (Minshall, Winakor & Swinney, 1982).

Not all clothing is acquired new and ready-made. Recent data are not available, but data from a 1965–1966 study give some indication of the sources used (Britton, 1975). According to that study, about 14 percent of clothing acquired by a low- to moderate-income family in a one-year period was acquired used or handed down. The percentage varied by age-sex groups, being the highest (one third of the total) for infants and declining to about 14 percent for female heads of households, 9 percent for adult married women, and 6 percent for adult married men.

Home sewing is another means of acquiring clothing. The American Home Sewing Association estimated that about 63 percent of women sew, and an additional 17 percent make minor repairs to garments. Data from the 1972–1973 Consumer Expenditure Survey indicated that 85 percent of all households own a sewing machine and about 44 percent had some expenditures for home sewing during a one-year period (Courtless, 1982a). A 1978 study of employed Wisconsin and Illinois women found that 15 percent of the women reported sewing during a one-week period, and 40 percent said they sometimes sewed. Women who spent the most time sewing were likely to be married and have low earnings (Courtless, 1985).

Doing laundry is a weekly chore in most households. A 1977–1978 study (Purchase, Berning & Lyng, 1982) indicated that nearly 80 percent of American families wash more than three loads per week. Over 90 percent do their laundry at home. Those who use coin-operated laundries average fewer loads per week— four compared with eight for families who do their laundry at home.

Expenditure Trends and Patterns

Prices and Specific Costs. The CPI for apparel and upkeep stood at 115.4 in 1988, lower than the all-items index. In the period from 1970 to 1988, the apparel and upkeep index nearly doubled; however, the all-items index tripled in that period. Thus, price increases in apparel and upkeep were relatively low, probably due in part to increases in imported apparel. Most of the price increase occurred during the high-inflation 1970s (U.S. House of Representatives, Table C-59).

Although most garments are purchased ready-made, some are constructed at home, often at a substantial difference in cost. Britton (1975) compared the cost of ready-to-wear dresses and two-piece costumes with the cost of home-constructed counterparts. Cost of the ready-to-wear garment was its purchase price; cost of the home-constructed garment encompassed cost of the pattern, fabric, trimming, and notions (such as thread, fasteners, tape, or interfacing). Cost of equipment (sewing machine, iron, ironing board) and electricity was ignored, since it is a negligible part of the cost of a single garment. Cost of the home sewer's time was not included, since both the amount of time and cost are highly variable depending on the skill of the sewer and price of her or his time. Britton found that the cost of materials used in a home-constructed one-piece dress ranged from 20 to 100 percent of the cost of its ready-to-wear counterpart, and the cost of materials for a two-piece costume ranged from 16 to 193 percent. She estimated that construction time might range from 3 to 12 hours.

Since apparel is a durable, purchase price is only part of the cost of consumption. Another cost is time spent in caring for clothing. Amount of time that employed women spend on wardrobe maintenance—that is, washing, drying, ironing, and mending clothes—has been studied. The data were collected in late fall of 1978 from 378 women in Wisconsin and Illinois who worked for pay or on a family farm or home business. Almost all the women performed some kinds of wardrobe maintenance during the survey week, spending an average of 3 ½ hours. Women aged 35 to 44 averaged the most time. The average amount of time was higher for married than for single women and increased with number of children (Courtless, 1988).

Equipment and supplies are also used in caring for apparel. The estimated cost of doing a load of laundry at home (Courtless, 1982b), in 1988 prices, was $1.25. About one-fourth of the cost was for the washer and dryer (purchase price and maintenance allocated over expected service life and average number of loads of laundry per year).

An analysis of energy consumption in producing and caring for garments provides some indication of the magnitude of the cost of maintenance in relation to the original cost of apparel. Polyzou (1979) compared two types of men's shirts—all-cotton and a polyester-cotton blend—with respect to the amount of energy consumed to produce the garment and maintain it during its wear life. Energy was measured in kilowatt-hour equivalents. The total energy required to produce the fiber was 5 kwh (kilowatt-hour) for the all-cotton shirt and 9.6 for the polyester-cotton. Energy used in fabric production and construction of the garment brought the kwh totals to 26.3 for the all-cotton and 32.6 for the polyester-cotton shirt. Maintenance—laundering and ironing—consumed two to three times as much energy (more for the all-cotton than for the polyester-cotton garment, because of the need for hot water and ironing). When the shorter wear life was taken into account, total energy was 115.5 kwh for the all-cotton shirt and 72.4 kwh for the polyester-cotton.

Expenditures. Spending on apparel has exhibited a long-term increase measured in dollars but has decreased as a share of the household budget. In 1901, apparel and services comprised 15 percent of the consumer unit budget (Figure 4.3). The budget share increased to 18 percent during the war years of 1917–

Figure 4.3
Budget Share Spent for Apparel, 1901–1987

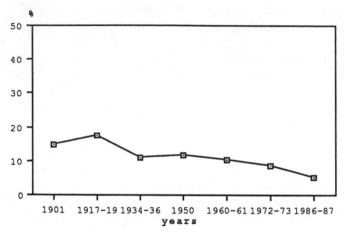

Source: Jacobs & Shipp (1990, p. 22).

1919, held steady at about 11 percent during the depression and post–World War II period, and then declined to 5 percent in 1986–1987.

Consumer units averaged about $1,500 per year in 1988 for apparel and services (Table 4.4). Approximately 13 percent of apparel and services expenditures went for footwear and about 17 percent for other apparel products and services, leaving over two-thirds for clothing.

Apparel expenditures increase with income. Consumer units in the highest income quintile spent more than five times as much as those in the lowest quintile. Apparel expenditures have an elasticity greater than one with respect to total expenditures (Norum, 1989; Dardis, Derrick & Lehfeld, 1981), suggesting that much of the expenditure for apparel should be considered luxury spending.

Multivariate analysis of data collected in 1972–1973 (Dardis et al., 1981), 1980–1981 (Norum, 1989), and 1986–1987 showed the following pattern:

• Income. As income increases, both the dollar amount and budget share for apparel increase.

• Age of householder. Household expenditure for apparel declines with age of householder. Chung and Magrabi (1990), for example, found that households in which the householder was 65 or older spent about $166 less per year on clothing and clothing services, other factors being equal, than did younger households. Norum found that young consumer units (householder aged 25 or less) spent 73 percent more on apparel in spring 1981 than did elderly units (householder aged 65 or over).

• Education of householder. Dollar expenditure increases with years of education (Norum, 1989; Dardis et al., 1981).

• Occupation. Compared with units in which the householder was employed in a service

Table 4.4
Apparel Expenditures, 1988

	All Consumer Units	Income quintile				
		Lowest 20%	2nd 20%	3rd 20%	4th 20%	Highest 20%
Apparel and services (total)	1,489	574	901	1,356	1,826	3,025
Men and boys	388	124	211	323	453	892
Men, 16 and over	311	102	150	253	349	738
Boys, 2 to 15	77	21	60	70	103	154
Women and girls	587	238	377	543	731	1,154
Women, 16 and over	492	204	318	464	597	965
Girls, 2 to 15	95	34	59	79	134	189
Children under 2	62	26	38	62	92	99
Footwear	196	98	135	214	251	322
Other apparel products & services	257	89	140	213	299	559

Source: U.S. Bureau of Labor Statistics (1990).

occupation (e.g., sales worker, food preparer, or beautician), consumer units in which the householder was in a blue-collar occupation spent less and devoted a smaller budget share to apparel. Consumer units in which the householder was in a managerial occupation, retired, or not working did not differ from service worker consumer units. Employed units spent more on apparel than did households in which the householder was unemployed or retired (Norum, 1989).

• Race. Black households spent more money (Dardis et al., 1981) and devoted a larger budget share to apparel than other households.

• Household size. Dardis et al. (1981) found a low but positive relationship between household size and expenditures for apparel in 1972–1973. This relationship did not appear in the 1986–1987 data, although budget share for apparel increased with number of members. Norum's analysis of data from 1980–1981 suggests that the age-sex composition of the consumer unit may have a greater effect on apparel expenditures than the number of members.

• Family type. One-person consumer units and units consisting of husband and wife plus one or more children older than 17 spent more on apparel than did units consisting of husband and wife only; budget share, however, was about the same. Husband-wife families with children under age 6 did not differ from all husband-wife families in dollar amount for apparel but did devote a smaller share of their budget to apparel.

• Home-sewing activity. Norum (1989) found that consumer units who reported expenditures for home-sewing materials spent more on apparel than did nonsewing units. This expenditure increase was greater for higher-income home sewers than for low-income home sewers.

• Season. Norum found evidence that expenditure pattern varies by season. Fall seemed to be associated with increased apparel expenditures for boys and girls aged 5 to 12, presumably because of back-to-school purchases. Teenage boys (aged 13 to 17) were likely to have higher purchases in winter and spring than in other seasons. Presence of a teenage girl or adult female in the household appeared to be associated with higher apparel expenditures regardless of season.

• Urbanization. Dardis et al. (1981) found evidence that households in rural areas spend slightly less on apparel than do urban households.

Apparel services—away-from-home laundry and dry cleaning services and repair of shoes, clothing, watches, and jewelry—are a component of apparel consumptions. Over half (57 percent) of the consumer units surveyed by the Bureau of Labor Statistics in 1985 reported expenditures for one or more apparel services, with an average expenditure of $187. The service most frequently purchased (by 52 percent of the consumer units) was laundry or dry cleaning. About 6 percent each spent money for shoe repair or apparel repair; about 4 percent purchased watch or jewelry repair (Courtless, 1989).

Both the percentage purchasing and the amount spent increased with income. Percentage purchasing declined with age of householder, but amount spent had an inverted U curve, with the highest average expenditure at ages 45 to 54, when consumer units averaged the highest expenditures for apparel as a whole. Black consumer units, who averaged lower total expenditures for apparel, had higher expenditures for apparel services. Husband-wife-earner families were no more likely than employed-male-only families to purchase apparel services, and they spent about the same amount of money. Consumer units in which the only earner was a female were slightly more likely than husband-wife-earner families to purchase apparel services, but they spent less. The lowest frequency of purchase and expenditure was among the very elderly and no-earner consumer units. Those most likely to have expenditures for apparel services had one or more of the following characteristics: black, high income, renter, householder less than 25 years old, or householder with more than four years of college (Courtless, 1989).

Impact on Well-being

Types of Impacts. Apparel affects the physical well-being of the wearer and the economic well-being of the household, and it plays an important role in defining and communicating the social identity of the wearer.

Apparel affects physical well-being by helping the wearer to keep dry and maintain a comfortable body temperature, and it provides protection from environmental hazards, such as rough or sharp surfaces, toxic substances, or sunburn. It affects the comfort of the wearer by being loose or binding, scratchy or soft. Apparel also may carry health or safety hazards through its flammability, absorption of chemicals, or bacterial contamination. Household textiles affect physical well-being in similar ways: by performing a drying function, helping to maintain the interior temperature of the dwelling, or controlling the light; by being comfortable or uncomfortable in use; and by the health and safety hazards they may entail.

The economic impact of apparel is the impact of apparel expenditures on the budget. Textile products are durables in that they can continue to perform useful functions over a period of months or years. The longer the wear life is of the item and the more frequently it is used, the greater is the benefit reaped from ownership. The characteristics of items in the household's apparel inventory affect the useful wear life of the items. McCullough and Morris (1980) grouped these characteristics under the headings durability, colorfastness, comfort, and appearance. Relationship of the item to the fashion cycle is also a factor in the useful wear life of the item (Winakor & Lubner-Rupert, 1983). An item that appears dated and unfashionable may be taken out of service long before it becomes unusable with respect to other characteristics.

The role of apparel in conveying social status and other cultural meanings has been identified by a number of social scientists, and its relationship to well-being is supported by evidence from a number of studies. Douglas (1980) drew on the relative income hypothesis in explaining the apparent contradiction between the relatively high income elasticity of apparel and declining share of total consumer spending out of rising real incomes. She hypothesized two interactions between the household and the community, which she called the leveling effect and the differentiating effect. The leveling effect is the tendency of all households to consume at a level near the mean for the community because of their desire to avoid the appearance of being different. Existence of this effect seems to be supported by an empirical study by Buckley (1983), who found that subjects rated other individuals as more attractive if they were wearing clothing similar to that worn by the subject. The differentiating effect stems from the desire to communicate one's position in the social system.

McCracken (1988, Chap. 4) described the kinds of cultural meaning conveyed by consumer goods, especially apparel. They include time (time of day, season, age of wearer, and perhaps whether the user of the product is abreast of interests and fashion trends in the community), place (nature and location of occasion in which the costume is worn), and person (role of the individual in the occasion and also role and social status in the community).

Standards. Some scientifically based standards for the safety of apparel and household textiles exist but do not cover the full range of impacts on health and safety. An example is the flammability standards mandated by the federal government for certain products. Most textiles are flammable in some degree and therefore present a hazard to users, either directly from burns or indirectly from smoke inhalation, which prevents the individual from escaping the fire. Some synthetic fibers melt (and may adhere to the wearer's skin) or give off noxious fumes. For this reason, flammability standards have been established for some specific textile products, such as children's sleep wear (Schwenk, 1984).

No generally accepted standards exist for economic impacts of apparel, although McCullough and Morris (1980) proposed a model for quality grading of textile products. Standard budgets for clothing were developed by Britton (1973) but were based on 1960–1961 data and are thus out of date.

Although cultural norms or standards undoubtedly exist and are generally well understood by members of the social group, they are rarely formalized or written down. Exceptions are the dress codes that apply to members of the military or certain organizations, or to pupils in some schools.

Evidence of Impact. There is substantial evidence that apparel affects the well-being of individuals and households. Johnson and Roach-Higgins (1987) found that college recruiters rated individuals (as portrayed in photographs and biographical information) as more or less employable depending on the appropriateness of the costume worn. Lennon (1990) found similar results for clothing attractiveness. Forsythe, Drake, and Cox (1984) found that the characteristics of the apparel worn by a young woman were associated with personnel interviewers' perceptions of the woman as being forceful, self-reliant, dynamic, aggressive, and decisive.

Some evidence is available regarding health effects of textile use. An example is a 1987–1988 study of the frequency of dermatological problems associated with textile use (Davis, Markee, Dallas, Harger & Miller, 1990). Over half of those interviewed reported that they had at some time in their lives experienced a dermatological-related problem with textiles. The most frequent problems were skin irritation, respiratory problems, or eye problems.

TRANSPORTATION

Acquisition and Use

Vehicle Ownership and Use. Private transportation is a preferred transportation mode for most Americans. In 1982 there were over 125 million automobiles in the United States (Chandler, 1985a, p. 24). Privately owned vehicles include cars, trucks, campers, trailers, motorcycles, and private planes. Consumer units in the United States owned an average of two vehicles per consumer unit. About 15 percent own no cars, trucks, or vans, but 9 percent own three or more (Census & HUD, 1989, p. 46).[5] Number owned varies by other characteristics of the consumer unit (pp. 46–47):

- Income. Consumer units in the highest income quintile owned an average of three vehicles; those in the lowest quintile owned slightly less than one (0.9) per unit. Forty-three percent of consumer units below the poverty level owned no cars, trucks, or vans.

- Age. Consumer units in the youngest age group owned just over one vehicle per unit. Number of vehicles increased to a peak (2.6 vehicles) at ages 45 to 54 and then declined to a low of one in units in which the householder was 75 or older. About one-fourth of elderly consumer units (65 or over) owned no car, truck, or van.

- Size of consumer unit. Number of vehicles increased from an average of one in one-person units to nearly three (2.7) in four-person units. The average in consumer units of five or more persons was only slightly lower (2.6).

- Consumer unit type. The largest number of vehicles was found in husband-wife families in which there were one or more children 18 or over. Some consumer units owned more than one vehicle per adult on the average: units with husband-wife only (2.3) and units with husband, wife, and children under age 6 (2.2). One-parent units with one or more children under 18 averaged the fewest vehicles (1.1).

- Number of earners. In general, the average number of vehicles exceeded the number of earners while also increasing with consumer unit size. Thus, while one-earner single consumers averaged 1.2 vehicles and one-earner units with two or more persons averaged 1.9 vehicles, units with two earners averaged 2.6 vehicles. Consumer units with three or more earners averaged 3.5 vehicles. Nonemployed single consumers averaged less than one vehicle per household, but no-earner consumer units with two or more persons averaged 1.5 vehicles.

- Housing tenure. Home owners owned substantially more vehicles per consumer unit (2.5) than did renters (1.3). About one-fourth of renter units owned no cars, trucks, or vans.

- Race and ethnic group. White consumer units averaged one more vehicle per unit than black units (2.1 compared with 1.1). Nearly one-third of all black consumer units and one-fourth of Hispanic units owned no cars, trucks, or vans.

- Region. Vehicle ownership was the highest in the Midwest and West and lowest in the Northeast. About one-fifth of all consumer units in the Northeast owned no car, truck, or van compared with 12 percent in the West and 13 percent in the Midwest. The percentage that owned three or more vehicles was somewhat higher in the West than in other regions.

* Urbanization. Urban consumer units averaged fewer vehicles (1.9) than rural units (2.6). About 16 percent of urban consumer units owned no car, truck, or van compared with 11 percent of rural units. The percentage owning three or more vehicles was the highest in the suburbs.

* Occupation. Vehicle ownership was the highest (2.9) in consumer units in which the householder was employed as a construction worker or mechanic. It was also high (2.6) among self-employed-worker units. Service worker and retired units averaged the fewest vehicles (1.6 and 1.5, respectively).

Automobiles are equipped with safety devices, such as seat belts, but usage is low. In 1988, 16 states had seat belt laws, but in 1985 only about a third of all adults wore seat belts "most of the time when they were in automobiles" (NCHS, 1990, p. 53). Three-fourths of infants were correctly restrained when riding in an automobile.

Use of public transportation depends, in part, on availability, which varies considerably among areas. Chicago, for example, averaged 101 trips by public transportation per person in 1983, while Dallas averaged only 22 (Lowe, 1990a, p. 17).

American adults average the equivalent of more than one workday per week in travel. According to one study (Kimbrell, 1989), men spend an average of 11 hours per week in travel, while women average 9. Most trips (about 80 percent) are made by automobile.

The most important single use of household vehicles is for earning a living. According to a 1970 survey (Courtless, 1981), about 35 percent of trips made by households were work related, accounting for about 40 percent of the miles driven by household members. About 70 percent of householders drive to work alone. The next most frequent mode of transportation to work is carpooling (16.2 percent), followed by mass transportation (5.4 percent). About 6 percent walk or work at home. Average distance to work was 11 miles in 1979 and average travel time 23 minutes (*Family Economics Review*, 1983). About 80 percent of full-time workers and nearly half of part-time workers begin their workday between 7 and 9 A.M., which accounts for the heavy rush-hour traffic in cities during that period. Quitting times are almost equally concentrated. Most full-time workers end their workday between 4 and 6 P.M., while 38 percent of part-time workers end their work between 3 and 5 P.M. (*Family Economics Review*, 1987).

Related Consumption. Owning and operating an automobile requires consumption of other commodities as well: gasoline and oil, repair and maintenance services, insurance, and provisions for parking. According to a 1980 report (Courtless, 1981), about two-thirds of all gasoline used in transportation is used in household-owned vehicles. Average miles per gallon is 16, lower than in other industrialized countries (Chandler, 1985a, p. 24). The fuel used in public transportation per passenger is much lower—less than one-third of that used by automobiles—than that used in private transportation, except for airlines, which use more than twice the energy per passenger than private automobiles (Chandler, 1985a, p. 27).

About three-fourths of all households had vehicle insurance in 1985—85 percent of those who owned a vehicle (Scoon, 1990). Uninsured vehicle owners tended to have lower income and less education than other vehicle owners. About one-third of those with no insurance were in the under–25 age group; about one-fifth were single. Lack of insurance was more frequent among black than among white vehicle owners and in rural than in urban areas. The percentage with expenditures for vehicle insurance increased with number of vehicles owned and was higher for husband-wife families than for other family types.

Over half (56 percent) of all occupied dwellings had a garage or carport. An additional 32 percent had some off-street parking (Census & HUD, 1989, p. 6).

Expenditure Trends and Patterns

Prices. The CPI for transportation increased by a slower rate than the all-items index from 1970 to 1988. In 1988, it stood at 108.7, just under three times the index for 1970, with most of the increase occurring before 1981 (U.S. House of Representatives, 1990, Table C-59).

Expenditures. The average consumer unit expenditure for transportation in 1988 was $5,093, one-fifth of total expenditures (Table 4.5). Of this, nearly half (46 percent) was for purchase of vehicles, and nearly one-fifth (18 percent) was for gasoline and motor oil. Maintenance and repairs comprised 11 percent of transportation expenditures, vehicle insurance 10 percent, and vehicle finance charges 6 percent. Public transportation accounted for 5 percent of transportation expenditure.

Transportation expenses have steadily increased as a share of the consumer unit budget. In 1917–1918, they comprised only 3 percent of the budget; by 1986–1987 the share was 26 percent (Figure 4.4). The increase was due to increased expenditures for private, rather than public, transportation. In fact, after 1934–1936, budget share for public transportation declined—from 2.6 percent in 1934–1936 to 1 percent in 1986–1987.

Average expenditures increased with income, from $1,660 among consumer units in the lowest income quintile to $9,158 in the highest quintile. Although transportation increased as a percentage of total expenditures, it declined as a percentage of income. The elasticity of transportation with respect to total expenditures is less than one, suggesting that households regard it as a necessity. Short-run demand for gasoline also has low elasticity, with respect to both price and total expenditures, although the elasticities vary with number of cars owned and total expenditure level of the household (Archibald & Gillingham, 1980). Expenditure elasticity was found to be higher for multicar than for one-car

Table 4.5
Transportation Expenditures, 1988

	All Consumer Units	Income quintile				
		Lowest 20%	2nd 20%	3rd 20%	4th 20%	Highest 20%
Transportation (total)	5,093	1,660	3,142	4,881	6,844	9,158
Vehicle purchases (net outlay)	2,361	588	1,422	2,282	3,334	4,308
Cars and trucks, new	1,355	300	625	1,230	1,912	2,886
Cars and trucks, used	982	287	782	1,022	1,386	1,376
Other vehicles	23	1	15	29	36	46
Gasoline and motor oil	932	459	659	926	1,204	1,420
Other vehicle expenses	1,521	501	912	1,452	2,023	2,870
Vehicle finance changes	284	60	116	259	403	585
Maintenance and repairs	553	215	387	540	702	998
Vehicle insurance	508	176	317	508	667	904
Vehicle rental, licenses, etc.	177	50	93	144	251	383
Public transportation	279	112	149	222	283	560

Source: U.S. Bureau of Labor Statistics (1990).

Figure 4.4
Budget Share Spent for Transportation, 1917–1987

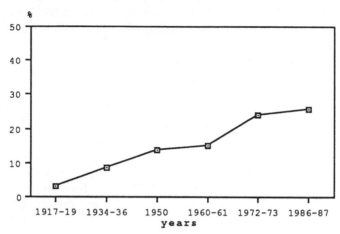

Source: Jacobs & Shipp (1990, p. 22).

households and was lower among households with a high total expenditure than among low-expenditure households.

Price elasticity for gasoline ranged from $-.39$ to $-.47$. Among one-car households, price elasticity was near -1 ($-.92$ to $-.99$) in households with low total expenditures and near 0 ($-.1$) in the high-expenditure group. Multicar households showed a similar pattern with respect to price elasticity, although there was less difference between the low- and high-total-expenditure groups (Archibald & Gillingham, 1980).

Private transportation expenditures, according to multivariate analysis, were higher among those 25 to 34 than in other age groups, other factors being equal. Budget share for private transportation was higher in the 25 to 34 and 55 to 64 age groups, compared with other age groups. Expenditures and budget share declined as education level increased but increased with income. Expenditures (but not budget share) were lower for managers than for other occupational groups. Those not employed devoted a smaller share of their budget to private transportation than other households but did not spend significantly less. Larger households devoted a smaller budget share to private transportation than did smaller households. No differences among racial groups appeared when other factors were equal. A comparison of family types showed that private transportation expenditures (both dollar amount and budget share) were higher for husband-wife households with one or more children age 18 or older and lower for single consumers, compared with other family types.

Expenditures for public transportation, which includes air fares as well as travel by train, bus, or subway, also increased with income. Multivariate analysis revealed no differences among age, household size, or occupational groups.

Expenditures increased, however, in both dollar amount and budget share, as education increased. Black consumer units spent more (both dollar amount and budget share) on public transportation than did white units. Compared with husband-wife-only families, two-parent families with a child under age 6 spent less on public transportation.

Impact on Well-being

Types of Impacts. Transportation is a facilitating area of consumption. It is most frequently undertaken for the purpose of enabling household members to carry on other household activities—work, school attendance, shopping, other errands, visiting, or recreation. As such it has three general types of impacts: effectiveness in performing its facilitating role, that is, in transporting household members, their belongings, and others traveling with them to the desired destination; efficiency with respect to use of resources; and impact on the comfort and safety of household members. Of these impacts, safety is the one most frequently studied and the only one on which national data are available.

Standards. No standards are available regarding minimum or optimum amount of transportation needed by households, efficiency, or comfort; however, a variety of standards intended to preserve the safety of travelers are promulgated by government—for example, requirements that automobiles include various safety devices such seat belts and regulations regarding the safe operation of vehicles.

Evidence of Impact. Traffic accidents are a leading cause of death and injury. In 1987, the motor vehicle death rate was 19.8 per 100,000 population. The rate was the highest among those aged 15 to 24 years and was more than twice as high for males as for females (NCHS, 1990, p. 137). Years of potential life lost from all causes in 1987 was 56.5 per thousand population. About 12 percent of the potential years lost was due to motor vehicle accidents (p. 125). Nearly 5 million persons (2 percent of the population) suffered traffic-related injuries in 1987, averaging about one and one-half days in bed per person (NCHS, 1988).

HEALTH CARE

Acquisition and Use

Health care refers to goods and services acquired for the purpose of curing or alleviating health problems. It also includes some items (such as routine visits to the doctor or dentist) that are intended to prevent health problems from developing or detect them at an early stage.

Well-being in the area of health does not entirely depend on the amount of health care received. If that were true, a chronically ill person who saw a doctor every week would be said to be better off than a healthy person who never visited a doctor or hospital. However, well-being as related to health care is associated with amount and quality received in relation to need, that is, in relation to likelihood or incidence of health problems.

Health Problems. Health problems encompass illness, injury, or impairment. They can be classified as acute conditions and chronic conditions. The National Health Interview Survey (NCHS, 1988, p. 3) classifies a condition as acute if it has lasted, or can be expected to last, less than three months and is sufficiently severe as to require at least one visit to the doctor or one day of restricted activity. Conditions that persist or can be expected to persist for more than three months are classified as chronic (p. 5).

Americans averaged nearly two acute conditions per year in 1987 (NCHS, 1988, p. 15). Acute conditions include infective and parasitic diseases (e.g., chicken pox), respiratory conditions (e.g., the common cold or pneumonia), digestive system conditions (e.g., "tourist's disease"), injuries, eye conditions, ear infections, headache, skin conditions, and so forth. Respiratory conditions, especially influenza and the common cold, were the most common. About one-fourth of the population in 1987 suffered some kind of injury, the most common being strains and sprains and open wounds and lacerations. Other common acute conditions were viral infections and acute ear infections.

Frequency of acute conditions varies with economic and demographic characteristics:

- Age. The incidence of acute conditions declined with age, from about three and one-half per year among children under 5 years old to about one per year among those aged 45 or older. Respiratory conditions were common at all ages, but infective and parasitic diseases were less frequent among older persons than among children, and injuries were more frequent (NCHS, 1988, p. 15).

- Sex. Although injuries were more common among males than females, females averaged a larger total number of acute conditions per year (nearly two per person compared with about one and one-half for males) (NCHS, 1988, p. 16).

- Race. White persons averaged more acute conditions per year than blacks (about 1.8 compared with 2.4 per person). The only category in which blacks were higher was in digestive conditions (NCHS, 1988, p. 17).

- Income. Acute conditions were somewhat more common among those with family income less than $10,000 (average about two conditions per year) than among higher-income groups. Low-income persons had a higher rate of injuries and digestive system conditions but a slightly lower incidence of infective and parasitic diseases (NCHS, 1988, pp. 18–19).

- Place of residence. Among regions, the highest incidence of acute conditions was in the West, with about two per person per year (NCHS, 1988, p. 20).

Chronic conditions include skin and musculoskeletal conditions (for example, arthritis and dermatitis), various kinds of impairments (such as visual or hearing impairments), and some digestive conditions (such as ulcers). The most frequent in 1987 were chronic sinusitis (afflicting 13 percent of the population), arthritis

(13 percent), high blood pressure (12 percent), deformity or orthopedic impairment (12 percent), hay fever or allergic rhinitis (10 percent), hearing impairment (9 percent), heart disease (8 percent), chronic bronchitis (5 percent), hemorrhoids (4 percent), migraine headache (4 percent), asthma (4 percent), dermatitis (4 percent), and visual impairment (about 3 percent) (NCHS, 1988, pp. 84–85).

- Age. Many chronic conditions become more frequent with age. Arthritis, for example, afflicted nearly half of all persons aged 65 and over. Other common conditions among the elderly were high blood pressure (37 percent); heart disease (30 percent), hearing impairment (30 percent), deformity or orthopedic impairment (17 percent), and cataracts (16 percent) (NCHS, 1988, pp. 84–85).

- Sex. Incidence of chronic conditions varies by sex. For example, the incidence of diabetes and heart disease are higher among elderly males than females, while elderly females were more prone than males to arthritis, cataracts, high blood pressure, or a deformity or orthopedic impairment (NCHS, 1988, pp. 86–87).

- Race. Incidence also varies by race. For example, whites were more likely than blacks to have cataracts, hearing impairment, and heart disease. Blacks had a higher incidence of arthritis, diabetes, and high blood pressure (NCHS, 1988, pp. 88–89).

- Income. In general, chronic conditions were more frequent among those with family income less than $10,000 than in higher-income groups. Exceptions were asthma and cataracts (NCHS, 1988, pp. 90–93).

- Place of residence. There appeared to be little variation by place of residence (NCHS, 1988, pp. 94–95).

Use of Services. Americans visit doctors frequently. About three-fourths of those interviewed in 1987 had seen a physician within the past year; less than 4 percent had not seen a physician within the previous five years (NCHS, 1988, p. 118). The average for the total population was over five contacts per year. More than half of these contacts took place in the doctor's office; some contacts were in a hospital (while not an overnight patient) or other location or by telephone. Frequency of visits to physicians varied with a number of factors (NCHS, 1988, pp. 116–119):

- Age. Frequency of physician contacts varied by age, with small children and the very elderly averaging the most doctor contacts. Children under age 5 averaged nearly seven (6.7) contacts per year, with 93 percent having seen a physician within the past year. The number of contacts declined to just over three per year among children aged 5 to 17 years old and then increased gradually over the life span to a high of nearly 10 per year among those 75 and over.

- Sex. Females averaged nearly two more physician contacts per year than males (6.2 compared with 4.5). The age-related pattern was somewhat different for males than for females. Among males, the lowest frequency of physician contacts was at ages 18 to 44, while among females the frequency increased steadily after childhood. Number of contacts was higher for females than for males at all ages.

- Race. Whites averaged somewhat more physician contacts than blacks—5.5 per year compared with 4.9—although this was not true at every age level. Whites averaged more contacts than blacks up to age 44; among those aged 45 and older, blacks averaged more physician contacts.

• Income. Number of physician contacts declined as income increased. Those with family income under $10,000 averaged 7.1 contacts per year, an average of two more than among those with incomes over $20,000. The age-related pattern differed among income groups. Among children under 18, number of contacts averaged about four to five per year, with the fewest contacts in the $10,000–20,000 group (who may have had less access to free or low-cost health care than those with less income) and the highest number in the highest-income group. Among those in the under-$10,000 range, the highest number of physician contacts was in late middle age (45 to 64), where the average in this income group was over 10 per year, slightly more than among those aged 65 and over. In other income groups, as in the population as a whole, number of contacts increased over the life span. Among the elderly (ages 65 and over), physician contacts averaged about eight to 10 per year, but, as in the case of children, the lowest number was in the middle-income group (in this case, $10,000–35,000).

• Place of residence. Among regions, the highest average was in the Midwest and the lowest in the South. The number appeared to increase with urbanization, with the highest average in major cities.

Hospital stays, unlike doctor visits, are rather infrequent. In 1987, 92 percent of the population had not been hospitalized during the year. Stays in the hospital were somewhat more frequent among the elderly and children under age 5 than in other age groups and among females than among males. Low-income persons were somewhat more likely to have a hospital stay than those with higher incomes (NCHS, 1988, pp. 120–121).

Expenditure Trends and Patterns

Prices. The CPI for medical care stood at 138.6 in 1988, the highest of the subindexes. Unlike prices of other commodities, the rate of growth did not decline after 1979. During the 1970s, medical care prices nearly doubled, and they more than doubled again from 1979 to 1988 (U.S. House of Representatives, 1990, Table C-59).

Expenditures. Health care expenditures in 1901 comprised just 3 percent of the consumer unit budget. This percentage increased to a high of 6.6 percent in 1960–1961 and then declined to 4 percent in 1986–1987 (Figure 4.5).

Average consumer unit expenditure for health care in 1988 was $1,298, about 5 percent of total expenditures (Table 4.6). About one-third of the amount spent for health care was for health insurance, 41 percent for medical services, 17 percent for drugs, and about 5 percent for medical supplies.

Expenditures increased as income increased, from $831 in the lowest income quintile in 1988 to $1,550 in the highest quintile. Percentage of the budget declined with income quintile, from 8 to 3 percent in 1988. The income elasticity

Figure 4.5
Budget Share Spent for Health Care, 1901–1987

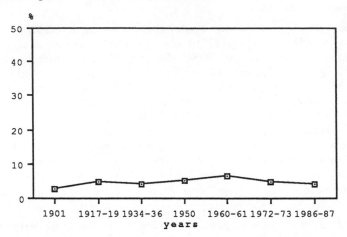

Source: Jacobs & Shipp (1990, p. 22).

of health care expenditures was slightly greater than 1 (1.11) (Abdel-Ghany and Foster, 1982). Expenditures for health care also vary with other factors:

- Age. Health care expenditures increase with age, other factors being equal, in both dollar amount and budget share. This shows in the averages for age groups. Average expenditures in 1988 increased from a low of $523 per year among consumer units in the youngest age group to $2,230 among those with a householder aged 75 and older, in spite of the fact that average income was lower in the 75-and-over group than in any other age group. Composition of expenditures also changes somewhat with age. Among younger consumer units, medical services was the most important category of expenditure, accounting for about 55 percent of health care expenditure among those with a householder under age 25 and about half among those in the 25 to 44 age group. Among the elderly (householder aged 65 or older), health insurance and medical services were of about equal importance.

- Education. Health care expenditures (but not budget share) tend to be higher among consumer units with higher levels of education, other factors being equal.

- Occupation. There appears to be no relationship between occupation and health care expenditures, other factors being equal. Also, consumer units in which the householder was not employed did not differ from nonemployed units.

- Race. White consumer units spend more and devote a larger budget share on health care than black units, other factors being equal.

- Consumer unit size and type. Single consumers spend less on health care and devote a smaller budget share to it than do other family types. Otherwise, there was little evidence that size and type were associated with health care expenditures when other factors were equal.

Table 4.6
Health Care Expenditures, 1988

	All Consumer Units	Income quintile				
		Lowest 20%	2nd 20%	3rd 20%	4th 20%	Highest 20%
Health care (total)	1,298	831	1,320	1,286	1,425	1,550
Health insurance	474	346	469	512	524	516
Medical services	529	271	552	480	564	697
Drugs	223	173	242	239	247	225
Medical supplies	71	41	57	55	89	112

Source: U.S. Bureau of Labor Statistics (1990).

Assistance Programs. Government-sponsored programs include Medicare and Medicaid. Medicare provides hospital and medical insurance to persons aged 65 or older and to younger disabled persons receiving cash benefits under the social security or railroad retirement programs. It is financed in part by employer and employee contributions and in part by monthly premiums paid by those enrolled in the program. In 1985, 31.1 million persons received Medicare benefits. Medicaid provides medical assistance to low-income persons. There were 21.8 million Medicaid recipients in 1985 (Schwenk, 1990).

Impact on Well-being

Types of Impacts. Health care is a factor in extending the life span, improving the productivity of human resources, and improving quality of life; however, this is true of other areas of consumption. More specific impacts include degree and duration of physical impairment and survival rates of those who have incurred a health problem.

Standards. In theory, all who need health care should receive it in amounts and quality that are adequate to achieve the beneficial impacts to the degree possible, given the present state of knowledge. That is a very high standard. No generally accepted standards of minimal adequacy exist; however, there are accepted indicators that can be used to compare the adequacy of health care provided to different population groups. These include access to health care, productivity of workers, life expectancy, and health status.

The most direct measure of access to health care is the proportion of health problems that receive treatment. An indirect measure is availability of resources needed to obtain health care. In the United States, health care insurance is the predominant means of ensuring adequate access to needed health care and is regarded as the crucial factor. Other factors include numbers of adequately trained health care workers, stock of health care facilities and equipment, and presence of medical personnel and facilities within a convenient distance of members of the population.

Productivity may be estimated by days lost from work due to illness or by incidence of disabling conditions that reduce productivity or ability to work. Life expectancy or mortality rates can be used as indicators of the adequacy of health care, although they also reflect exposure to an unsafe or unhealthy environment. Like life expectancy or morbidity, health status is related to health care but is affected by other factors as well.

Evidence of Impact. According to the National Health Interview Survey of 1987 (NCHS, 1988, pp. 27–32), about 62 percent of all acute conditions receive treatment in the United States. An acute condition, by definition, is a short-term health problem that results in one or more days of restricted activity, as well as those medically attended. Among those conditions most likely to receive medical attention, in order of likelihood, were acute urinary infections, skin conditions, eye or ear conditions, delivery and conditions associated with pregnancy, injuries, and infective and parasitic diseases. Influenza was least likely to receive medical attention.

Percentage receiving treatment varies with characteristics of the individual:

- Age. Nearly 80 percent of the acute conditions suffered by children under age 5 and about 76 percent of those suffered by the elderly received medical attention. Children aged 5 to 17 were least likely to receive medical attention; only about half of their episodes were treated.
- Sex. Females were somewhat more likely than males to have treatment for acute conditions.
- Race. Acute conditions reported by blacks were more likely to have received medical treatment than those reported by whites.

Another indicator of access to health care is health insurance coverage. In 1987, approximate 85 percent of the United States population had some kind of health insurance coverage (Schwenk, 1990). Employment-related coverage was the most important source of health insurance; nearly two-thirds were covered by health insurance connected with employment of a family member. An additional 10 percent had other private health insurance, 10 percent had coverage from public sources, such as Medicare or Medicaid or other public assistance, and the remaining 15.5 percent had no health insurance. Coverage varied by age and other factors:

- Age. Coverage was the highest among the elderly (with less than 1 percent not covered) and lowest among those aged 19 to 24.
- Sex. Males were slightly less likely than females to have some form of health insurance coverage. Males were slightly more likely than females to have employer-related coverage; females were more likely than males to be covered by public sources.
- Race. The highest percentage of persons not covered by health insurance was Hispanics, with nearly one-third without any kind of health insurance coverage, followed by blacks (22 percent not covered). About 88 percent of whites had some kind of health insurance coverage.
- Marital status. Coverage was lowest among those never married, separated, or divorced.
- Region. The South and West had the highest incidence of persons without health insurance coverage.

Health status is a major cause of unemployment or loss of work time. In 1986 among poor households, 12 percent of householders either did not work or worked only part of the year because they were ill or disabled (*Family Economics Review*, 1990).

Adults in the United States averaged 17 activity-restricted days due to acute or chronic conditions in 1987. Number of days lost increased with age, was higher for females than for males and for blacks than whites, and tended to decline as income increased. Adults in the lowest income group averaged about

30 activity-restricted days per year, three times the number in the highest income group. Number of days lost from work or school averaged about five per year and showed a similar pattern (NCHS, pp. 112–113).

One approach to assessing the adequacy of health care is to look at the excess mortality ratio (EMR), the number of preventable deaths expressed as a percentage of the minimum achievable death rate. The estimated EMR for the United States in 1985 was 31.7, meaning that the death rate was 31.7 percent higher than the minimum death rate that could have been achieved. When only those under age 65 were considered, the EMR for females was much higher than for males—about 82 compared with 73; however, the reverse was true for all ages (Uemura, 1989, p. 33).

Another aspect of health status is life expectancy. In 1985, life expectancy at birth was 71.2 years for males and 78.2 for females (NCHS, p. 6). Disability-free life expectancy has also been calculated. According to Robine (1989), males can expect 7.1 years of restricted activity (10.7 percent of their life span) and females 4.9 years (8.8 percent of their life span).

Respondents in the 1987 National Health Interview Survey were asked to assess their own health status. Two out of five regarded their health as excellent. This percentage declined with age, however; only 15 percent of the elderly assessed their health as excellent. Fewer females than males and blacks than whites rated their health as excellent. The percentage with excellent health increased with income. Over half of those in the highest income group reported that their health was excellent compared with one-fourth of those in the lowest income group. Twenty-two percent of the poorest group had health rated fair or poor compared with 4 percent in the high-income group (NCHS, pp. 114–115).

OTHER COMMODITIES

Expenditure Patterns and Trends

Housekeeping Services. A wide variety of housekeeping services are available: domestic services (cleaning, home laundering, and cooking), gardening (lawn cutting, lawn fertilizing, pruning, and tree removal), care of invalids in the home (including handicapped and elderly persons), appliance and furniture repair, other housekeeping services (water softening, moving, storage, freight, laundry and dry cleaning of household textiles, equipment rentals, and security services), baby-sitting, and day care. Nearly half (45 percent) of all consumer units purchased one or more household services in 1985 (Schwenk, 1989). Mean expenditure was $651, about 3 percent of total expenditures.

The types of services most frequently purchased were appliance and furniture repair (13 percent of all consumer units) and gardening and lawn care services (13 percent). Only 6 percent purchased domestic services. Baby-sitting and day care were purchased by 8 and 5 percent, respectively. Less than 1 percent of all consumer units paid for the care of invalids in the home. Purchase of all types of services was most frequent among the very elderly (75 and over).

Purchase of domestic services increased with income. About 4 percent in the lowest income group purchased such services, compared with 14 percent in the highest income range. Frequency of purchase was much lower than average (1 percent) among young consumer units (householder under age 25) and much higher than average (13 percent) among the very elderly (75 or over). Those most likely to purchase services were white (compared with black), home owners, husband-wife families with children, and two-earner consumer units.

About one-fourth of all consumer units with children purchased some form of child care in 1985. This proportion was about the same for husband-wife families as for single-parent families; however, child care expenditures in single-parent families were higher. Expenditure was related to employment of the mother. Among husband-wife families, over one-fifth of the two-earner units purchased child care services, compared with 8 percent of consumer units in which only the husband was employed. Among units in which the wife only was employed or the female, single householder was employed, about 8 percent incurred child care expenses; however, the average expenditure was about as high as that in two-earner consumer units.

Personal Care. Personal care, which includes personal care services, such as haircuts and electrical appliances for personal care, averaged $334 in 1988, about 1 percent of total expenditures (Table 4.7). This expenditure increased with income.

Alcoholic Beverages. Consumer units in 1988 averaged $269 on alcoholic beverages, about 1 percent of total expenditures. Over half of all persons aged 12 and over reported some consumption of alcohol in a one-month period in 1988 (NCHS, 1989, p. 70). The percentage was higher (about 15 percent) among those aged 18 to 34. Among teenagers, about one-fourth used alcohol, with the percentage slightly higher for males and lower for females. A larger percentage of whites (55 percent) than blacks (44 percent) or Hispanics (49 percent) used alcohol. The amount consumed per capita increased slightly from 1978 to 1980–1981 and then declined to about 2.5 gallons per capita in 1987.

Expenditure for alcohol tends to increase with income and decline with increases in consumer unit size, other factors being equal, but budget share does not increase. The highest expenditures was in younger households (under 35) and lowest in older households (65 or older). Black households spent less on alcohol than white, when other factors were held constant. Compared with husband-wife-only households, alcohol expenditure was higher among single consumers and lower in households (either two-parent or female headed) with children.

Tobacco. Use of tobacco in the United States declined from 1979 to 1987. In 1979, 33 percent of the adult population used tobacco; in 1987, the percentage had dropped to 28.8. The percentage of teenagers who smoked also declined.

Table 4.7
Other Expenditures, 1988

	All Consumer Units	Income quintile				
		Lowest 20%	2nd 20%	3rd 20%	4th 20%	Highest 20%
Entertainment	1,329	448	768	1,096	1,547	2,880
Fees and admissions	353	119	145	275	430	790
Television, radios, sound equipment	416	188	286	398	502	736
Pets, toys, & playground equipment	230	92	148	207	335	428
Other supplies, equipment & services	330	50	188	216	279	926
Personal care products & services	334	154	233	310	423	608
Reading	150	67	96	136	190	273
Education	342	254	170	164	310	723
Tobacco products & smoking supplies	242	179	226	260	284	263
Miscellaneous	578	243	366	546	719	1,112
Cash contributions	693	165	342	545	768	1,827
Personal insurance & pensions	2,249	268	808	1,850	3,402	6,321
Life & other personal insurance	314	110	182	269	395	665
Pensions & Social Security	1,935	159	626	1,580	3,007	5,656

Source: U.S. Bureau of Labor Statistics (1990).

Smoking was more common among men than among women (NCHS, 1989, p. 66).

Expenditures for tobacco and smoking supplies averaged $242, less than 1 percent of total expenditures. Like other commodities, amount spent tended to increase with income; however, unlike other commodities, expenditures in the highest income group were lower than in the next-highest. Expenditures were the lowest among the very old households.

Use or nonuse of tobacco affects other expenditures as well. In 1987, most life insurance companies and some health insurance carriers offered health behavior–related discounts (NCHS, 1989, p. 66).

Drugs. While the percentage using marijuana declined from 1977 to 1988, the percentage using cocaine increased. About 19 percent of young adults (aged 18 to 25) reported frequent use of marijuana in 1977 but only 7 percent in 1988. A survey of the 1988 high school senior class showed that 3.4 percent had used cocaine in the previous month (NCHS, 1989, p. 71).

Entertainment and Reading. Since 1901, when entertainment accounted for less than 3 percent of the budget, consumer unit allocation to entertainment has generally increased (Jacobs & Shipp, 1990, p. 22). Entertainment accounted for about 5 percent of total expenditures in 1988, or $1,329. Expenditure increased with income, in both dollar amount and budget share. Among consumer units with householders less than 55 years old, expenditure for entertainment averaged 5 to 6 percent of total expenditures but declined to 3 percent among the very elderly. White consumer units allocated a larger share to entertainment than did blacks.

Reading, which includes purchase of newspapers, magazines, periodicals, books, encyclopedias, and reference materials, accounted for less than 1 percent of the budget in 1988. The most common type of reading material purchased by consumer units, according to a 1984 study (Schwenk, 1988), is newspapers; over two-thirds of all consumer units purchased newspapers in that year. Thirty-eight percent purchased magazines or periodicals.

Education. Before 1960, education accounted for about half of 1 percent of the current consumption expenditures of consumer units; from 1960 to 1988 it comprised about 1 percent. Average expenditure in 1988, including tuition and purchases of books and school supplies for students at all levels, was $342 per consumer unit. Expenditures for reading and education increased with income and educational level of the householder (Schwenk, 1988).

College tuition is the largest educational expense among those who have it. In 1984, college tuition averaged $2,610 among the 7 percent of the sample reporting this expense, with the maximum amount reported being $60,500 (Schwenk, 1988). Three percent reported expenditures for elementary or high school tuition; amounts averaged $1,813 but ranged up to $18,000 per year. In addition to expenditures by consumer units, there was an annual expenditure from public funds of $3,182 per student enrolled in a public elementary or secondary school. About one-fourth of federal, state, and local taxes were spent on education in 1984.

Cash Contributions. Cash contributions averaged $693 in 1988, about 3 percent of total expenditures. Such expenditures included contributions for the support of persons not living in the household, alimony, and child support.

Personal Insurance and Pensions. Personal insurance and payments to pension funds (including life insurance, endowments, annuities, and other nonhealth personal insurance) accounted for $2,249 per consumer unit in 1988, about the same amount as was spent for food at home. Most of this was spent for pensions and social security. Expenditure increased with income. Among family types, it averaged higher among husband-wife families than among other families.

When other factors were held constant, expenditures and budget share for personal insurance were lower among younger consumer units (householder under age 35) than among older units and among single than among married or single-parent units. Husband-wife families with children under the age of 6 had higher expenditures than families with other children. There was no difference among occupational or household-size groups. Black consumer units, however, spent significantly more and allocated a higher budget share to personal insurance than white units, other factors being equal.

Impact on Well-being

The types of impacts vary in this miscellaneous group of commodities. Consumption of entertainment, alcohol, and tobacco is associated with pleasure. Expenditures for retirement and insurance yield financial security. Housekeeping services ease the load of work at home, enable family members to engage in other activities, and maintain the appearance and functioning of the home. Personal care is associated with maintaining and communicating role and status. Cash contributions fulfill obligations to others.

Consumption of two commodities, alcohol and tobacco, is known to have detrimental as well as pleasurable effects on the consumer and might be classified in Hoyt's category of destructive consumption. Education (and, perhaps, reading) could be classified as expansive. Services that enable household members to engage in other worthwhile activities may also have an expansive impact. Other commodities might be regarded as protective.

Standards are lacking for consumption of these commodities, but some information is available on the health impacts of tobacco, alcohol, and drugs. Use of tobacco was responsible for about 19 percent of all deaths in the mid-1980s (Chandler, 1986, p. 13)—about 390,000 deaths in 1989 (NCHS, 1989, p. 66). About half of all traffic fatalities in 1988 were alcohol related. Deaths from cirrhosis were about 10.8 per 100,000 population (NCHS, 1989, p. 71). In total, about 4.7 percent of all deaths in 1984 were related to use of alcohol. Use of illegal drugs accounted for an additional 1.3 percent (Chandler, 1986, p. 13).

CONSUMPTION RESIDUES

Situation and Trends

Solid Waste. Inevitably the process of consumption results in residues or wastes that must be disposed of: solid waste in the form of packaging and containers, food waste, yard waste, and discarded durable goods. It also includes liquid wastes that enter the sewer system and gases that enter the atmosphere. Household wastes are mingled with wastes from commercial establishments, such as offices, retail stores, and restaurants, and from institutions such as schools and hospitals.

According to the Congress of the United States (CUS), 3.6 pounds of solid waste per capita per day were discarded in the United States in 1986, not including automobiles or debris from construction or demolition of buildings (1989, p. 4). From 1970 to 1986, the amount generated increased by about 0.7 percent annually (p. 77).

Paper and paperboard comprise the largest proportion of materials discarded, accounting for 41 percent of the total weight of discarded materials (before materials recovery). Yard wastes (leaves, grass clippings, weeds, and prunings) account for 20 percent of the total, followed by food waste (9 percent), metals (9 percent), glass (8 percent), plastics (7 percent), and wood, rubber, leather, textiles, and miscellaneous organic substances. When classified by type of product, containers and packaging account for 31 percent of the total, nondurable goods 25 percent, and durable goods 14 percent (CUS, 1989, p. 5).

Harmful substances are included in solid wastes. These include harmful metals, such as lead (from solder in steel cans and electronic components, automobile batteries, ceramic glazes and inks, and plastics), mercury (from household batteries, fluorescent light bulbs, thermometers, and mirrors), and cadmium (from rechargeable household batteries and plastics). Other hazardous household wastes include cleaning products, automobile products, home maintenance products (such as paint), personal care products, and yard maintenance products (such as pesticides, insecticides, and herbicides) (CUS, 1989, pp. 86–88).

About 10 percent of solid waste was recycled in 1986. Twenty-two percent of paper and paperboard were recycled, 25 percent of aluminum (about 55 percent of aluminum cans are recycled), 8 percent of glass, 4 percent of iron and steel, and 1 percent of plastics. A negligible amount of yard and food waste is recycled (CUS, 1989, p. 28).

Composition of solid waste has changed over the years. Paper and paperboard increased as a percentage of total solid waste from 1970 to 1986, as did wood and textiles. The largest increase was in plastics, which nearly tripled as a percentage of the total. Discards of metals, glass, and food waste declined as a percentage of total solid waste (CUS, 1989, p. 28).

By the year 2000, the amount of solid waste per capita is expected to total nearly 4 pounds per year. Increases of 10 percent or more are expected in discards of furniture and furnishings, books and magazines, office papers and commercial printing papers, beer and soft drink cans, aluminum foil and closures, corrugated boxes, and plastic containers and other plastic packaging (CUS, 1989, pp. 80–81).

Among the factors believed to be associated with amount of waste generated are the following:

- Household size. Some studies indicate that small households generate more solid waste per person than do larger households.

- Demand for convenience products. Single-serving packaging increases the amount of packaging waste.

- Socioeconomic status. Evidence suggests that higher-income households discard more waste, especially newspapers and yard waste, than do lower-income households; however, the evidence is mixed.

- Urbanization. Residents in rural areas may discard less solid waste per capita than those in urban areas (CUS, 1989, pp. 77–78).

Indoor Air Contaminants. Air contaminants come from several sources. Materials used in constructing the home may be sources of radon, formaldehyde, or asbestos. Appliances that are unvented or not vented properly may emit carbon monoxide, oxides of nitrogen, sulfur dioxides, water vapor, and particulate. Furnishings may give off odors.

Human beings and their activities also are a source of air pollution. Metabolism produces carbon dioxide and odors. Other pollution-causing activities include smoking, use of aerosol sprays, and use of some cleaning products (Morris & Eichner, 1986, p. 106).

Impact on Well-being

Several impacts can be identified: cost of disposing of waste, estimated at $60 per capita (CUS, 1989, p. 56); use of resources (some nonrenewable), including use of land for landfills; and hazards to health and safety from dangerous substances entering the environment.

NOTES

1. Relatively nutritious was defined as providing significant amounts of folacin, vitamin B6, pantothenic acid, magnesium, vitamin A, calcium, iron, and vitamin E1. The definition was based on a 1976 survey of members of the Society for Nutrition Education. Individuals consuming foods that provide recommended amounts of these eight nutrients are likely to be consuming sufficient amounts of other nutrients as well.

2. Estimated by the Center for Housing Studies of Harvard University, based on median value of house purchased by a first-time buyer aged 25 to 29 in 1977 (data from the Annual Housing Survey), indexed by Department of Census, Construction Reports C-27 Constant Quality Home Price Index.

3. Payments assumed a 25-year mortgage with a 20 percent down payment.

4. Estimated by the Center for Housing Studies of Harvard University, based on median 1977 contract rent plus fuel and utilities, property taxes, and insurance.

5. Figures on average number of vehicles owned are from the 1988 Survey of Consumer Expenditures and pertain to all vehicles. Figures on percentages owning vehicles are from the 1987 *American Housing Survey* and pertain to cars, trucks, and vans only.

5

Consumption Patterns in the United States

This chapter provides a profile of different types of spending units—for example, one-parent families, black families, or families with both husband and wife employed. Included in the profile are population characteristics; resources, described in terms of time, income, and durable goods; and spending patterns.

In these profiles, spending is summarized in two ways. First, the mean allocation of expenditures among major categories is presented. This provides a useful description of how such consumer units actually behave on the average. It does not tell us, however, whether their behavior is due to the identifying characteristic (for example, the race of the consumer unit) or to differences in income or other factors. To answer that question, a second expenditure summary is provided to identify expenditure pattern as it uniquely relates to the identifying characteristic.

Data have been drawn from several sources. For this reason, the definitions do not always match. While expenditure data are summarized for consumer units, income and population data are provided by the Bureau of the Census for families and households or, in some cases, individuals. In reading the profiles, keep in mind the differences among these units. Another limitation concerns the year to which data pertain. Where possible, 1988 data have been used throughout; however, some information was available only from earlier years. Unless otherwise noted, all data pertain to 1988. Expenditure data are from the 1988 Survey of Consumer Expenditures, public use tapes, except where otherwise noted.

ALL HOUSEHOLDS

Population Trends

In 1985, there were nearly 87 million households in the United States. The number is expected to increase, although at a declining rate. By the year 2000 there are expected to be about 106 million, a 22 percent increase (U.S. Bureau of the Census [Census], 1986b, p. 1).

Increases in numbers of households will occur exclusively among middle-aged and elderly households, while the numbers of younger households are expected to decline. Households in which the householder is less than 35 years old, 29 percent of the population in 1985, will comprise only 21 percent by 2000. Households in the 35 to 64 age range will increase from 50 to 57 percent of the population. The very elderly, householder aged 75 and over, will increase from 8 to 11 percent of the population, but those in the 65 to 74 age range will decline slightly as a share of the population (Census, 1986, p. 3).

Seventy-two percent of the households in 1985 were families, that is, "a group of two persons or more (one of whom is a householder) related by birth, marriage, or adoption and residing together" (Census, 1986, p. 7). Married-couple families comprised 58 percent, families with a female householder but no spouse 12 percent, and families with a male householder but no spouse 3 percent of the total. Nonfamily households (28 percent of the total) included 16 percent female and 12 percent male householders. By the year 2000, the proportion of families in the population is expected to decline to about 68 percent and the nonfamily component to increase correspondingly. The proportion of male householders is expected to increase among families with only one parent present and among nonfamilies (Census, 1986, p. 2).

An increasing number of households include adult children. Consider the case of young men and women aged 18 to 24. In 1970, 54 percent of men and 41 percent of women in that age range were living in the parental home; in 1988, the percentages had increased to 61 and 48 percent, respectively. In 1970, 35 percent of the men and 47 percent of the women were living in their own homes; in 1988 the percentages were 25 and 38 percent, respectively (Census, 1989f, p. 7).

Except among the elderly, most households have at least one employed member, but employment varies by age, sex, and marital status. About half of all families with earners had two or more earners in 1988 (Census, 1990g, p. 410). Among those currently married and living with their spouse, 79 percent of the men and 57 percent of the women were in the labor force in 1988. The participation rate varies by age, however. Among married men under age 45, over 90 percent were employed in 1988, with the highest participation rate among those aged 25 to 34. The rate dropped to 82 percent among those aged 45 to 64 and then to about 18 percent among those aged 65 and over. Participation rates among women follow a similar pattern, with the peak (73 percent) at ages 35 to 44, declining to 7 percent among married women aged 65 and over (Census, 1990g, p. 384).

Labor force participation rates among married men were higher than among single men (79 percent compared with 72 percent in 1988), while rates among single women were higher than among their married counterparts (65 percent compared with 57 percent). The age-related pattern was similar to those of

Table 5.1
Trends in Median Income

Year	Median family income	
	in current dollars	in 1988 dollars
1967	7,143	25,300
1968	7,743	26,322
1969	8,389	27,041
1970	8,734	26,630
1971	9,028	26,371
1972	9,697	27,444
1973	10,512	28,008
1974	11,197	26,868
1975	11,800	25,947
1976	12,686	26,375
1977	13,572	26,495
1978	15,064	27,332
1979	16,461	26,823
1980	17,710	25,426
1981	19,074	24,823
1982	20,171	24,728
1983	21,018	24,964
1984	22,415	25,522
1985	23,618	25,967
1986	24,897	26,873
1987	26,061	27,139
1988	27,225	27,225

Source: U.S. Bureau of the Census (1990g, pp. 7, 9).

married persons. Men who were widowed, divorced, or separated had a participation rate of 67 percent, while women in this category had a rate of 46 percent. Among married men, labor force participation rates have declined, from 87 percent in 1970 to 79 percent in 1988. The participation rates among single men have increased, however, as have the rates for women in all marital categories (Census, 1990g, pp. 384–385).

Resource Ownership

Income. Trends in household income are shown in Table 5.1. The real income (in 1988 dollars) of all households increased slightly from $26,630 in 1970 to $28,008 in 1973, declined to a low of $24,728 in 1982, and then increased to $27,225 in 1988 (Census, 1990h, p. 7). The distribution of income also changed. The share of aggregate income received by households in the highest income quintile increased between 1970 and 1988, while the share received by those in the lowest three quintiles declined (Census, 1990h, p. 9).

- Race: Median income was the highest among white households ($28,781) in 1988 and lowest among black households ($16,407). Households of Hispanic origin were in between, with a median income of $20,359 (Census, 1990h, p. 9).

- Age: Median income followed an inverted U-shaped curve, with the peak among households in the 45 to 54 age range and the lowest income among those aged 65 and over (Census, 1990h, p. 11).

- Marital status: Median income was the highest among married-couple households ($36,436 in 1988). Other types of households ranked as follows, by income: male householder, no wife present; single male; female householder, no husband present; and single female (Census, 1990h, p. 10).

- Household size: Median household income increased with size of household, up to four persons (Census, 1990h, p. 12).

- Education: Median income increased with years of school completed by the householder (Census, 1990h, p. 13).

- Region: Median income of households was the highest in the Northeast ($30,425 in 1988) and lowest in the South ($24,607) (Census, 1990h, p. 10).

The share of household income received from different sources has changed over the past few decades. In 1918, about 97 percent of the income received by a white laborer came from earnings, while the corresponding percentage in 1980 was only 84 percent. Transfer payments (social security, pensions, and other assistance) not available in 1918 comprised 13 percent of the income of a white laborer in 1980 (Brown, 1987, p. 20). Over 1983–1986, 15 percent of the population received part of their income from one or more major assistance programs (food stamps, rent assistance, Medicaid, or cash assistance) (Census, 1989a, p. 1). The importance of other sources of income has changed as well. In 1960, only 37.7 percent of women were in the labor force; in 1988, 56.6 percent were (Census, 1990g, p. 380).

The distribution of income varies by a number of factors. On average, income is low for young adults, increases to a peak at about ages 45 to 54, and drops substantially after retirement; however, this pattern varies by education and occupation group, with the college educated and those in professional and managerial occupations reaching their peak later and maintaining it longer than other groups. Earned income varies by sex of earner, with females receiving lower pay, on the average, than males. Income varies by race and ethnic group. For example, median before-tax income of white households was $33,915 in 1988, compared with $19,329 for blacks and $21,769 for those of Hispanic origin (Census, 1990h, p. 17). It also varies by geographic area. In 1988, median income of households was the highest in the Northeast ($30,425) and lowest in the South ($24,607) (Census, 1990h, p. 10). Average after-tax income of households is the highest in the suburban portions of major metropolitan areas ($24,658 in 1986) compared with the inner city ($18,412), other metropolitan areas ($20,621), or nonmetropolitan areas ($17,834). Larger households have higher incomes than smaller households. The median income of two-person households was $27,075, for example, compared with $39,051 for four-person households (Census, 1990h, p. 21).

In 1983, families received an estimated $446 billion in noncash income plus an additional $49 billion in return on equity in an owned home. Of the $446 billion, nearly three-fourths ($323.7 billion) consisted of employer contributions for private health and pension plans and federal and state social insurance programs. Government programs accounted for $122 billion, with somewhat less than half ($55 billion) earmarked for the poor (McNeil, 1985). As these figures show, the largest share of noncash income goes to households in which one or more members are employed. Employee benefits have been increasing as a share of total compensation to the employee—from 12.6 percent in 1950 to 28.5 percent in 1983 (Hefferan, 1985).

A 1990 report of the Bureau of the Census estimated the impact of benefits and taxes on income distribution in 1989. Mean household income after deducting state and federal income taxes and social security payroll taxes, but including capital gains and health insurance supplements to wage or salary income, was $28,829. After including benefits (cash transfers from government and the value of Medicare, Medicaid, school lunches, and other means-tested government noncash transfers), the mean was $32,444. Including the net imputed return on equity in own home resulted in an increase to $36,319. Thus, benefits added more than $7,000 to the average household income. They also resulted in somewhat greater equality in the income distribution (Census, 1990e, p. 5).

Assets. Median net worth of households in 1988 was $35,752. Net worth varies by income and household characteristics. Median net worth of whites was somewhat higher than for all households, $43,279, while that for blacks was $4,169 and for households of Spanish origin $5,524. Net worth increased with income. The median for households in the lowest income quintile was less than $20,000; in the highest quintile, the median net worth was nearly 18 times as much. Married-couple households had a median net worth of $57,134, much higher than that of female householders ($13,571) or male householders ($13,053). Net worth increased with age—from about $6,000 in the youngest group to about $80,000 among households in the 55-to-64 age group (Census, 1990d, pp. 8–10).

The most important single asset to most households is their equity in their home (the value of the home minus the amount owed). If home equity were excluded, median net worth would have been only $9,840 in 1988 (Census, 1990d, p. 6). Home equity comprised 43 percent of total net worth—68 percent for black households and 58 percent for households of Spanish origin. Other assets, in declining order of magnitude, were interest-earning assets at financial institutions (14 percent), business or profession (9 percent), rental property (8 percent), and stocks and mutual fund shares (7 percent) (Census, 1990e, p. 10). Median value of owned home was $43,070 (Census, 1990d, p. 15).

The assets most frequently owned were motor vehicles (owned by 86 percent of all households) and homes (owned by 64 percent) (Census, 1990d, p. 4).

Although motor vehicles were most frequently owned, equity in them accounted for just 6 percent of total net worth of households. Home equity accounted for the largest single source of net worth—43 percent of the total. Home equity was especially important to low-income households. In the lowest income group, home equity accounted for over half (59 percent) of total net worth; it accounted for only 37 percent in the highest income group (Census, 1990d, p. 5). In 1979, 44 percent of total household assets were owned by households in the top 20 percent of the income distribution. Those in the lowest 40 percent owned only 22 percent of the total assets. For those in the top 20 percent, financial assets or equity in own business or farm comprised the largest share of their assets; for those in the lowest 40 percent, the most important assets were equity in home or automobile (Hefferan, 1983).

A major purpose of asset accumulation is to provide for consumption during retirement. To find out how the economic situation of households changes during retirement, the Social Security Administration has conducted a longitudinal study of men and women who were aged 58 to 63 in 1969. Hogarth (1989) examined their patterns of saving and dissaving from 1971 to 1979. In 1971 the respondents owned an average of $39,078 in assets, 39 percent of it housing equity. Mean assets had increased to $55,087 in 1979, with an increase in housing equity accounting for most of it. Over half of the respondents (54 percent) had been dissaving during the period; they had lower financial assets in 1979 than in 1971. These tended to have lower incomes than those whose financial assets increased and were more likely to be single, female, have lower educations, and have lost their spouses during the period. Hogarth estimated that nearly one-fifth of the respondents were dissaving at rates that could not be maintained during their expected lifetimes.

Debt. Use of consumer credit has been increasing in the United States. In 1970, credit outstanding was 131.6 percent of disposable personal income. The percentage increased steadily and in 1988 was 728.9. The largest segment of consumer debt was automobile installment credit. In 1988, each household owed an average of $7,104 for automobile installment loans, $3,029 for revolving credit, and $2,192 in other loans. Over 100 million persons had credit cards. They charged an average of $3,663 on their credit cards and had an average of $1,661 in credit card debt (Census, 1990g, p. 506).

Human Capital. About one-fifth of all adults (25 years and over) had a college degree in 1988. That percentage has been rising, from 11 percent in 1970, while the percentage who did not graduate from high school declined, from 48 percent in 1970 to 24 percent in 1988. Twenty-one percent of whites had a college degree compared with 11 percent of blacks and 10 percent of Hispanics. Thirty-seven percent of blacks and 49 percent of Hispanics had not completed high school in 1988 (Census, 1990g, p. 133). Educational attainment is highly correlated with income. In 1987, the average monthly income of a non–high school graduate was $761. A high school graduate received 1.5, a person with a bachelor's degree 2.8, and a person with a professional degree over 5.5 times this amount (Census, 1990c, p. 33).

Durables. The two major durables for most consumer units are the automobile or other vehicle and the home. In 1988, consumer units owned an average of two vehicles per household, including cars, trucks, campers, motorcycles, trailers, and airplanes. The number increased with income, from just under one per consumer unit in the lowest income quintile to three in the top quintile. Average number also increased with size of consumer unit and number of earners. The average number increased with age of householder up to ages 45 to 54 and thereafter declined. Among the different family types, the highest average number of vehicles was found among husband-wife consumer units with the oldest child aged 18 or over (3.5 vehicles) and the lowest (an average of one per household) among one-parent consumer units. Blacks averaged fewer vehicles per consumer unit, perhaps because, like one-parent units, their income was lower than the average. Vehicle ownership was the highest in the West and Midwest and lowest in the Northeast.

About 62 percent of all consumer units were home owners in 1988. The pattern was similar to that for vehicle ownership with respect to income, family type, and number of earners (except for no-earner units, who are mostly elderly and showed a high rate of home ownership) and race but increased with each increase in age of householder up to age 75. The highest rates of home ownership were in the Midwest and South and the lowest in the West and Northeast. Although rate of home ownership was much lower among one-person consumer units than among larger units (40 percent compared with over 68 percent), there appeared to be no consistent pattern of variation by number of members among units with two or more persons.

Expenditure Patterns

The largest component of expenditure for all consumer units in 1988 was housing, which comprised 31 percent of total expenditures. Over half of the housing expenditure went for the dwelling itself, while utilities, fuels, and public services accounted for about one-fifth, furnishings and equipment about one-sixth, and relatively small amounts for household operations and supplies. The pattern of housing expenditure varied between home owners and renters. Home owners allocated a slightly smaller share of the total to housing but within the housing area allocated about half to the dwelling, nearly one-fourth to utilities, and about 15 percent to furnishings and equipment. Renters allocated a slightly larger share of their total expenditures to housing (33 percent compared with 30 percent), but about two-thirds of this went for the dwelling. Compared with home owners, renters spent a smaller share of their housing budget on utilities (some utilities are often provided as part of the rental agreement) and much less on household furnishings and equipment.

One-fifth of total expenditures was allocated to transportation. Within this category, about 95 percent was spent on private transportation.

Food was the next largest category of expenditure, comprising about 14 percent of the budget, with more than half of the food budget going for food at home.

About 5 percent each was allocated to apparel, health care, and entertainment and about 3 percent to cash contributions (which included child support and alimony, as well as contributions to religious, educational, charitable, or political organizations). Personal care took about 1 percent of the budget, as did life and other personal insurance, alcoholic beverages, and education. Reading and tobacco each comprised less than 1 percent of the total.

Expenditure pattern varied with income of the consumer unit. Compared with the highest income group, units in the lowest income quintile spent a larger share of their budget on housing, food, health care, education, personal care, tobacco, and alcoholic beverages and a smaller share on transportation, apparel, entertainment, personal insurance, and cash contributions.

As a means of identifying expenditure patterns in the population of all consumer units, units were grouped into clusters according to similarity of budget allocation among expenditure categories.[1] Four distinctively different clusters appeared. The mean allocation of total expenditure in major expenditure categories in each cluster is presented in Table 5.2. Based on the main features of the clusters, they were designated as homebound pattern, shelter-dominated pattern, service-using pattern, and private-transportation-dominated pattern.

Homebound Pattern. Twenty-six percent of the total sample belonged to this cluster. Compared with the total sample of consumer units, those in the homebound cluster averaged higher proportions of expenditures devoted to food at home, tobacco, personal care, utilities, house furnishings and equipment, health care, reading materials, and miscellaneous items. The means for consumer units in this cluster for food at home and tobacco were more than 45 and 48 percent higher, respectively, than the corresponding means for the total sample. For utilities and health care, the means were 56 and 68 percent higher than those for the sample as a whole. The remaining means were moderately higher than those for the total sample.

While the mean allocations to utilities and health care in this cluster were about 56 and 68 percent higher, the means for domestic services and shelter were about 46 and 54 percent lower, respectively, than those of the total sample. For food away from home, education, and public transportation, households in this cluster averaged about 20 percent lower proportions of expenditures, and for alcoholic beverages and private transportation, they averaged about 25 percent lower proportions than the total sample of consumer units. The mean proportions allocated to apparel and services and entertainment were somewhat lower than the means for the total sample.

Food at home accounted for the largest share of total expenditure, followed by utilities and health care. Since consumer units in the cluster averaged a large proportion to health care, implying low mobility, and to food at home and

Table 5.2
Four American Consumption Patterns

Consumption categories:	Patterns			
	1	2	3	4
	budget share as a % of average for all consumers			
Food at home	45	-12	-22	-26
Food away from home	-19	7	23	-1
Alcoholic beverages	-26	22	1	-20
Tobacco	48	-12	-38	-23
Apparel & services	-3	1	49	-14
Shelter	-54	47	-35	-41
Utilities	56	-18	-18	-24
Domestic services	-46	-23	535	-43
House furnishings & equipment	4	-5	47	-7
Personal care	25	-9	20	-17
Public transportation	-21	31	-19	-47
Private transportation	-24	-25	-32	114
Health care	68	-27	30	-33
Entertainment	-8	1	30	0
Reading materials	16	0	7	-24
Education	-18	13	-35	3
Miscellaneous items	19	-15	88	-14
Percentage of sample:	26	50	6	18

Source: Chung (1990).

utilities, implying they spent much time at home, the name *homebound pattern* seems justified.

Shelter-dominated Pattern. Fifty percent of the total sample belonged to this cluster. Consumer units in this cluster had higher proportions of expenditures than average for the total sample devoted to food away from home, alcoholic beverages, apparel and services, shelter, entertainment, education, and public transportation. The proportions of expenditures on food away from home and education in this cluster were moderately higher; the proportions of expenditures on public transportation and shelter were about 31 and 47 percent higher than the means for the total sample, respectively. The proportion of expenditure on apparel and services was slightly lower than that of the total sample. The proportion of expenditure on reading materials in this cluster was the same as the mean for the total sample.

The mean proportions of expenditures devoted to food at home, tobacco, personal care, utilities, house furnishings and equipment, and miscellaneous items for consumer units in this cluster were somewhat lower than the means for the total sample. The mean proportions of expenditures devoted to apparel and services and entertainment were slightly lower than those of the total sample. However, consumer units in the cluster had about 25 percent lower proportions of expenditures on health care, domestic services, and private transportation than the average expenditure allocations of the total sample.

Compared with consumer units in other clusters, those in the shelter-dominated cluster averaged a high proportion on shelter (31 percent of total expenditure).

Service-using Pattern. Only 6 percent of the total sample belonged to this cluster. Compared with the total sample, consumer units in this cluster averaged higher proportions of expenditures for food away from home, alcoholic beverages, apparel and services, personal care, domestic services, house furnishings and equipment, health care, entertainment, reading materials, and miscellaneous items. The mean proportions of expenditures on health care and entertainment were 30 percent higher, and the means for apparel and services and house furnishings and equipment were about 49 percent higher than those of the total sample. The mean proportion of expenditure on domestic services was much higher—536 percent higher—than the mean for the total sample. Also, the mean for miscellaneous items was higher than that of the total sample. The remaining means were moderately higher than those for the total sample.

The proportions of expenditures on food at home, utilities, and public transportation in the cluster were about 20 percent lower, and the means for shelter, education, and private transportation were about 35 percent lower than those for the total sample.

Since consumer units in the cluster allocated a high proportion of their total expenditure to domestic services, the cluster was designated as service using.

Private-Transportation-Dominated Pattern. Eighteen percent of the total sample belonged to this cluster. The mean proportion allocated to private transportation was 114 percent higher than the mean for the total sample. Except for education and private transportation, consumer units in this cluster had lower proportions of expenditures in almost every category than the average allocations of the total sample. The mean proportion of expenditure on entertainment was the same as the mean for the total sample.

Consumer units in this cluster allocated about 25 percent less on food at home, tobacco, utilities, and reading materials and 43 percent less on domestic services, on the average, than did the total sample. Also, the mean proportions of expenditures on health care, shelter, and public transportation in this cluster were substantially lower than the means for the total sample. The proportion of expenditure on foods away from home averaged slightly lower (less than 1 percent lower) than that of the total sample.

THE ELDERLY

Population Trends

The elderly (persons aged 65 and older) are increasing in both numbers and as a percentage of the population. In 1970 they comprised 10 percent of the population; by 1987 the percentage had increased to 12 percent. By 2080, one in every four persons is expected to be elderly (Census, 1989f, p. 9).

Of those who were not institutionalized, about two-thirds were living with a spouse or other relative. About 30 percent were living alone, a slightly larger proportion than were living alone in 1970. The likelihood of living alone increases with age. Of those aged 75 or over, 40 percent were living alone in 1988 compared with 24 percent of those in the 65 to 74 age range. Elderly women were much more likely to live alone than elderly men. Forty-one percent of women aged 65 and over lived alone in 1988 compared with 16 percent of men (Census, 1989f, p. 10). The higher proportion of women than men among the very elderly who live alone can partly be attributed to the longer life expectancy of women and the fact that men who are widowed are more likely to remarry than are women who lose their spouses.

Relatively few of the elderly are in the labor force after age 65, although the percentage is higher for men than for women. Among ever-married men, the participation rate declined between 1970 and 1988: from 30 to 18 percent for married men and from 17 to 12 percent for men who were widowed, divorced, or separated (Census, 1990g, p. 384). The participation rate among single women also declined slightly (from 18 to 11 percent) but remained about the same for ever-married women (about 7 percent for those currently married and 8 percent for those widowed, divorced, or separated) and single men (about 21 percent).

Resource Ownership

Income. Median income of households in the 65-and-over range is lower than that of any other age group—$14,923 in 1988 (Census, 1990h, p. 11). However, some of the changes that occurred in the income distribution during the 1970s and 1980s favored the elderly, who, as a result, experienced a higher rate of increase in real household income, adjusted for family size, than other age groups. Real income in this group was 40 percent higher in 1988 than in 1970, in marked contrast to the gains of 10 percent or less in the 35-to-64 range and declines among younger households. Thus, the elderly of 1988 were, on average, at least as well off as other age groups and were expected to continue to be so during the next several decades (Hurd, 1989a).

Not all of the elderly, however, are affluent. In 1985, about half of all elderly households had incomes below twice the poverty line, compared with fewer than one-third of young households (Leonard, Dolbeare & Lazere, 1989). Hurd (1989a, 1989b) identified two groups of elderly who should be objects of concern: the many "near poor," whose incomes are just high enough to disqualify them for social programs but not high enough to cover high-expenditure health care needs, and elderly widows, who have an especially high rate of poverty.

Durables. Although number of vehicles owned tends to decline after middle age, the average does not drop below one per consumer unit. In 1988, units with a householder aged 65 to 74 owned an average of 1.7 vehicles, lower than the overall average of two per consumer unit. The very elderly (householder aged 75 or over) owned an average of one vehicle per consumer unit. Among units with a householder in the 65-to-74 age range, the percentage owning at least one vehicle was about the same as for all consumer units (87 percent), but over one-third of the very elderly aged 75 and over owned no vehicle.

Home ownership was the highest among consumer units in the 55-to-74 age bracket, with nearly 80 percent owning their own home, but dropped somewhat (to 73 percent) among the very elderly.

Expenditure Pattern

Compared with all consumer units, units in which the householder was aged 65 or older allocated a much larger share of their total expenditures to health care (Figure 5.1). They also allocated larger shares to housing, food at home, and personal insurance. They allocated smaller budget shares than younger households to private transportation, food away from home, apparel, entertainment, reading and education, alcohol, and tobacco.

Differences in income and other household characteristics account for some differences in expenditure patterns between older and younger consuming units. When these were taken into account, the pattern remained basically the same, except that the difference in allocation to personal insurance disappeared and a higher allocation to public transportation was evident (Figure 5.2). Some differences, such as the higher allocation of older households to housing and food at home, were accentuated.

In summary, elderly consumer units allocate their expenditures somewhat differently than do younger units with similar income, household size, housing

Figure 5.1
The Elderly: Average Budget Allocation among Consumption Categories

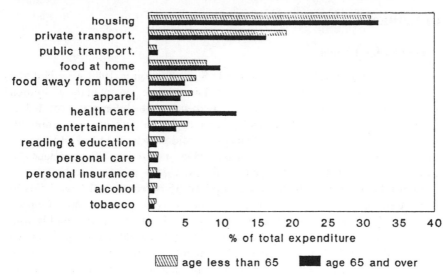

Source: U.S. Bureau of Labor Statistics (1988).

Figure 5.2
The Elderly: Estimated Budget Allocation, Holding Income and Other Factors Constant

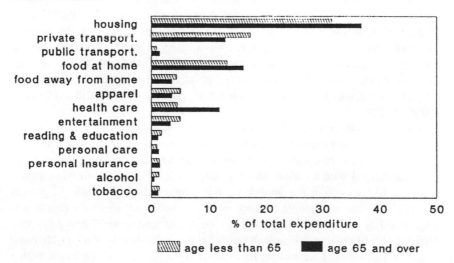

Source: U.S. Bureau of Labor Statistics (1988).

tenure, and other characteristics. Housing, health care, and food at home dominate their budgets. Many belong to the home-bound pattern of consumption.

CHILDREN

Population Trends

About one-fourth (26 percent) of the U.S. population in 1988 were children under the age of 18 (Census, 1989e, p. 38). Twenty-nine percent of those children were under the age of 5. By 2000, the percentage of children is expected to decline to 24 percent, with a smaller percentage (26 percent of all children) being under the age of 5. The percentage of children who are black (15 percent in 1988) is expected to increase (Census, 1989e, p. 16). The life expectancy of children born in 1990 was 75.6 years (Census, 1989e, p. 34).

Family households with children comprised 35 percent of all households in 1988 (Census, 1990b, p. 34). No-child families were most common (Census, 1990b, p. 8). Single-parent families comprised 23 percent of households with children. The percentage of children living in single-parent households doubled from 1960 to 1980 (from 9 percent to 20 percent) and by 1985 had increased to 23 percent (Census, 1990b, p. 35). School enrollment rates are high: 97 percent for children aged 5 to 14 and 44 percent for those aged 15 to 24 (Census, 1990b, p. 20).

A necessary consumption item for children is care and supervision. Much of this is provided by parents. It is relevant, therefore, to consider whether children live with one or both parents, since one-parent families, especially if the parent is employed, have less total time available for child care.

About three-fourths of all children lived with both parents in 1988. Of those living with only one parent, the majority (88 percent) lived with the mother. The percentage living with both parents was slightly higher for younger children and slightly lower for older children. Percentages living with both parents differed by racial group. While 81 percent of white children lived with both parents, only 42 percent of black children and 69 percent of Hispanic children did so (Census, 1989f, p. 20).

Nearly half (46 percent) of all children living in one-parent families in 1988 resided with a parent who was employed full time, 9 percent lived with part-time-employed parents, and 8 percent with a currently unemployed parent. Only 37 percent lived with a parent who was not in the labor force. Single mothers were less likely to be in the labor force than single fathers. In 1988, 42 percent of children living with single mothers were in families in which the parent was employed full time and 10 percent part time, compared with 70 and 7 percent, respectively, of children living with single fathers. Children in black or Hispanic single-parent families were more likely than white children to be living with a parent who was not in the labor force (Census, 1989f, p. 23).

Some employers have work schedule or leave policies that can aid employed parents in caring for their children. Such arrangements might include flextime, voluntary part time, job sharing, work at home, or flexible leave. About 61 percent of employers had such policies in 1987 (Hayghe, 1988).

Resource Ownership

Income. Median income of families does not increase with number of children. According to Census figures, the highest median income is for families with two children; thereafter, median income tends to decline with each additional child. In 1986, for example, families with no children had a median income of $30,018, families with one child had $29,081, two-child families had $30,421 (the highest of the child-number groups), families with three children had $27,501 and families with six or more children had $14,354. A similar pattern appeared in earlier years. Median income for families with no children was slightly higher than the median for all families; median for families with children was slightly lower (Census, 1990h, p. 22). Per capita median income declines substantially with size of family, from $13,538 in two-person households in 1988 to less than $4,500 in families with seven or more persons (Census, 1990h, p. 21).

Economies of scale and the lower consumption needs of small children compared with adults can be expected to offset partially the lower per capita income associated with the presence of children. Although expenditures for food at home and utilities tend to increase with size of household when income and other factors are taken into account, size of household does not appear to be associated with higher expenditures in other areas. In fact, expenditures for some other commodities, such as food away from home, alcohol, and shelter, are likely to decline.

A few employers (about 11 percent, according to a 1987 study) provide direct child care benefits in the form of day care, assistance with child care expenses (e.g., vouchers to defray child care expenses or agreements with child care providers to give discounts to employees), child care information and referral, and counseling services (Hayghe, 1988).

Incomes tend to be especially low among young families with children. In 1986, 30 percent of families with children in which the householder was under the age of 30 had incomes below the poverty threshold, more than double the poverty rate of children in older families (Johnson, Sum & Weill, 1988, pp. 40–41). Over half of all children in families with a householder under the age of 25 were poor. From 1973 to 1986, the poverty rate among young families increased by more than 50 percent.

The poverty rate among children in the United States is high compared with that in other industrialized countries. According to Smeeding and Torrey (1988), the 1979 poverty rate among children in the United States was higher than in Sweden (which had the lowest poverty rate), West Germany, Canada, the United

Kingdom, and Australia. In 1988, 20 percent of children in the United States under the age of 16 were in poverty (Census, 1990f, p. 9).

Poverty rates vary by age, education, and householder marital status. Families most likely to be poor are those in which the householder is young (under the age of 30), female, a high school dropout, and has children (Johnson et al., pp. 39–42).

About one-third of women with children under the age of 18 whose fathers are not present were below the poverty level in 1987. The average child support payment was $2,710. The majority, however, received no child support from the absent father. Of those with dependent children, father absent, 59 percent had been awarded child support payments; of these, slightly over half received the full amount, one-fourth received partial payment, and nearly one-fourth received no payment in 1987 (Census, 1990a).

Children themselves have income; most of it (83 percent) comes from their families and about 17 percent from other sources. In 1989, the average annual income of children aged 4 to 12 was $230. Sixty percent of the children received an allowance, which accounted for about half of the total. Gifts from parents, relatives, or friends accounted for 20 percent, 15 percent came from work inside and 12 percent from work outside the home. Children save nearly one-third of their income, according to McNeal. The highest savings rate was among 4 year olds and the lowest among 7 year olds (McNeal, 1990).

Durables. Vehicle and home ownership among consumer units with children varies, depending on whether there are one or two parents present. Compared with all consumer units, husband-wife units with children averaged more vehicles per consumer unit, and one-parent units averaged fewer. Almost all (96 percent) of the husband-wife consumer units with children owned at least one vehicle, compared with 64 percent of one-parent consumer units. The pattern for home ownership was similar, with about three-fourths of husband-wife units and one-third of one-parent units being home owners. Although the percentage of home owners among husband-wife consumer units with children under the age of 6 was about the same as the average for all units (59 percent compared with 62 percent), the percentage was higher (76 percent) among those with children aged 6 to 17 and nearly 90 percent among those with older children living at home.

An estimated 450,000 children were homeless in 1989, about one-fourth of the total number of homeless. An estimated 2 million additional children are "precariously housed and at imminent risk of homelessness" (National Law Center on Homelessness and Poverty, 1990, p. 1). One of the serious consequences of homelessness for children is that it hinders them from getting an education. A 1987 survey of eight cities indicated that 43 percent of homeless children do not attend school.

Expenditure Patterns

Families spend at least $4,545 per year (in 1989 dollars) on children, according to one estimate (Lino, 1990a). Since the amount will vary depending on the

Table 5.3
Annual Expenditures on Children

Age of Child	Total	Housing	Food	Transpor- tation	Cloth- ing	Health	Education, Child Care, & Other
Income: Less than $28,300							
0-2	4,100	1,680	630	560	300	210	720
3-5	4,400	1,630	710	610	330	200	920
6-8	4,400	1,630	910	660	360	210	630
9-11	4,260	1,510	1,030	590	370	220	540
12-14	4,890	1,450	1,100	890	610	220	620
15-17	5,220	1,430	1,250	1,130	570	230	610
Total	81,810	27,990	16,890	13,320	7,620	3,870	12,120
Income: $28,300 - $46,900							
0-2	5,850	2,230	790	940	390	270	1,230
3-5	6,190	2,170	910	990	420	250	1,450
6-8	6,170	2,180	1,150	1,070	450	270	1,050
9-11	6,020	2,060	1,300	1,000	460	280	920
12-14	6,700	2,000	1,370	1,300	760	280	990
15-17	7,120	1,980	1,530	1,540	720	300	1,050
Total	114,150	37,860	21,150	20,520	9,600	4,950	20,070
Income: More than $46,900							
0-2	8,330	3,340	950	1,290	480	330	1,940
3-5	8,800	3,280	1,150	1,340	520	320	2,190
6-8	8,680	3,290	1,380	1,450	550	330	1,680
9-11	8,500	3,170	1,550	1,380	560	350	1,490
12-14	9,280	3,110	1,690	1,680	900	350	1,550
15-17	9,770	3,090	1,790	1,920	860	370	1,740
Total	160,080	57,840	25,530	27,180	11,610	6,150	31,770

Source: Lino (1990a).

income level of the family, estimates are provided at three income levels (see Table 5.3). The largest share of expenses is for housing, followed by food (in the low- and middle-income groups) and then transportation. Annual costs at different ages reflect the average situation of families with such children, which may help to account for the fact that some expenditures, such as for housing, appear to decline with age of child. Families with younger children are likely to have purchased a home more recently than families with older children, which probably explains the apparent decline in housing expenditures with age. Homes purchased more recently are probably purchased at a higher price than older homes; also, mortgage payments on recently purchased homes include a smaller proportion of payment on principal (counted as savings rather than expenditure).

Expenditures for food and clothing, for which age-specific data are available, increase with age of child.

Estimated child-rearing expenses vary by region and urbanization. They are higher in urban than in rural areas and, among regions, highest in the urban West and lowest in the urban Midwest.

Families spend slightly more (about 3 percent) on the oldest child than on the second. Economies of scale are also evident. In comparison with husband-wife families with two children, similar families with one child spend 21 percent more and families with three or more children spend 22 percent less per child.

Espenshade (1984, pp. 35–38) estimated "parental expenditures on children" at three cost levels—low, medium, and high—based on education and occupation of the "household head" and other household characteristics. Unlike the Lino estimates, the level of living (indicated by percentage of consumption allocated to food) varies, declining until the oldest child reaches the age of 18 and then beginning to increase (Espenshade, 1984, pp. 72–73). Separate estimates were provided for each child in one-, two-, and three-child families, for employed- and nonemployed-wife families, and for blacks and whites.

Estimated annual expenditure per child at the medium level with the wife employed full time, in 1988 prices, was $7,880 in a one-child family, $6,097 in a two-child family, and $5,073 in a three-child family. Costs at the high level were 12 percent higher, and those at the low level were 6 percent lower than the medium level. Expenditures on children were about 17 percent higher for white than for black families at the high level and about 3 percent higher at the medium and low levels. The difference in racial groups was the lowest among one-child families and highest among three-child families. Expenditures on children were higher in full-time-employed-wife families than in families in which the wife was not employed. For example, expenditures in one-child families with an employed wife were 15 percent higher at the high level, 24 percent higher at the medium level, and 28 percent higher at the low level.

Two other, lower, estimates are available. Lazear and Michael (1988, p. 122) estimated the average annual amount spent on a child, in 1988 prices, as $3,438. Beller and Graham (1990) estimated the cost of maintaining a child at the poverty level at $2,726, in 1988 prices.

In summary, the annual costs of rearing a child range from less than $3,000 at the poverty level to nearly $8,000 for an only child in a high-socioeconomic-status, working-wife family. Costs per child increase with age of child, decline with number of children, and are lower for black than for white families and for nonemployed-wife than for working-wife families.

The initial cost of child rearing is the cost of having a baby. A 1982 survey by the Health Insurance Association estimated the average costs of a maternity hospital stay plus professional services at approximately $2,092 ($3,135 at the 1988 price level) for a normal birth and $5,004 (in 1988 prices) for a cesarean delivery. Other costs (in 1988 prices) were estimated at $1,004 for layette, nursery, and bath items and $277 for a maternity wardrobe (*Family Economics Review*, 1984, p. 19).

Child care costs deserve special attention as a component of child rearing costs, since child care has become a necessity for many families with preschool children. According to a 1986 Census survey (1989b), most children under the age of 5 whose mothers were employed were cared for either in their own home (28 percent) or in someone else's home (42 percent). About 18 percent were cared for in an institutional setting (day or group care center, nursery school, preschool, kindergarten, etc.). The average child care cost was $45 per week.

It is also worth considering what children themselves spend their money for. The largest item of expenditure (about one-third of the total amount of children's income) is for candy, soft drinks, and snacks, followed by toys, games, and crafts. Other items are clothing, movies and other spectator events, and video games (McNeal, 1990).

The cost of a college education is a major item associated with child rearing. In 1988, the average annual cost for undergraduate tuition and fees at a public university (in-state tuition) was $1,750 with an additional $3,010 for dormitory room and board. Costs at a private university were $8,770 and $4,560, respectively (National Center for Education Statistics, 1988, p. 252).

THE POOR

Population Trends

The poor are a persisting and increasing segment of population in the United States. The number of poor persons increased from 25.9 million in 1975 to 31.5 million in 1989. The percentage of poor persons fell from 22.2 percent of total population in 1960 to 12.1 percent in 1969 and remained approximately the same during the 1970s and 1980s. The poverty rate in 1989 was 12.8 percent (Census, 1990e, p. 10; Littman, 1989, p. 16; Sawhill, 1988, pp. 1082–1083).

In 1959, about 72 percent of the poverty population was white, with blacks making up around 25 percent of the population. The majority of the poor in 1959 were either under 18 years or elderly. These characteristics have changed. In 1989, blacks made up almost 30 percent of the poor, although whites still made up a large majority (66 percent). The most striking change in the demographic characteristics of the poverty population was the increase in the number of female-headed households and the decrease in the number of elderly. In 1989, female-headed households made up 37 percent of the poverty population compared to 17.8 percent in 1959; only 10.7 percent of the poor were elderly, compared to 31.2 percent in 1959. Persons under 18 years still made up a big proportion of the poor in 1989 (39.9 percent), although the percentage had decreased from 44.5 percent in 1959 (Census, 1990f, pp. 57–59). Poverty rates among young families headed by persons under age 30 nearly doubled between

1973 and 1986, jumping from 12 to 22 percent. About one out of three families headed by persons under age 25 was poor in 1986 (Census, 1990f, pp. 57–59; Johnson et al., p. 39).

Several longitudinal studies have investigated the dynamics of poverty. Using data from the Panel Study of Income Dynamics, Levy (1980) found that the absolute chance that a person from a poverty household would continue to be poor was about 30 percent. Using the same data set, Duncan (1984) found substantial turnover in the poverty population during the decade 1969–1978. Nearly one-quarter of the total U.S. population had been poor at least once during the decade, but only 2.6 percent of the population were persistently poor.

Several studies found differences in the demographic characteristics of the temporarily and the persistently poor. The persistently poor were defined as "people in poverty for more than 8 or 9 years" (Coe, 1978; Hill, 1981; Duncan, 1984). Blacks made up a majority of the persistently poor (60 to 77 percent), and female heads with children made up 60 percent of the persistently poor (Coe, 1978; Hill, 1981). Households whose head worked fewer than 500 hours annually made up 70 percent of the persistently poor. The elderly made up approximately 16 percent of the persistently poor (Hill, 1981).

Poor householders were less likely to be in the labor force and more likely to be unemployed than nonpoor householders. About 53 percent of poor householders were in the labor force in 1989, compared with 85 percent of nonpoor householders. Among those in the labor force, 21 percent of the poor were unemployed, compared with 5 percent of the nonpoor. Twenty-two percent of householders in working-poor families worked year round, full time, compared with 60 percent of nonpoor working householders. The main reasons for not working among householders in poverty were family responsibilities (44 percent) and illness or disability (24 percent); retirement was the main reason of the nonpoor family householders for not working (58 percent). Reason for not working varied by family structure. Poor female householders without a husband usually gave family responsibilities as a reason for not working (66 percent); only 12 percent of the householders in married-couple poor families cited this as a reason. Seventy-three percent of married-couple poor families who did not work reported retirement, illness, or disability as the reason (Census, 1990f, pp. 67–70).

Resource Ownership

Income. The poverty threshold for a family of three was $9,885 in 1989. Most of the families who were poor that year had incomes well below this level; more than a third had incomes of less than $5,000. Trends in the relative distance of money income of the poor from the poverty level showed the aggravation of poverty. In 1979, the percentage of the poor persons whose income was less than half the poverty threshold was 30 percent. This figure increased to about 33 percent of the poor in 1979 and reached 38 percent in 1989. The proportions of both male- and female-headed families with an income of less than half of the poverty threshold increased between 1975 and 1986, from 25 percent to 30 percent for male-headed, and from 35 percent to 48 percent for female-headed families (Census, 1990f, p. 67; Littman, 1989).

In 1989, the average amount of money needed to raise the income of each poor family to its respective poverty threshold was $4,969, a figure that had remained unchanged since 1982 but was higher than in the mid- to late 1970s. The average income deficit for poor families with female householder, no husband present ($5,412), was higher than that for married-couple families ($4,424) in 1989. Deficit per family member was $1,650 in 1989 for female-headed families, compared with $1,147 for married-couple families. Both male- and female-headed poor families experienced relatively large decreases in the average deficit during the 1960s, but the average deficit for female-headed poor families began the decade $1,000 higher than the deficit for male-headed poor families ($5,200 versus $4,200 in 1959) and remained higher through the 1970s and 1980s, despite the fact that average family size is smaller for poor families headed by females (Census, 1990f, p. 77; Littman, 1989).

Noncash benefits are another important form of resources of the poor. Between 1970 and 1986, direct outlays on noncash benefits in the form of food stamps, Medicaid, subsidized housing, and school lunches more than doubled in real terms, representing almost two-thirds of total assistance to the poor (Sawhill, 1988, p. 1078). However, growth in noncash benefits does not explain much of the increase in the income deficit. Although noncash benefits have increased in the aggregate from $96.6 billion to $135.7 billion between 1979 and 1986 (in 1986 dollars), the average market value of noncash benefits for poor families was actually less in 1986 than in 1979 in real terms. The average market value of noncash benefits received by poor families decreased from $4,221 in 1979 to $3,662 in 1981 before recovering to $4,088 in 1986. Particularly the average market value, in real terms, of housing benefits of poor families substantially decreased (from $2,837 in 1979 to $1,777 in 1986, in 1986 dollars) and food benefits decreased moderately (from $1,674 to $1,479), while medical benefits somewhat increased (from $3,400 to $3,463) (Littman, 1989).

Durables. Poor households averaged a lower rate of vehicle ownership than did nonpoor households in 1987. Average number of vehicles for the poor was 0.9, compared with 2.2 for the nonpoor; 44 percent owned no vehicles.

In 1985, about 40 percent of the poor were home owners. Poor home owner households were more likely to be headed by an elderly person, to have no children, and to be married. Two-fifths of all poor home owner households were headed by an elderly person, while just one-third had children. The typical head of a poor home owner household was aged 62. In contrast, poor renter households were more likely to be younger, to have children, and to be headed by a single parent. Only about one-fifth of poor renter households were headed by an elderly person, and more than half of all poor renter households had children. Thirty-eight percent of the poor renters were female-headed households, and 35 percent

Figure 5.3
The Poor: Average Budget Allocation among Consumption Categories

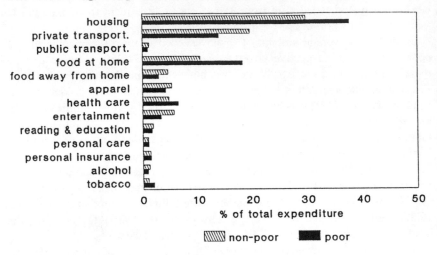

Source: U.S. Bureau of Labor Statistics (1988).

were single households. The typical head of a poor renter household was aged 38. Blacks and Hispanics are less likely to own their homes than are whites. In 1985, about 22 percent of Hispanic poor households and 28 percent of black poor households were home owners, while 46 percent of white poor households owned their homes (Leonard et al., 1989, pp. 46–47, 51).

Poor households are more likely to live in substandard or overcrowded housing than the nonpoor. In 1985 more than 20 percent of poor renters—and one in every six poor home owners—lived in housing having physical deficiencies. By contrast, 10 percent of nonpoor renters—and fewer than one in 20 nonpoor home owners—lived in housing units with deficiencies. About 8 percent of poor households lived in overcrowded conditions, compared with 2 percent of the nonpoor (Leonard et al., 1989, pp. 19–23).

Expenditure Patterns

The mean allocation of expenditures among the poor and the nonpoor is presented in Figure 5.3. Compared with nonpoor households, poor households averaged higher proportions of expenditures devoted to food at home, housing, public transportation, health care, and tobacco, with the largest average proportion to housing. They allocated lower budget shares to food away from home, alcoholic beverages, apparel, private transportation, entertainment, and education. For personal care and insurance, the average proportions of expenditures were about the same between poor and nonpoor households.

When differences in age, family size, and home ownership were considered

Figure 5.4
The Poor: Estimated Budget Allocation, Holding Other Factors Constant

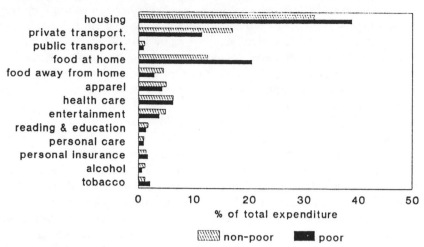

Source: U.S. Bureau of Labor Statistics (1988).

(Figure 5.4), poor households were still found to allocate higher proportions of expenditures on food at home, housing, and tobacco. There was no difference in public transportation, health, and education when household characteristics were taken into account.

The high burden of housing expenditures on the poor was found in many studies (Schwenk, 1988; Cha, Chung & Magrabi, 1989; Leonard et al., 1989; Scoon, 1989; Cha 1991). In 1985, 45 percent of renter households and one-third of home owners in poverty paid at least 70 percent of their incomes for housing costs, while the typical household with an income of $20,000 to $25,000 spent 19 percent of its income for housing (Leonard et al., 1989, pp. 2–4). According to Leonard et al., housing cost burden had sharply increased since the mid-1970s. For example, the percentage of poor renters who paid at least 60 percent of their incomes for rent and utilities increased from 44 percent of all poor renters in 1978 to 60 percent in 1985, while the proportion of poor owners in that situation increased from 31 percent to 38 percent. Leonard et al. pointed out that the increasing housing cost burden of the poor could be attributed to the increasing number of households with low income and the decreasing number of low-rent units available during the period (pp. 5–9). Expenditures by the poor for nonessential housing was low, however. Schwenk (1988) found that households in the lowest income bracket (under $10,000) spent le·s on lodging away from home (including rental of hotel and motel rooms, expenses for vacation homes, and housing for someone at school) than households in the highest income bracket ($40,000 and over).

According to Stone (1990), housing expenditure is one of the most nondiscretionary of budget items, and hence the one to which nonhousing expenditures usually adjust. He argued that households paying more than they can afford for housing tend to suffer from deprivation of nonshelter necessities resulting from the squeeze between incomes and housing expenditures and labeled such households "shelter poor." He pointed out that many low-income households and large households (containing three or more persons) are likely to be shelter poor even when they pay less than 25 percent of their incomes, because they still do not have enough left over after paying for housing to be able to obtain minimum levels of nonshelter necessities (pp. 50–51).

The general conclusion is that poor households tend to spend more on basic needs and less on higher needs. Andreasen (1975, pp. 31–54) pointed out that a major problem for the poor is that although they have needs that are in many respects not unlike those of the nonpoor, they lack both the level and the stability of income to satisfy those needs. Since their limited incomes usually go for basic needs or requirements, the proportion of income that is discretionary is much smaller among the poor than among the nonpoor. Andreasen believed that this explains why many poor people use dissaving or credit in order to acquire even a small proportion of the standard American package of goods and services. He also pointed out the problem of lack of information in purchasing. The poor are less likely to read newspapers, comparison shop, patronize supermarkets, or buy lower-priced private brands, despite their greatest interest in saving money.

HUSBAND-WIFE FAMILIES

Population Trends

In 1985, married-couple families comprised 58 percent of all households in the United States. This percentage declined from 72 percent in 1970 and is expected to decline further, perhaps to about 53 percent in the year 2000. The number of such households is expected to increase, however, from about 50 million in 1985 to 56 million in 2000 (Census, 1990g, p. 45).

Nearly half (47 percent) of married-couple households had one or more children under 18 years of age living in the household (Census, 1989f, p. 30). The percentage of such households that included only the biological children of both spouses was 77 percent in 1985, a decline from 79 percent in 1980. One family in five was a "blended" family in 1985, containing stepchildren of one parent. About 2 percent included adoptive children. Among black households, the percentage of blended families was much higher than the average—about 36 percent (Census, 1989f, p. 31). An increasing percentage of married women are employed in the labor force and thus have less time available for work in the home. Over half (57 percent) of all married women were in the labor force in 1988 compared with 41 percent in 1970. The percentage of married women with children who were employed was 57 percent for those with children under the

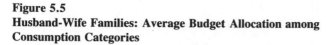

Figure 5.5
Husband-Wife Families: Average Budget Allocation among
Consumption Categories

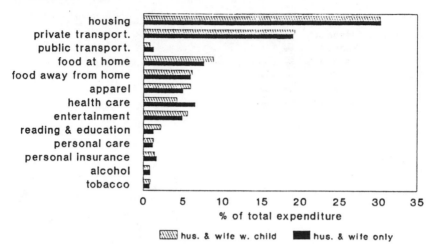

Source: U.S. Bureau of Labor Statistics (1988).

age of 6 and 73 percent for those with older children (Census, 1990g, pp. 384–385).

Resource Ownership

Income. The median income of married-couple families in 1988 was $36,389, about 13 percent higher than the median income for all families (Census, 1990h, pp. 14, 18). The rate of increase since 1960 was higher for married-couple families than for all families.

Durables. Husband-wife consumer units averaged a higher rate of home and vehicle ownership than did all consumer units in 1988. Average number of vehicles was 2.6 compared with 2 for all units, with 96 percent owning at least one vehicle. Seventy-eight percent were home owners, compared with 62 percent of all consumer units.

Expenditure Patterns

The general expenditure pattern for husband-wife consumer units was similar to that for all units, although there were some differences among the different types of husband-wife units. Compared with husband-wife units without children, those with children allocated a larger share of their budget to food at home, apparel, entertainment, and education and a smaller share to health care and personal insurance (Figure 5.5). The share allocated to many expenditures tended

Figure 5.6
Husband-Wife Families: Estimated Budget Allocation, Holding Income and Other Factors Constant

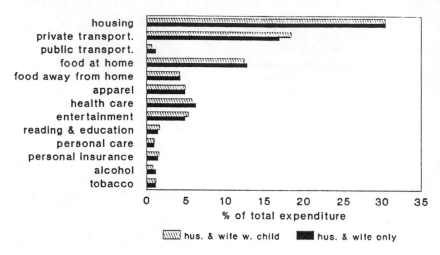

Source: U.S. Bureau of Labor Statistics (1988).

to increase with age of child. These included food (especially food away from home), apparel, transportation, health care, personal care, education, tobacco, and cash contributions. The share for housing and entertainment tended to decline.

Some of the apparent differences among types of husband-wife consumer units can be explained by factors other than the presence of children, among them, differences in income, household size, and whether or not the wife is employed. When other factors are taken into account, husband-wife families with young children allocate a higher budget share (in comparison with those with no children) to private transportation, entertainment, and personal insurance and lower shares to food at home, health care, and alcohol (Figure 5.6). Families with older children allocate a higher proportion to apparel, private transportation, and education and a lower proportion to shelter and health care than do those with younger children.

In summary, child care and insurance appear to be especially important to families with young children; apparel, private transportation, and education are especially important when the children grow older.

WORKING-WIFE HOUSEHOLDS

Population Trends

In 1988, 57 percent of all wives (husband present in the household) were in the labor force (Census 1990g, p. 385), an increase over the 45 percent in the labor force in 1975. The rate was only slightly lower for married women with small children. Over half of married women with children 1 year old or younger and nearly three-fourths of those with school-aged children were in the labor force in 1988.

Working-wife households have two adults present in the home, but, with the wife employed, there is less time available for household activities than in similar households in which the wife is not employed. Some time pressures and shortages are inevitable. The family may adjust in two ways: by adjusting employment schedules and housework time.

Employed workers may choose to work less than full time. In 1987, 32 percent of employed wives were in part-time jobs compared to 13 percent of total employed women and 7 percent of employed husbands (Census, 1990g, pp. 387, 455). Another possibility for easing time pressures is flexible work schedules, which may permit an employed husband or wife to meet both work and family obligations. In 1987, 13 percent of employed married men and 10 percent of employed married women were on flexible work schedules. Among employed married women, the percentage on flexible schedules was slightly higher (about 14 percent) if they had children under 14 years of age (Census, 1990g, p. 388).

An alternative to adjusting employment hours is to adjust housework time. Several studies have shown that employed wives spend less time on household activities than do wives who are not employed. Robinson (1977), for example, found that employed wives in urban areas spent an average of 3.6 hours less per day on family work than did nonemployed wives. The data were from a nationwide survey conducted in 1965–1966. Major reductions in work time appeared in the areas of child care, cooking, laundry, and such chores as meal cleanup, house cleaning, and outdoor work. Employed wives also had less leisure time than nonemployed wives.

Although they may reduced the amount of time they spend on housework, employed wives nevertheless work long hours. Another study, conducted in 1967–1968, found that wives employed full time (more than 30 hours per week) worked about 10 hours per day on housework and paid employment, longer than the 8.6 hours worked by full-time homemakers (Walker & Woods, 1976). Similar results were found in a 1975–1976 study (Pleck, 1985). Employed wives spent an average of 3.4 hours per day on housework compared to nonemployed wives' 5.6 hours. On total work—housework and paid employment—employed wives worked about 9 hours per day, longer than the 6.8 hours worked by nonemployed wives. Employed wives also had less sleep time than nonemployed wives.

Resource Ownership

Income. Working-wife households average a much higher income than non-working-wife households. The median income of working-wife households in 1988 was $42,709, or about 57 percent higher than the $27,220 median income for nonworking-wife households (Census, 1990g, p. 453). The rate of increase since 1970 was higher for working-wife households than for nonworking-wife households. In 1987, the mean earnings of wives was $16,603 for full-time employed wives and $5,959 for part-time employed wives. The mean earnings in 1987 of all employed wives ($13,250) were less than half that of all employed husbands ($29,150) (Census, 1989c, p. 2). In 1987, working wives contributed about 36 percent of their family's income (BLS, 1990).

Durables. Vehicle and home ownership were higher in 1988 among two-earner households than among those with only one earner or among all households (BLS, 1990). Nearly all two-earner households owned at least one vehicle. The average was 2.6 vehicles per household, compared with 2 for all households. Seventy percent were home owners, compared with 62 percent of all households.

Expenditure Patterns

Working-wife households have expenditure patterns that differ from those of nonworking-wife households. They need to spend extra money for work-related expenses and also may purchase more market goods and services that save time for housework. Working-wife households spend more money on work-related expenses, such as clothing, transportation, and personal care, and on some time-saving services for housework, such as food away from home, personal care, and domestic services (Bellante & Foster, 1984; Jacobs, Shipp & Brown, 1989; Yang & Magrabi, 1989). On the other hand, working-wife households spend less on time-consuming goods such as food at home and entertainment (Yang, 1991).

Compared with nonworking-wife households, working-wife households allocate a larger share of their budget to food away from home and private transportation (Figure 5.7). More than 10 percent of the budgets in working-wife households was spent on vehicle purchase. Working-wife households allocated lower budget shares to food at home, housing, apparel, public transportation, health care, tobacco, and personal insurance.

Some of the differences in expenditure pattern between nonworking- and working-wife households can be explained by differences in income and other household characteristics. For instance, the wife is more likely to be employed if she is younger, more highly educated, and in a smaller household. When these factors are taken into account, working-wife households spend a larger share of their budget on private transportation and a smaller share on food at home, housing, public transportation, and health care (Figure 5.8). There was little difference between working- and nonworking-wife households in other expenditures.

SINGLE-PARENT HOUSEHOLDS

Population Trends

In 1988, over one-fourth of all family groups with children had only one parent present. Twenty-four percent of such groups included the mother only; 4 percent

Figure 5.7
Working-Wife Families: Average Budget Allocation among
Consumption Categories

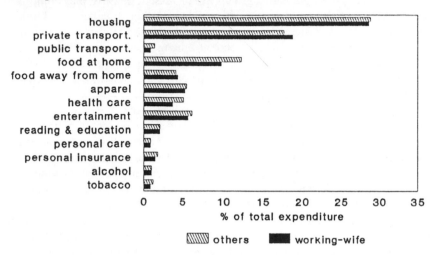

Source: U.S. Bureau of Labor Statistics (1988).

Figure 5.8
Working-Wife Families: Estimated Budget Allocation, Holding Income and Other
Factors Constant

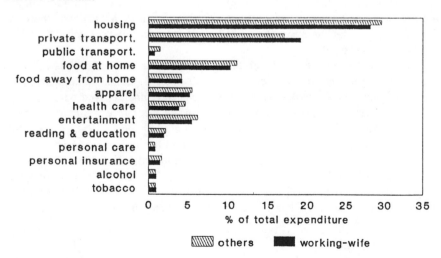

Source: U.S. Bureau of Labor Statistics (1988).

included the father only. Most of these single-parent groups maintained their own households, but about 22 percent lived with relatives or an unrelated person. Father-only families were somewhat more likely to maintain a separate household than were mother-only families (Census, 1989f, p. 13).

The percentage of single-parent groups has increased. In 1970, they comprised only 13 percent of all family groups with children. Although father-only families were few, the number increased at a faster rate than the mother-only families. Single-parent families were more frequent among blacks and Hispanics than among whites. In 1988, over half (59 percent) of black and 44 percent of Hispanic families with children contained only one parent, compared with 21 percent of white families (Census, 1989f, p. 15).

Divorce was the most frequent reason for the absence of one parent, accounting for about 40 percent of the single families, but about one-third of the single mothers and one-fifth of the single fathers had never been married. Among black and Hispanic one-parent families, never-married parents were more common (accounting for 56 percent of the black and 36 percent of the Hispanic families) compared with those who were divorced (accounting for 18 and 30 percent, respectively) (Census, 1989f, p. 16).

Age of the parents has implications for their ability to earn income and perform necessary household functions. A middle-aged parent, for example, is likely to be earning substantially more than a teenaged parent. Single parents tended to be somewhat younger than parents in two-parent situations (Census, 1989f, p. 17). Also, single mothers tend to be older than single fathers, and black single parents tend to be younger than whites.

Single-parent households have substantially less time available to perform household tasks than do two-parent households. This is especially true if the parent is employed. In 1988, 70 percent of divorced women with children under the age of 6 and 53 percent of mothers separated from their husbands were in the labor force, an increase from 63 and 45 percent, respectively, in 1970 (Census, 1990g, p. 384).

Nearly half (46 percent) of all children living in one-parent families in 1988 resided with a parent who was employed full time, 9 percent lived with part-time employed parents, and 8 percent with a currently unemployed parent. Only 37 percent lived with a parent who was not in the labor force. Single mothers were less likely to be in the labor force than single fathers. In 1988, 42 percent of children living with single mothers were in families in which the parent was employed full time and 10 percent part time, compared with 70 and 7 percent, respectively, of children living with single fathers. Children in black or Hispanic single-parent families were more likely than white children to be living with a parent who was not in the labor force (Census, 1989f, p. 23).

Resource Ownership

Income. Although income in single-parent families is on average lower than that of married-couple families, it tends to be higher than that of single con-

Figure 5.9
Single-Parent Families: Average Budget Allocation among
Consumption Categories

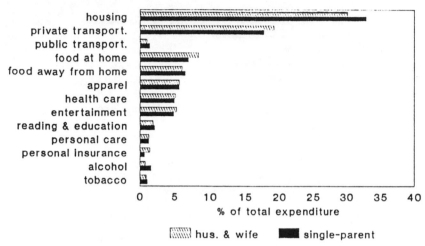

Source: U.S. Bureau of Labor Statistics (1988).

sumers, many of them elderly. In 1988, the median income of single-father families was $28,642 and that of single-mother families was $16,051—79 and 44 percent, respectively, of the median income for husband-wife families (Census, 1990h, p. 10). Compared with their one-person-household counterparts, single-father families had incomes 57 percent higher and single-mother families 72 percent higher.

Durables. Vehicle and home ownership are low among single-parent consumer units compared with all consumer units or with other family types. In 1988, about two-thirds owned a vehicle. Only one-third owned homes.

Expenditure Pattern

Compared with two-parent families with children (Figure 5.9), one-parent consumer units allocated a much larger share of their expenditures to necessities: housing (38 percent compared with 30 percent) and food (except for food away from home). They also allocated slightly larger percentages to alcohol and tobacco. Some necessities, however, received a smaller allocation. One-parent consumer units allocated less to private transportation, health care, and personal insurance than did two-parent units. They also allocated smaller shares to entertainment and cash contributions.

When differences in income and other characteristics were taken into account, the picture changed only slightly (Figure 5.10). Allocations to entertainment and apparel were slightly higher than that in two-parent families, and allocation to

Figure 5.10
Single-Parent Families: Estimated Budget Allocation, Holding Income and Other Factors Constant

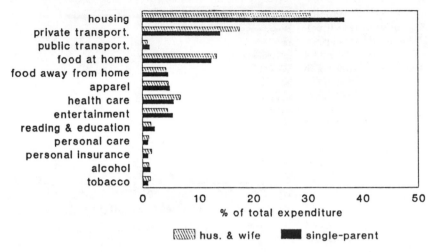

Source: U.S. Bureau of Labor Statistics (1988).

tobacco was lower. Some differences—for example, higher allocation to housing and lower allocation to private transportation—were accentuated when other factors were considered.

The income elasticities of expenditures by single-parent consumer units are lower than those found for husband-wife units (Lino, 1990b): housing, 0.27; transportation, 0.28; food, 0.24; and clothing, 0.36. Lino attributed this to the high degree of income uncertainty experienced by many single parents.

SINGLE CONSUMERS

Population Trends

Over one-fourth (28 percent) of all households in 1985 were nonfamily households, that is, single men or women living alone or with persons to whom they were not related (Census, 1986, p. 2). This percentage is expected to increase to about 32 percent by the year 2000. The householder in over half of these households (54 percent) was female.

The majority of single consumers under the age of 65 were in the labor force (Census, 1990g, p. 384). Thus, time is likely to be something of a constraint. Offsetting this is the smaller household size and absence of children.

Resource Ownership

Income. On average, the income of single consumers tends to be quite low, reflecting the substantial numbers of elderly in this group. In 1988, the median

Figure 5.11
Single Consumers: Average Budget Allocation among Consumption Categories

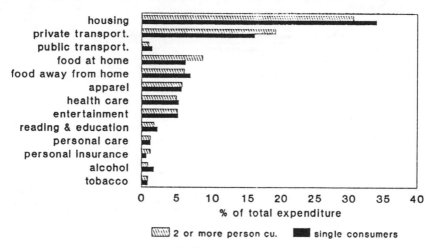

Source: U.S. Bureau of Labor Statistics (1988).

income of single-person households was only $13,982, less than half (38 percent) that of married-couple households. Median income of single males was higher than that of single females ($18,284 compared with $11,622) (Census, 1990h, p. 10).

Durables. About three-fourths of single consumers owned at least one vehicle in 1988. Only 44 percent were home owners.

Expenditure Pattern

The profile of the one-person consumer unit, compared with units of two or more members, can be summarized (Figure 5.11). Higher proportions of their expenditures go to housing, public transportation, food away from home, health care (probably because this group includes many elderly persons), reading and education, and alcoholic beverages. Their allocation is also higher for cash contributions (perhaps because the group may include many who are paying alimony or child support). Lower-than-average proportions go to private transportation, food at home, and personal insurance (presumably because they do not have dependents).

When differences in income, age, and other characteristics are taken into account, the differences in allocation to private transportation narrow, and single consumers spend a lower budget share than other consumer units on tobacco and a higher share for entertainment (Figure 5.12). They tend to allocate lower shares of expenditures to apparel and health care than other units.

Use of convenience foods by single-person households is similar to that by

Figure 5.12
Single Consumers: Estimated Budget Allocation, Holding Income and Other Factors Constant

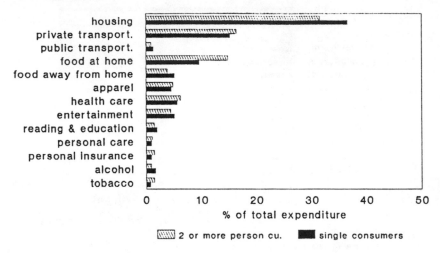

Source: U.S. Bureau of Labor Statistics (1988).

multiperson households (Richardson, Pearson & Capps, 1985). Both types of households allocated 45 percent of their expenditures for food at home to convenience foods in a 1977–1978 study. Food purchased by single-person households tended to provide higher levels of food energy and more nutrients per nutrition unit[2] than food purchased by multiperson households; however, there may have been greater food waste in the smaller households, making actual intake about the same.

BLACK HOUSEHOLDS

Population Trends

Black persons in 1988 comprised about 12 percent of the population in the United States (Census, 1989e, p. 38). The proportion is expected to reach about 13 percent by 2000 (Census, 1990g, p. 16). The largest rise will be in black children, expected to increase from 15 percent of all children in 1988 to 21 percent in 2000. If present patterns continue, this means a substantial increase in one-parent households, since over half of all black children live with only one parent (Census, 1989e, p. 18).

Resource Ownership

Income. Median income of black households was $16,407 in 1988, about 71 percent that of white households (Census, 1990h, pp. 7–8). About one-third (34

Figure 5.13
Black Consumer Units: Average Budget Allocation among
Consumption Categories

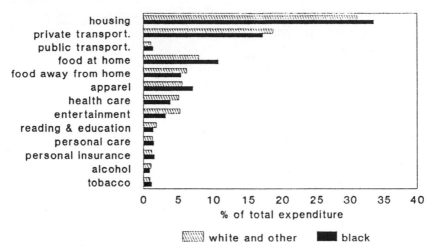

Source: U.S. Bureau of Labor Statistics (1988).

percent) of black households had income less than $10,000, compared with 15 percent of white households. At the other end of the income scale, while only 10 percent of black households had incomes over $50,000, 22 percent of white households were in that income bracket.

Durables. Home and vehicle ownership were relatively low among black consumer units in 1988. Sixty-three percent owned one or more vehicles, compared with 86 percent of all consumer units. Less than half (41 percent) were home owners.

Expenditure Patterns

The pattern of budget allocation of black consumer units differed from that of white units in many areas of expenditure, although some of the differences seem to be due to their lower average income and other differences. Compared with white consumer units, and even when taking income and other characteristics into account, they tend to allocate a larger share of the budget to housing, public transportation, food at home, apparel, personal care, and insurance (Figures 5.13 and 5.14). A smaller share is allocated to food away, private transportation, health care, entertainment, reading and education, and alcohol. Average allocation to tobacco is slightly higher but slightly lower when household characteristics are held constant.

Figure 5.14
Black Consumer Units: Estimated Budget Allocation, Holding Income and Other Factors Constant

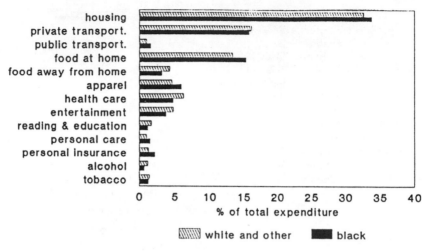

Source: U.S. Bureau of Labor Statistics (1988).

RURAL AND URBAN HOUSEHOLDS

Population Trends

Slightly over one-fourth (27 percent) of the U.S. population lived in rural areas in 1988, about the same percentage as in 1970 (U.S. Bureau of the Census & Department of Agriculture, 1989). According to data from the Bureau of Labor Statistics (BLS, 1990), average household size was not different between rural and urban households in 1988, being 2.6 in both groups. Average age of householder was somewhat older among rural residents, however. Black households were less frequent in rural than in urban areas, as were households with a female householder. Less than 8 percent of the rural population lived on farms.

Resource Ownership

Income in rural areas averaged lower than in urban areas in 1988—$22,132 compared with $29,543. Rural consumer units averaged more vehicles per unit in 1988 than did urban consumer units—2.6 compared with 1.9. Ninety-one percent of rural consumer units owned at least one vehicle. Few rural residents were renters, with about three-fourths owning their dwelling (BLS, 1990).

Expenditure Pattern

Differences between the expenditure patterns of rural and urban consuming units appear to reflect differences in prices, particularly of housing, greater

Figure 5.15
Rural and Urban Consumer Units: Average Budget Allocation among Consumption Categories

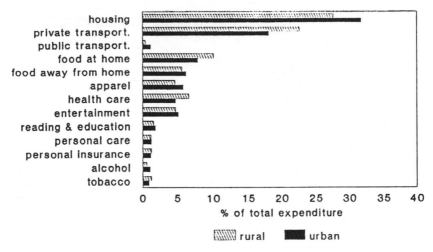

Source: U.S. Bureau of Labor Statistics (1988).

distances to travel for shopping and other errands, lack of public transportation, and perhaps a more casual life-style. Compared with urban residents, and even when holding income and other characteristics constant, rural consumer units showed a higher budget allocation to private transportation, health care, and tobacco and a lower allocation to housing, apparel, public transportation, entertainment, and reading and education (Figures 5.15 and 5.16). On the average, rural consumer units allocated a larger budget share to food at home, but the reverse was true when income and other characteristics were taken into account.

OCCUPATIONAL GROUPS

Population Trends

The greatest difference related to occupation is likely to be between those who are employed and those who are not employed. In 1988, 62 percent of the adult population in the United States (men and women age 16 and over not living in an institution) were employed (Census, 1990g, p. 380). An additional 4 percent were unemployed, and the remainder were not in the labor force. The percentage not in the labor force steadily declined from 1950 through 1980, partly because of the increased participation of married women in the labor force. This trend is expected to continue to the year 2000, with the participation rate of men declining slightly (from 76 percent in 1988 to 75.5 percent in 2000) and the participation rate of women increasing (from 56 to 62.6 percent). Whites

Figure 5.16
Rural and Urban Consumer Units: Estimated Budget Allocation, Holding Income and Other Factors Constant

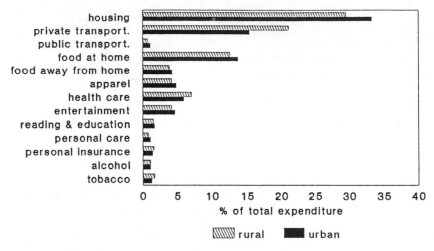

Source: U.S. Bureau of Labor Statistics (1988).

had a slightly higher rate of participation in the labor force than blacks (Census, 1990g, p. 378).

The largest group of workers (31 percent) were employed in technical, sales, or administrative positions in 1988 (Census, 1990g, pp. 389–390). An additional 25 percent were in managerial or professional occupations. The remainder were employed as operators, fabricators, and laborers (15 percent); service occupations (13 percent); precision production, craft, and repair (12 percent); and farming, forestry, and fisheries (3 percent). The largest increases in employment from 1986 to 2000 are expected to be among technicians and related support workers; service workers (except private household workers, where employment is expected to decline); sales workers; executive, administrative, and managerial workers; and professional workers (Silvestri & Lukasiewicz, 1987, p. 47).

Availability of time for household activities may vary with occupation. Those not employed have the largest amount of time potentially available for such a use, followed, probably, by part-time workers. Although the normal workweek is 40 hours, many workers put in many additional hours of paid and unpaid overtime, a pattern that varies to some extent by occupation. In some occupations—for example, school teaching—employment is seasonal. Some occupations require frequent travel.

Resource Ownership

Income. Median earnings of all workers in 1988 were $20,612 for males (Census, 1990h, pp. 44–45). Median earnings of females were much lower

($11,096). Part of the difference can be attributed to the greater incidence of part-time employment among females. When median earnings of men and women were compared for full-time workers only, females earned about two-thirds as much as males. The highest median earnings were in executive, administrative and managerial, and professional specialty occupations. The lowest median earnings were in farming, forestry, and fisheries (about one-third of the median for all occupations), followed by service occupations (about half of the median).

Durables. Three broad occupational groups were identified in the Survey of Consumer Expenditure: self-employed, wage and salary earners, and retired. Consumer units were classified by the occupation of the householder. Compared with consumer units in which the householder was employed, retired-householder units were somewhat less likely to own a vehicle (79 percent compared with 92 or 91 percent). Over three-fourths of the self-employed or retired consumer units owned their own homes, but home ownership was somewhat less frequent among wage and salary workers (about 60 percent). About three-fourths of the wage and salary home owners had a home mortgage compared with about 60 percent of the self-employed and about 19 percent of the retired home owners.

Wage and salary earners are not a homogeneous group. They may be divided into managers and professionals, clerical workers (including technicians and sales workers), service workers, and blue-collar workers (including precision production, craft and repair workers, operators, fabricators, and laborers). Vehicle ownership, high in all these occupational groups, was the lowest among service workers, who were also least likely to own their own homes. Clerical workers were better off in these respects but were not so likely to be vehicle or home owners as managers and professionals or blue-collar workers.

Expenditure Pattern

Although home ownership and frequency of home mortgages differed among occupational groups, budget share for housing was approximately the same— just under one-third. Some differences did appear in the components of housing expenditure, with the nonemployed allocating a larger budget share to utilities (even when income and other differences were taken into account) and managers and professionals allocating more than other occupational groups to household operations (which included child care) and furnishings and equipment. (Comparisons between working and nonworking households are summarized in Figure 5.17.)

Next in importance was transportation, which averaged about one-fifth of the total budget. The lowest budget share was among the retired, the highest among blue-collar workers. Differences tended to disappear, however, when income and other factors were taken into account (Comparisons between working and nonworking households are summarized in Figure 5.18.)

Differences in budget share for food at home appear to be strongly influenced by income, with the lowest income group (retired) allocating the largest budget

Figure 5.17
Occupational Groups: Average Budget Allocation among Consumption Categories

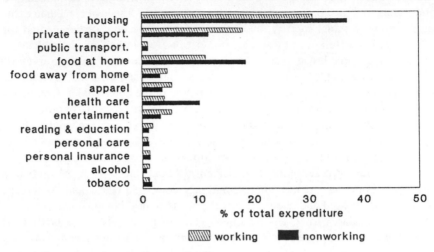

Source: U.S. Bureau of Labor Statistics (1988).

Figure 5.18
Occupational Groups: Estimated Budget Allocation, Holding Income and Other Factors Constant

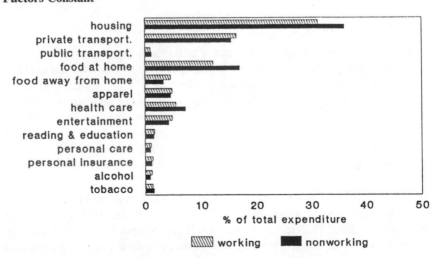

Source: U.S. Bureau of Labor Statistics (1988).

share to food at home and the highest income group (managers and professionals) allocating the smallest share. However, even when income and other factors were taken into account, nonemployed consumer units were found to allocate a larger share to food at home than did employed units. Retired consumer units, who averaged the lowest income, allocated the smallest budget share to food away compared with other occupational groups, even when income and other factors were taken into account. Service workers, whose income was only slightly higher, allocated the largest budget share to food away, but differences among employed groups were not significant when income and other household characteristics were taken into account.

Retired consumer units allocated a larger budget share to health care than other occupational groups, probably because of their older age. Of the employed groups, the self-employed averaged a higher budget share for health care than wage and salary workers, probably because health insurance is often provided by employers. When differences in age, income, and other factors were taken into account, there was no difference among occupational groups with respect to health care allocation.

Occupational groups can also be compared along other dimensions:

- Apparel. Managers and professional workers averaged the highest budget share for apparel and retired units the lowest. Differences among employed groups were not great, however, and appeared to be attributable mostly to income. When income and other differences were taken into account, the only difference that appeared among occupational groups was that blue-collar workers allocated a lower share to apparel than other groups, perhaps because of less formality in work attire or in life-style.

- Entertainment. Although retired consumer units have more time available for recreational activities than employed units, they averaged the lowest budget share for entertainment—about 4 percent of total spending compared with about 5 to 6 percent among employed units.

- Life and other personal insurance. Although differences among occupational groups were not great, it may be worth noting that the allocation was higher among the retired and self-employed than among salary and wage earners.

- Cash contributions. Retired consumer units, whose average income was the lowest, allocated a higher percentage of their budget to contributions—5 percent—compared with about 3 percent for the self-employed, managers, and professionals (who had the highest average income) and about 2 percent among other occupational groups.

A comparison of the profiles in Figures 5.17 and 5.18 suggests that expenditure allocations of nonworking consumer units are distinctly different from those of units in which the householder is employed. Most differences were somewhat smaller, however, when income and other household characteristics were taken into account.

NOTES

1. Data from the 1986 Consumer Expenditure Survey were used to identify expenditure patterns for all consumer units. Data for consumer units who were interviewed for four quarters during this period were merged and their expenditures summed to provide total annual expenditures for each household. After all adjustments were made, the sample consisted of 1,717 households. Cluster analysis, a procedure for clustering a large number of cases into a requested number of groups, was used to identify consumption patterns (Aldenderfer & Blashfield, 1984). The variables used for clustering the households were budget shares allocated to consumption categories.

2. A nutrition unit is "the sum of the RDA for a given nutrient for persons eating in the household (adjusted for meals eaten away from home) divided by the RDA for the adult male" (Richardson, Pearson & Capps, 1985, p. 16).

6

Consumption in Other Countries

The most important reason to study the consumption patterns of countries other than our own is that this knowledge provides us with a standard of comparison and thus enables us to make a better assessment of the level and quality of consumption in our own country, leads us to raise questions about the reason for and value of specific consumption practices, and generally gives us a better understanding of our own behavior.

Practical reasons can be advanced also. Some may look forward to travel or living in other countries and will find it useful to identify in advance those aspects of consumption that are likely to differ from their own. Some may have philanthropic reasons and desire information about problems and needs. Some may expect to be involved in business dealings with foreign markets and need general information about ways of life in those regions.

Finally, we should note that knowledge of consumption patterns in other countries provides us with a wider range of behavior to study—extreme poverty, isolated rural communities, subsistence economies, households relying on earnings of migrant members, and so on. This wider range of data can help us gain a better understanding of the fundamental relationships that shape consumption.

Consumption patterns vary greatly even within a single country. Clearly the task of summarizing consumption patterns worldwide is an impossible one, even were data available. In the sections that follow, two kinds of data will be summarized: average data on selected social indicators, available through the United Nations, World Bank, and other sources, and information about selected countries. The first sections deal with population, resources, and other general characteristics. The remaining sections are concerned with consumption patterns.

GENERAL CHARACTERISTICS

Population

The world population is large and growing. In 1988, it was about 5.1 billion, 15 percent higher than in 1980 (World Health Statistics Quarterly [WHSQ], 1989b, p. 192). By the year 2000, it will have increased by nearly a billion (Brown, 1990, p. 5).

Much of the expected growth will be in poor countries (low-income and lower-middle-income countries), which are characterized by large and growing populations. With about one-fourth of the land area of the world, they have over half the total population (World Bank, 1989). The highest-income group of countries occupies about one-fourth of the land area but has only about 15 percent of the world's population. Thus, poor countries average a higher population density than high-income countries—an average of 76 and 36 people per square kilometer in low-income and lower-middle-income countries, respectively, compared with 23 in high-income countries (World Bank, 1989).

The population growth rate was also the highest in the poorest countries— 2.0 and 2.2 percent per year in the two poorest groups compared with 0.5 in high-income countries. High rates of population growth are likely to have a negative impact on economic development. Kelley, after reviewing the empirical evidence, concluded that "economic growth (as measured by per capita output) in many developing countries would have been more rapid in an environment of slower population growth, although in a number of countries the impact of population was probably negligible, and in some it may have been positive" (1988, p. 1715).

The population growth rate was slightly higher in lower-middle-income countries than in low-income countries. Kristensen (1982) noted that countries in the next lowest income group may be somewhat worse off in some respects than those with the lowest incomes, possibly because the rate at which development efforts take effect differs, depending on the nature of the effort. For example, provision of safe water supplies, vaccination, and better sanitation may have an immediate impact in the form of lower mortality rates among infants and small children and increased life expectancy, but programs to increase labor productivity or introduce new income-earning opportunities may take many years to produce results.

High rates of population growth and increased life expectancy affect the age-dependency ratio (the ratio of persons under 15 or over 64 years of age to the working-age population). The lower-middle-income group of countries had the highest percentage of the population under the age of 15 and the highest ratio of dependents of the four income groups. The age dependency ratio was .74 in the lower-middle-income group, about the same (.65 to .66) in the low-income and middle-income groups, and .49 in the high-income group. The low-income group of countries averaged about 35 percent of the population in the 14-and-under group and about 4 percent aged 65 and over. In the high-income group the percentages were 21 percent and 13 percent, respectively (World Bank, 1989).

Although the elderly are a minority, they comprise the most rapidly growing segment of the population worldwide. In 1988, persons aged 65 and over comprised about 4 to 5 percent of the population in Latin America (excluding the Caribbean) and 3 percent in Africa and Asia (Kinsella, 1988, p. 1). By the year 2020 the percentages are expected to be 6 percent in some countries and 4 percent in Africa. Over half of the elderly in the world live in developing countries; by 2020 the percentage is expected to be 72 percent—over a billion people.

The quality of human resources is affected, among other things, by health status and educational attainments. Life expectancy is low and infant mortality rates high in developing countries. In 1988, the life expectancy of men and women in the poorest group of countries was 60 years; in the high-income countries, life expectancy of men was 73 and of women 79 years (World Bank, 1990, pp. 240–241). Infant mortality rates were 72 per thousand in the low-income countries and 9 per thousand in the high-income countries. Literacy rates tend to be low in poor countries. About 57 percent of the adult population in low-income countries were able to read and write simple sentences, according to the World Bank (1989). About 74 percent in lower-middle-income and 78 percent in middle-income countries were literate.

More than half (59 percent) of the people of the world lived in rural areas in 1984; by the year 2000, that percentage is expected to decline to about 52 percent. The degree of urbanization varies considerably among countries. In developed countries, three-fourths of the population lived in urban areas in 1984, while in developing countries only 30 percent did (Kinsella, 1988, p. 53). In India, for example, about three-fourths of the population lived in rural areas in 1981; in Malawi (in 1977) about 91 percent were rural (Kinsella, p. 8). Overall, the percentage in rural areas was 66 percent in the lowest income group, with the percentage declining to 22 percent in the highest income group (World Bank, 1989).

Income

The World Bank (1989), in its summary of social indicators of development, grouped countries of the world into four groups based on per capita gross national product (GNP).[1] The low-income group contained countries with per capita GNP of $545 or less. Of the 50 countries in this group, the majority were in Asia or sub-Saharan Africa (Table 6.1). Mean per capita GNP in this poorest group was $310.

The lower-middle income group of countries contained those with a per capita GNP of $546 to $2,200. The majority of countries in Latin America and the Caribbean were in this group. Mean per capita GNP was $1,270.

The upper-middle-income group contained those with per capita GNP of

Table 6.1

Countries of the World, Grouped by Income and Region

Low-income ($545 or less)	Lower-middle-income ($546-2,200)	Upper-middle-income ($2,201-6,000)	High-income ($6,001 and above)
Sub-Saharan Africa	Sub-Saharan Africa	Sub-Saharan Africa	Asia
Benin	Angola	Gabon	Hong Kong
Burkina Faso	Botswana	Reunion	Japan
Burundi	Cameroon	Seychelles	Singapore
Central African Rep.	Cape Verde		
Chad	Congo, People's Rep.	Asia	Europe, Middle East,
Comoros	Cote d'Ivoire	Korea, Rep.	North Africa, and
Equatorial Guinea	Djibouti		Others
Ethiopia	Mauritius	Latin America &	
Gambia	Senegal	Caribbean	Australia
Ghana	South Africa	Antigua & Barbuda	Austria
Guinea	Swaziland	Argentina	Bahamas
Guinea-Bissau	Zimbabwe	Barbados	Bahrain
Kenya		Brazil	Belgium
Lesotho	Asia	French Guiana	Bermuda
Liberia	Fiji	Guadeloupe	Brunei
Madagascar	Kiribati	Martinique	Canada
Malawi	Malaysia	Panama	Cyprus
Mali	Papua New Guinea	Puerto Rico	Denmark
Mauritania	Philippines	St. Kitts & Nevis	Finland
Mozambique	Thailand	Suriname	France
Niger	Tonga	Trinidad & Tobago	French Polynesia
Nigeria	Vanuatu	Uruguay	Germany, Fed. Rep.
Rwanda	Western Samoa	Venezuela	Iceland
Sao Tome & Principe			Ireland
Sierra Leone	Latin America	Europe, Middle East	Israel
Somalia	Caribbean	and North Africa	Italy
Sudan	Belize	Algeria	Kuwait

Tanzania
Togo
Uganda
Zaire
Zambia

Asia
Bangladesh
Bhutan
China
India
Indonesia
Kampuchea
Lao,PDR
Maldives
Myanmar
Nepal
Solomon Islands
Sri Lanka
Viet Nam

Latin America & Caribbean
Guyana
Haiti

Europe, Middle East and North Africa
Afghanistan
Pakistan
Yemen, PDR

Bolivia
Chile
Colombia
Costa Rica
Dominica
Dominican Rep.
Ecuador
El Salvador
Grenada
Guatemala
Honduras
Jamaica
Mexico
Nicaragua
Paraguay
Peru
St. Lucia
St. Vincent & the Grenadines

Europe, Middle East and North Africa
Egypt, Arab Rep.
Jordan
Lebanon
Morocco
Poland
Syrian Arab Rep.
Tunisia
Turkey
Yemen Arab Rep.

Greece
Hungary
Iran, Islamic Rep.
Iraq
Libya
Malta
Oman
Portugal
Romania
Yugoslavia

Luxembourg
Netherlands
New Caledonia
New Zealand
Norway
Qatar
Saudi Arabia
Spain
Sweden
Switzerland
United Arab Emirates
United Kingdom
United States

Source: World Bank (1989, pp. 353–354).

$2,201 to $6,000, with an average of $2,940. Very few countries in Asia or sub-Saharan Africa were in this group (an exception was the Republic of Korea), but it included many countries in Latin America and the Caribbean and some in Europe, the Middle East, and North Africa.

The high-income group (per capita GNP over $6,000) contained countries in North America (except Mexico), northern Europe (except countries from the Soviet bloc), some oil-rich countries of the Middle East, and some Pacific Basin countries (Australia, New Zealand, Hong Kong, Singapore, and Japan). Israel is also a member of this group. Mean per capita GNP was $17,080.

Employment

Developing countries tend to be highly dependent on agriculture. Although agricultural land as a percentage of total land area was about the same in all four groups of countries (between 30 and 40 percent), population density on agricultural land varied greatly, from 211 per square kilometer in the lowest-income group to 62 in the highest-income group (World Bank, 1988). India, for example, had about 71 percent of the total labor force in agriculture. The United States, in comparison, had less than 4 percent of the labor force in agriculture. While agriculture accounted for about one-third of total gross domestic product (GDP) in low-income countries, it was only 3 percent in high-income countries.

Few workers in poorer countries have professional or managerial jobs. In Thailand, for example, about 5 percent of all workers were in this occupational category in 1980 (Kinsella, 1988, p. 52) compared with about 22 percent in the United States (Silvestri & Lukasiewicz, 1987, p. 47). Many work in the informal sector, earning small amounts as street sweepers, trash collectors, or whatever other opportunities are offered. Some engage in small enterprises, such as tailoring, making pottery, or offering a small stock of goods for sale on the sidewalk or the doorstep of their home (Kristensen, 1982, pp. 43–44).

Rates of unemployment and underemployment are high in poor countries. About 40 percent of workers in developing countries were underemployed in 1977 (United Nations Department of International and Social Affairs, 1986, p. 13).

Subsistence production adds substantially to the total real incomes of households in poor countries. This includes hunting and fishing, wild-food gathering, collection of firewood, and the manufacturing of furniture, farm tools, clothes, cooking utensils, and other items for use by the household. In rural Cameroon in 1974, for example, this was estimated at about 54 percent of the total real income of the household. In Nepal in 1980, subsistence income was estimated to comprise 70 percent of total real income (Goldschmidt-Clermont, 1987, pp. 47–48).

Many families obtain income through migration. While the women and children remain in the village, the husband or adult children migrate to cities or even other countries to work, sending most of their earnings home and returning periodically to visit. For example, on a visit to New Delhi in 1985, we noticed four or five taxis stationed near the hotel. The drivers lived in their taxis and obtained their meals and bathing facilities at the hotel. On inquiry we found that the drivers came from the same small village in Punjab and were supporting wives and families back home.

According to the International Labour Organization, there were about 2.6 million foreign workers in Iraq and Kuwait prior to the 1990 invasion of Kuwait by Iraq. Most of these workers came from Bangladesh, Egypt, India, Jordan, Pakistan, Philippines, Sri Lanka, Sudan, and Thailand. The wage remittances from these workers provided about 29 percent of the average imports of the economies in their home countries (Swoboda, 1990).

Poverty

Poverty rates are high in poor countries. In 1985, one-third of all persons living in developing countries—1 billion people—were poor; their annual consumption was less than $370 per person per year (World Bank, 1990, pp. 27–29). The highest concentrations of poverty were in South Asia (51 percent), sub-Saharan Africa (47 percent), and the Middle East and North Africa (31 percent). Poverty rates in other poor countries were somewhat lower: 20 percent in East Asia, 19 percent in Latin America, and 8 percent in Eastern Europe.

Poverty rates tend to be higher in rural than in urban areas. In Kenya, for example, 80 percent of the total population but 96 percent of the rural population are poor. The poorest households tend to be larger than average, with many elderly or children who are dependent on working members of the household for support. In some countries, especially southern Africa and Latin America, many poor households are headed by women (World Bank, 1990, pp. 28–31).

Income is divided very unequally in the world. Those in the richest income quintile had 58 percent of the total income of the world in 1985, about 15 times the share of the poorest quintile. The ratio (share of the richest to the poorest quintiles) was 12 for the United States and ranged from about 4 in Japan to 28 in Brazil. Income per capita in the poorest 40 percent of the population in 1985 averaged less than $1,000 (1980 U.S. dollars) in many countries, with amounts ranging from $90 in Malawi and $300 in India to $990 in Mexico (Durning, 1990, p. 138).

The disparity in wealth is even greater than that in income. In India, for example, those in the top income decile had 25 times as much income as those in the bottom decile but 250 times as much wealth (Durning, 1989, p. 124). Many of the rural poor are landless. In Africa, the landless and near-landless comprised 40 percent of the rural population in the mid–1970s; in Asia and Latin America, the percentage ranged from 51 percent (Mexico) to 92 percent (Dominican Republic) (Durning, 1990, p. 142).

Lipton (1988, pp. 4–8) differentiated between two groups of poor: the poor, who spend 70 percent or more of their income on food, and the ultra-poor, who, although spending 80 percent or more of their income on food, nevertheless fulfill less than 80 percent of their calorie requirements. One-fourth to one-half of the poor in developing countries may belong to the ultra-poor group.

The poor, and especially the ultra-poor, are highly dependent on earned income but are likely to be employed irregularly, with frequent periods of unemployment or underemployment. Seasonal variation in the availability of employment creates hardship, and wage rates fluctuate.

The poor have few assets. In rural areas, they are likely to be among the landless—those who own no land and work as unskilled agricultural workers or servants—or the near-landless—those whose landholdings are too small or unproductive to provide even one-third of the food needs of the household. They may, however, own some livestock—usually poultry or small animals or, occasionally, cows or other milk producers. Poor landowners are not likely to own a draft animal to help with the labor of cultivation and transportation. The assets most commonly owned are the dwelling and furnishings.

Education levels, and thus human capital, are low among the poor, limiting their opportunities for employment and their ability to use their own resources to best advantage. In India, for example, in the poorest income group, over 70 percent of the rural and urban women and rural men are illiterate and over 40 percent of the urban men. In the most affluent group, less than one-fourth of the rural men and urban women are illiterate and less than 10 percent of the urban men. In general rural residents have lower education levels than those living in urban areas, and women average lower levels than men (World Bank, 1990, p. 32).

Consumer credit is less available to the poor than to the better off, and the former are likely to pay higher interest rates. Nevertheless, many of the poor borrow to take care of emergencies or to tide them over periods of unemployment.

Contributions of Women

The contributions of women to the real income of the household deserve separate attention for two reasons: their contribution is substantial, and the impact of their earnings on household consumption is somewhat different from the impact of men's earnings.

Many women participate in the paid labor force. Their participation rate is about 35 percent in low-income and high-income countries, with lower rates of participation (22 to 24 percent) in the two middle-income groups (World Bank, 1989). Their earnings are lower, on the average, than those of men, partly because of lower wage rates. However, several studies of poor households indicate that women contribute a larger proportion of their earnings to the consumption needs of the family than do men (Blumberg, 1988, pp. 57–58). A study in two regions of India, for example, indicated that men in the sample contributed about three-fourths of what they earned, on the average, retaining the remainder for their own leisure or status activities, such as eating or drinking with friends. The women, whose average earnings were only 55 percent of their husbands' earnings, contributed about 90 percent of their earnings to the support of the family. Similar results were found in a Mexico City study.

In situations in which women are not obligated to contribute to the support of their families, they often use their earnings to purchase gold or silver jewelry. Jewelry, in countries in which banks are not readily accessible or safe, is often used in lieu of a savings account. It is portable, relatively easy to protect, and can be sold to provide needed cash.

Women also contribute labor to agriculture and subsistence activities. A study of women in Nepal showed that although the women in the sample contributed only 21 percent of the wage and salary income of their households, they contributed half of the household's real income (compared to 44 percent by men and 6 percent by children) (Acharya & Bennett, 1982, p. 63).

Women's participation in agricultural production varies among countries and also by other factors. A study of households in a Bangladesh village showed that while the amount of time contributed to agricultural work by an adult female (aged 22 to 59) in a large landowning household was about 90 percent of that contributed by an adult male, female contributions in small landowning households averaged 7 percent higher than that of males, and in landless households 37 percent higher (Dixon-Mueller, 1985, p. 48). In Botswana, the majority of the time contributed to crop husbandry, according to a 1976 study, comes from females (Goldschmidt-Clermont, 1987, pp. 81–82).

Still another area in which women contribute to the total real income of the household is in unpaid domestic work. The United Nations Economic Commission for Africa estimated that women in that region contribute 100 percent of the labor for child care, cooking, cleaning, grinding, and processing food and 90 percent of the labor for fetching water (Chandler, 1985b, p. 38). Women's contribution to labor for other activities was: fetching fuel, 80 percent; growing food, 70 percent; community projects, 70 percent; selling and exchanging produce, 60 percent; storing food, caring for animals, and house repairs, 50 percent; and house building, 30 percent. If the market value of such activities were taken into account, it might add 30 percent to total real income, according to a study in Cameroon (Goldschmidt-Clermont, 1987, p. 47).

Not surprisingly, the burden of work on women is heavy. In Nepal, for example, one study showed that while men worked an average of about 8 hours per day, women worked an average of 11 hours (Goldschmidt-Clermont, 1987, p. 145). Children also work long hours, sometimes under unhealthy conditions, either on the family farm or other home-based enterprises or in paid employment. Instances of children in bondage to pay off family debts are not uncommon (World Bank, 1990, p. 31).

TOTAL CONSUMPTION

Analysis of consumption patterns in one country, the United States, shows that the pattern varies with income and other sociodemographic factors. Do these same relationships appear when population groups are compared within and among other countries?

One form of evidence of consumption pattern is the distribution of private final consumption expenditures of a country. Table 6.2 shows the percentage distribution of consumption expenditures in eight countries (United Nations Statistical Office, 1988)—two from each of the four income groups identified by the World Bank.[2] The pattern with respect to share devoted to food is precisely similar to that found within the United States: countries with the highest per capital GNP devoted the smallest share of personal consumption expenditures to food. They spent the largest share on gross rent, fuel, and power, on medical and health expenses, and on personal transport equipment (except for Portugal).

Variation in some categories of consumption seems to reflect cultural or other differences among countries. An example is the high allocation to education in some countries. Korea, Jordan, and India allocated a larger percentage to education than did the United States. Variations in allocation to alcoholic beverages and tobacco may also reflect cultural differences.

A comparison of 1984 family budget data in high- and upper-middle-income countries was made by Poduska (1988).[3] Average family expenditure was the highest in the United States—somewhat higher than Switzerland (although Switzerland had a higher per capita GNP in 1980). Countries with total family budgets that were higher than the mean ($13,463) for the 18 countries were, in order of budget amount; United States (with average family budget nearly twice the mean), Switzerland, Australia, Canada, West Germany, Norway, Denmark, and Japan. Countries lower than the mean were the Netherlands, Belgium, Sweden, France, Finland, Great Britain, Greece, Ireland, Spain, and Italy. Italy had an average family budget less than half the mean.

Although the effect of income differences shows to some extent in the comparison of budget share allocation among the countries in this group, differences in price and other factors also play a part. For example, although the United States showed the lowest allocation to food of the countries in this group and the two countries with the lowest total expenditures (Spain and Italy) showed the highest allocation, two other countries (West Germany and Denmark) allocated about the same share to food as the United States, while Japan, with family expenditures at about the mean, allocated about the same portion as the two lowest-expenditure countries. Allocation to health care services varied, in part, with type of health care system. Great Britain, for example, with a national health care system, showed family allocation of expenditures to health care of less than 1 percent, the lowest in this group of countries. Variations in the price of gasoline probably affected allocation to transportation. Although the United States showed the largest percentage allocation to transportation (about 20 percent), the allocation in several lower-income countries was almost as high (19 percent in Norway and France). Gasoline prices in Europe average substantially higher than in the United States (Renner, 1988, p. 17). Japan, a small, highly

Table 6.2
Distribution of Personal Consumption Expenditures: Eight Countries

Countries	Per Capita GNP	Food & non-alcoh. beverages	Alcoholic beverages & tobacco	Gross rent fuel and power	Household furnishings & operation	Medical & health expenses	Personal transport equipment	Educa- tion
	$	%	%	%	%	%	%	%
High income:								
Switzerland	27,260	27.6	-	19.4	5.8	7.9	3.5	-
U.S.	19,780	13.6	2.9	20.6	6.2	12.1	4.6	2.0
Upper-middle income:								
Korea	3,530	40.2	7.2	9.9	4.8	3.7	0.2	4.8
Portugal	3,670	31.7	4.3	6.2	9.6	4.2	8.7	0.9
Lower-middle income:								
Ecuador	1,080	29.6	5.1	11.2	7.4	3.8	-	-
Jordan	1,500	43.3	3.7	6.7	5.4	4.0	-	3.0
Lower income:								
India	330	58.7	3.8	7.0	4.1	1.3	0.5	2.1
Sudan	340	61.5	1.7	4.3	4.3	4.5	-	0.9

Source: World Bank (1989).

urbanized country with a well-developed public transport system, showed a low share for transportation. Compared with low-income countries, households in high-income countries allocate lower budget shares to food and higher shares to housing and transportation (for example, see Hazell & Roell, 1983; Alderman & von Braun, 1984).

The relationship between income and consumption pattern is illustrated by 1974–1975 data from Brazil (Gray, 1982, p. 38). Families were grouped by per capita income. Compared with the highest 20 percent, the lowest 30 percent in the income distribution showed higher budget shares for food (59 percent compared with 16 percent) and a much lower share for nonfood expenditures. Among nonfood items, the low-income group spent a slightly larger share of the budget for clothing, health and hygiene, and tobacco, while the highest income group showed higher budget shares for transport (about 6 percent compared with about 1 percent), housing, education, recreation, taxes and workers' contributions, and net savings and investment.

Within income groups, differences appeared between rural and urban families (Gray, 1982). The average per capita income of rural families in Brazil was much lower than that of urban families at each income level. Rural families at each income level spent a much larger share of their total budget on food than did urban families and a slightly larger budget share on clothing. In the lowest income group, urban families spent a larger budget share on housing and all other nonfood items except clothing than did rural families. In the highest income group, urban families spent a larger budget share than rural families on housing, education, recreation, taxes, and workers' contributions, but high-income rural families spent a larger share on health and hygiene and transport. They also allocated a larger share to net savings and investment in spite of their much lower incomes (about half that of the mean per capita income of urban families).

FOOD

Patterns of Consumption

Food consumption varies with both economic and cultural factors.

Cultural Factors. Caliendo (1979, pp. 227–255) pointed out that patterns of food consumption are influenced by the social organization of a society and by the cultural meanings attached to food. Cultural influence appears in the delineation of the household group (who is included) and definitions of the roles of members. In India, for example, sons, especially the oldest son, generally continue to live in the parental home after their marriage, and thus brides go to live with their in-laws. Property is owned and controlled by the father-in-law; the operation of the household is controlled by the mother-in-law (Johnson & Shukla, 1987, p. 8). Gujral described the meal pattern of families in one part of rural India as follows: "Generally, members of the household do not eat simultaneously. The meal-eating sequence of a typical family of low socioeconomic status is: first the husband's father, then the husband, then the children, and finally, the mother, who is in attendance throughout and eats whatever remains" (1987a, p. 37). The male head of the family, according to Gujral, receives the largest share of the food supply. Both the mother and any small children in the family are generally deficient in calories and some nutrients. Khan, Anker, Dastidar, and Bairathi summarized findings regarding intrafamily distribution of food in another part of India as follows: "Throughout the entire life cycle, men are relatively more privileged than women as regards individual food intake. . . . Although all household members observed in this study ate the same basic meals, males (adults and children) received the lion's share of nutritious food" (1988, p. 414).

Food carries cultural meanings. Caliendo (1979) pointed out that food provides emotional and sociological security. It provides comfort and may also be used to relieve anxiety or cope with stress. It may be used "to gain acceptance and friendship, to influence others, to gain responses and change behaviors of others, to establish nonverbal communication with others, or to threaten, deprive, discipline, or cajole others into behaving in a certain way" (p. 237).

Many beliefs exist about the relation between nutrition and health. In some cases, the beliefs may have at least a partial foundation in scientific research; in other cases, they are traditional. One common belief in some parts of Latin America and Africa is that foods can be classified as "hot" or "cold," according to their effect on the body. A "hot" illness can be treated by eating a "cold" food, and vice versa. In Puerto Rico, for example, overconsumption of "hot" foods are believed to lead to illness such as diarrhea, rashes, or ulcers, while "cold" foods cause arthritis, menstrual problems, and colds (Caliendo, 1979, p. 241). Some foods may be taboo for certain groups, perhaps because they are regarded as ritually unclean or because of their relationship to the clan's totem. Consumption of some foods is restricted for some types of persons. For example, Vemury and Levine (1978) reported that in parts of Africa young girls are limited in their consumption of foods of animal origin. Women may limit their consumption of some foods (usually those of animal origin) during pregnancy because they fear harmful effects. In Central Asia the onset of puberty and menstruation are occasions that call for food avoidances (Vemury & Levine, 1978, pp. 156–172). Although many of these practices are intended to safeguard health, their actual impact is to limit diets further that are none too rich in nutritious foods. The restricted or prohibited foods are often those that provide needed protein, and the restrictions usually seem to apply to the most nutritionally vulnerable groups.

Economic Factors. Among the economic factors that influence food consumption, the principal ones are supply, price, and income. Per capita supply of a given food commodity is affected by the following:

1. Increase in total supply in relation to population increase. In the three decades 1950 to 1980, total world grain supply increased by more than 30 percent in each decade

(Brown & Young, 1990, p. 76). Because of population growth, however, per capita increases were less than half that amount. From 1980 to 1990, total grain production increase was estimated at 17 percent, and per capita change at −2 percent. The Worldwatch Institute estimated a 9 percent total increase and a 7 percent per capita decrease from 1990 to 2000.

2. Whether it is produced locally. Locally produced foods are generally cheaper than those that must be transported into the area. (An exception to the rule of higher prices on imported foods might be food aid.) Distribution and marketing of commodities in a wide geographic area require a transportation and marketing system, with their associated costs. In remote rural areas of poor countries, systems for transporting and marketing may not exist and locally produced foods may be the only foods available.

3. Seasonal variation. Commodities are usually cheapest and most readily available at harvest time. Between harvests, locally produced supplies must be preserved and stored, adding to the cost and risk of spoilage and loss.

4. Technology and facilities for food processing and storage. Unless food is eaten immediately after harvesting, it must be preserved and stored. Meat and fresh fruits and vegetables quickly spoil if not preserved by freezing, drying, canning, salting, pickling, or some other method. Grains must be dried and preserved from rodents, insects, and other contamination and spoilage. Processing and storage require appropriate equipment, facilitates, and materials, as well as trained labor to perform the work. This adds to the cost of the food and limits the consumption of some foods. Vemury and Levine, for example, in their analysis of factors that affect food consumption, noted that in Africa "lack of storage and preservation facilities results in high food losses" (p. 157) and that "lack of adequate storage facilities . . . inhibits consumption of fresh fruits, dairy and meat products" in Latin America (p. 144). In poor countries, advanced technologies for processing and storage of food are generally too costly. Especially in rural areas, households must rely on methods that are low in cost and can be implemented with locally available materials and knowledge. Postharvest food losses are usually high. In one part of rural India, grains (if not grown by the household) are usually purchased in bulk at harvesttime, when prices are low, and stored in the home in bags, earthenware pots, or metal containers. Preservatives are mixed with the grain to retard spoilage. Commonly used preservatives include dry leaves of the neem tree, ash or dried mud, castor oil, boric powder, and mercury tablets. Most fruits and vegetables are eaten fresh, but some may be sun dried or pickled (Gujral, 1987b).

The role of economic factors is illustrated by an analysis by Marks and Yetley (1987) of global patterns of demand for food. They focused on three groups of foods: least preferred, preferred, and most preferred. Least-preferred foods consisted of coarse grains (maize, millet, barley, and sorghum). Preferred foods consisted of wheat and rice and most preferred of meat (beef and buffalo, pork, poultry, sheep, and goat). To describe the impact of economic factors, they divided countries into six income groups. In the lowest income group, coarse grains comprised the largest proportion of the diet, followed by wheat and rice, with meat comprising the smallest share. In this group of countries, the elasticities of wheat and rice and of meat were positive, with the elasticity of wheat and rice being higher than that of meat. The income elasticity of coarse grains was negative (indicating that they are inferior goods). The implication is that as household incomes rise, households tend to shift from coarse grains to wheat and rice, while increasing their meat consumption only slightly. This finding may be compared with Lipton's conclusion that the "ultra-poor, when income goes up a little, spend as if their overriding priority were to obtain more (and inexpensive) calories" (1988, p. 4).

Consumption of wheat and rice as a percentage of food increases with average per capita income of the country, according to Marks and Yetley, reaching a peak in the middle-income groups and thereafter declining, while consumption of coarse grains declines with income increases. Consumption of meat increases with income, forming a larger share of the total diet than wheat and rice among high-income countries; however, the income elasticity of meat was negative in the highest income group of countries.

Marks and Yetley also estimated the relationship between composition of the diet and caloric adequacy. They found that at the point at which coarse grains and wheat and rice accounted for about equal shares of the diet, caloric intake was equal to the amount recommended for adequacy (p. 29). This also seems to indicate a strong desire on the part of consumers for some variety in the diet, since it appears that, in very poor populations, some degree of dietary variety (in the form of wheat and rice instead of coarse grains) will be purchased even before caloric needs are completely satisfied.

Overton (1990) reported similar results regarding food consumption but used finer groupings of commodities. The largest amount of food consumed per capita in 1986, according to Overton, was in the developed countries, with 2,031 pounds per capita. Consumption was about 1,900 pounds per capita in the Soviet Union and Eastern Europe, about 1,300 in Latin America and the Near East, and about 1,000 in China and Africa. Consumption was the lowest in the Far East (excluding China), with 878 pounds per capita. Overton also found differences in the composition of the diet. In the developed countries, the largest proportion of the diet, in pounds per capita, consisted of animal products, with the next-largest category being "other," including alcohol, beverage crops, fruits, nuts, spices, pulses, and vegetable oils. Relatively small shares were devoted to cereals, vegetables, starchy roots, and sweeteners. In the centrally planned countries (Soviet Union, Eastern Europe, and China), the largest share consisted of cereals, then animal products, and vegetables. In Africa, starchy roots comprised the largest share of the diet and meat the smallest. Cereals formed the largest share of the diet in the Near and Far East. Protein and energy consumption varied accordingly. Protein consumption averaged about 60 grams per capita per day in developing countries (about 50 grams in Africa) and nearly 100 grams in developed countries.

Although consumers in the United States do not have the highest per capita income among the countries of the world, they have long spent the lowest percentage of their incomes on food at home. In 1986, 10.4 percent of total personal consumption expenditures in the United States went for food at home. Switzerland, with higher per capita consumption expenditures, spent nearly twice that percentage (20.2) on food at home. Canada spent a slightly higher percentage than the United States. Several countries spent more than half of their personal consumption expenditures on food: Sudan (63 percent), Sierra Leone (58 percent), India (53 percent), and the Philippines (52 percent) (Korb & Cochrane, 1989, pp. 26–29).

Within countries, in which food habits and supplies are presumably somewhat similar for the entire population, differences appear. In Brazil, for example, families in the lowest per capita income group allocated a larger share of their food-at-home budget to cereals, roots, legumes, and sugar than the high-income group, who allocated a larger share to vegetables, fruits, meat, dairy products, and oils and fats. The percentage of food-at-home expenditures for beverages was about the same in the low- as in the high-income group. Differences also appeared between rural and urban families, with rural families at all income levels devoting a larger share of their food budget to roots and legumes than urban families. Percentage of the food budget spent on food outside the home increased with income and was higher for urban than for rural families (Gray, 1982, p. 38).

Hunger and Malnutrition

Nutritional scientists differentiate between undernutrition—the consumption of food in amounts insufficient for the physiological needs—and malnutrition— a deficiency in one or more specific nutrients. A third condition is also found: overnutrition, the consumption of food in amounts greater than is needed, usually with detrimental consequences to health. Food intake is only one factor that affects nutritional status. It is also affected by utilization of the food by the body. Thus, persons whose intake of food should be adequate may suffer from malnutrition because of impaired absorption, utilization, or transport of nutrients; increased excretion (for example, diarrhea due to a gastrointestinal upset); or increased requirements (for example, due to disease or parasitic infections). Evers and McIntosh (1977, p. 187) characterized the first type of malnutrition as primary malnutrition and the second as secondary malnutrition. Poor sanitary conditions may lead to malnutrition as surely as inadequate food intake.

Malnutrition is the most important cause of disability in the world, equal in importance to noncommunicable illnesses (Wood, 1989, p. 116). Caloric intake is the first concern. Variations in food energy supplies are strongly related to income. Average daily calorie supply per capita in 1986 was 2,384 in the low-income countries, 2,846 in the middle-income countries, 3,117 in the upper-middle income countries, and 3,376 in high-income countries. Averages per country ranged from 1,595 in Mozambique to 3,645 in the United States (World Bank, 1990, pp. 232–233).

The most widespread nutritional problem in rich countries is probably overnutrition. Average per capita consumption of calories in most industrial market economies is higher than needed. For example, per capita consumption in the United States in 1982 was 3,616 (Kaneko & Nidaira, 1988, p. 248). This caloric intake was more than enough, according to recommendations of the Food and Agricultural Organization, for a very active adult male (Tarrant, 1980, p. 191), and hence much higher than was needed for most members of the population. Substantial amounts of this oversupply of food are probably used for pets or wasted, but the incidence of obesity and diseases that have been linked to consumption of some types of foods indicates that nutritional problems exist.

In poor countries, undernutrition—inadequate intake of calories—is the greatest problem. Protein deficiency is also found; however, utilization by the body of protein and calories is linked in that if calorie intake is inadequate, protein will be converted into calories to help meet the shortfall. Studies have shown that almost all people whose calorie intake is adequate are consuming sufficient protein (Evers & McIntosh, 1977, p. 185; Tarrant, 1980, pp. 192–193).

Protein consumption also varies with income. In 1986, daily per capita supply of protein in two high-income countries, the United States and Switzerland, was 108 and 98 grams, respectively. In contrast, daily per capita supply of protein (in grams) was 65 in Sudan and 55 in India, two low-income countries (World Bank, 1989).

In poor countries, as many of half of the children under the age of 5 may be malnourished. In Ecuador, for example, 38 percent of this age group were malnourished in 1987. In Sudan and India the percentage in 1983 was 55 and 49, respectively (World Bank, 1989). This percentage varies by season. In Madagascar, surveys in 1982, 1983, and 1984 showed that the percentage of the under-age–5 group that were below 80 percent of the Harvard Standard Weight for Age was the highest (around 52 percent) in January through April, dropped to a low of about 44 percent in July through September and then rose again (Jolly, 1988, p. 84).

The high rates of malnourishment among children in developing countries have implications for the human resources of those countries. Murdoch summarized the consequences as a "massive cost" in the form of "human suffering . . . [and] effects upon death rates (especially childhood death rates) and upon economic welfare" (1988, p. 101).

Food Security

Developing countries as a group produced only about half of the food they consumed in the 1980s (Trostle, 1989). Indeed, their food self-sufficiency declined. In the early 1960s, developing countries produced about 55 percent of the food they consumed. During the period from 1960 to 1987, net cereal imports increased by more than 8 percent per year. Food aid also increased, with an annual rate of increase of 3.7 percent between 1975 and 1987. In 1987, food aid in the form of cereals accounted for one-fifth of total cereal imports in developing countries (Trostle, 1989; Nightingale, 1990).

The United States is a major food donor to developing countries. Food aid is provided under Public Law 480. About two-thirds of the total in 1986 was provided in the form of concessional sales (Title I), government-to-government agreements that specify interest rate, repayment period, and currency mix that may be used for repayment. In some cases, repayment is waived (Title III). Direct donations of food account for the remaining food assistance (Title II). The food donations are channeled to the needy through private voluntary organizations, governmental agencies in developing countries, and multilateral agencies, such as the World Food Program. Types of programs to which the donated food is directed include community health programs for mothers and infants, school feeding programs, food-for-work programs for unemployed adults, and programs for the destitute (Development Coordination Committee, 1979).

In 1986, the United States contributed $1.5 billion worth of food aid, including over 5 billion metric tons of cereal, over half of the total contributed by donor countries (Matsumoto & Smith, 1989). The largest share of U.S. food aid—over 40 percent—went to Africa in 1986–1988. About one-fourth each went to Asia and Latin America, with very small percentages to the Middle East and Europe. This allocation is substantially different from that in 1976–1978. During the interval between these two periods, there were substantial increases in shares going to Africa and Latin America and corresponding decreases in aid to other regions.

Within developing countries, food policies and programs to help the poor may take several forms: food price subsidies (for example, the Egyptian food rationing system, which involves the distribution of selected foods at low prices), food-linked income-transfer programs (for example, food stamps or supplementary feeding programs), or income-generation programs (for example, public works programs). The evidence for the effectiveness of such programs is mixed. For example, Chavez and Martinez (1981) compared the first-year school performance of children who had received food supplements from birth and whose mothers had received food supplements during the pregnancy (the supplemented group) with a group of similar children who had received no food supplements (the nonsupplemented group). They found marked differences between the two groups. The supplemented group scored better on tests, were more active and attentive, and participated more in classroom activities. Pinstrup-Andersen (1988, p. 147) examined the impact of such programs in general on the food security and nutritional status of the poor and concluded that some groups have benefited from the programs, while others have not benefited or have even suffered negative effects. He pointed out that improving the nutritional status of those in greatest need depends in large part on the effectiveness of targeting programs to those groups: "Inappropriately targeted subsidies and transfers, e.g., those available to all urban but no rural households, are not cost-effective in reaching the poor and malnourished because they include the better-off urban households and exclude the rural poor" (p. 164). Type and design of program are also important. For example, a food subsidy program in Brazil resulted in slightly lower consumption of calories by the poor recipients because the increase in the subsidized wheat consumption was more than offset by decreased consumption of rice and other foods (pp. 154–155). Policies that keep food prices low for urban consumers may lower the prices of agricultural products and thus result in lower real incomes for rural people.

HOUSING

The housing owned or rented by a household entails more than the structure of the dwelling and its furnishings. It is inextricably associated with a total social and physical environment, including access to income-earning opportunities and services, association with neighbors, air and water quality, and the possibility of environmental hazards. These aspects associated with housing are especially important in international comparisons since the range of variability is great.

Research on social indicators provides a framework for identifying aspects of housing that are regarded as important. Galster (1985), for example, examined 10 aspects in his study of Ohio families: dwelling quality, dwelling quantity, neighborhood, public services, modernity, interior condition, exterior condition, privacy, rooms, and yard. Whorton and Moore (1984) proposed six scales for assessing satisfaction with community: satisfaction with personal safety (i.e., frequency of crime), job availability, educational and health care facilities, housing (condition, availability, and affordability), and the community in general. St. John and Clark (1984) considered several additional aspects: location with respect to relatives, close friends, church, social services, shopping, jobs, schools, and recreational facilities; social services, shopping, jobs, schools, and recreational facilities; availability of public transportation; how well buildings are kept up; how crowded it is; and how noisy. Turner (1980) pointed out the need to consider water supply, drainage for storm water and wastewater, and human waste disposal.

The impact of housing on health is of special concern. The World Health Organization (World Health Organization [WHO], 1988, pp. 32–34) identified several features of the housing environment that have significant impacts on health:

• Housing materials, equipment, and condition of structure. The house needs to provide protection from heat and cold, noise, dust, rain, insects, and rodents. For example, Chagas disease is spread by insects that live in cracks in mud or wooden houses. Use of open fires or unprotected stoves increases the risk of burns.

• Access to water. Diseases transmitted by water include typhoid, cholera, hepatitis, poliomyelitis, dysentery, and infection by intestinal protozoa.

• Sewage disposal. According to the World Health Organization, "there is a direct link between absence of facilities for the safe disposal of excreta and solid wastes and the incidence of infections'' (p. 33). Food, water, or the hands may become contaminated, leading to the ingestion of pathogenic organisms, such as pinworm or hookworm.

- Land. If adequate sanitation facilities are not available, the land surrounding the dwelling may become contaminated with fecal material or chemical wastes. Inadequate drainage may facilitate the spread of malaria and hookworm.

- Overcrowding. A high number of persons per dwelling, especially if accompanied by poor ventilation, promotes the spread of communicable diseases, such as influenza or tuberculosis.

- Air. Smoke from open fires and unvented stoves contributes to respiratory infections (a leading cause of mortality in developing countries), particularly among women and children. Many urban areas have high levels of air pollution. In São Paulo, for example, levels of carbon monoxide in the air exceeded standards of the World Health Organization on 226 days in 1987 (*Der Spiegel*, 1989).

Housing needs and costs are affected by household size. High-income countries are characterized by small household size. Table 6.3, with eight selected countries grouped by income level, shows that the two highest-income countries each have an average of fewer than three persons per household while the four lowest-income countries average five or more. While the smaller household size in the higher-income countries is due in part to the lower birthrates and hence smaller number of children, it may also be affected by the opportunity afforded by higher incomes for living independently. Recent data on housing conditions are not available, but earlier data (from 1970 in most cases) indicate that higher-income countries average more rooms per house—about five, compared with about two in those low-income countries for which data are available. Combined with the smaller family size, this means fewer persons per room—fewer than 1 per room in higher-income countries and 2.5 to 3.0 in lower-income countries. Lower-income countries had a much larger percentage of homes without electricity or piped water in 1970. Some countries made considerable progress after 1970 in expanding the availability of electricity, piped water, and toilets, although some differential between low- and high-income countries persists.

Although some kind of housing is a near-necessity, it is less essential than food. We would expect, therefore, that countries in which food expenditures form a large percentage of personal consumption expenditures would spend a low percentage on housing. Data in Table 6.2 seems to bear this out. The rank order by housing expenditure is exactly the reverse of the rank order by food.

Housing and related conditions generally vary considerably between rural and urban areas; therefore, these will be discussed separately.

Rural Housing

In the world as a whole, 58 percent of the population lived in rural areas in 1988 (World Health Statistics Quarterly [WHSQ], 1989b, p. 193). Developing

Table 6.3
Indicators of Housing: Eight Countries

Countries	Housing expenditure as % of GDP	Population		Average number of persons per household	Average number of rooms	Average persons per room	% of housing units without	
		% urban	annual rate of growth				electricity	piped water
High income:								
Switzerland	12.4	60.9	0.5	2.5	4.8	0.6	–	6.7
U.S.	14.8	73.9	0.9	2.7	5.1	0.6	2.5	4.0
Upper-middle income:								
Korea	6.5	68.6	3.7	4.5	4.1	–	48.8	1.6
Portugal	6.3	32.3	1.7	4.0	4.5	0.8	52.3	39.5
Lower-middle income:								
Ecuador	4.4	54.6	4.8	5.1	2.1	2.6	84.9	86.8
Jordan	5.7	66.3	5.3	6.7	–	–	–	–
Lower income:								
India	7.1	26.8	4.4	5.2	–	2.8	–	–
Sudan	13.0	21.3	4.5	5.1	2.0	2.5	36.1	29.7

Source: World Bank (1989).

and developed countries differed, however. About one-fourth of the population in developed countries and 70 percent of the population in developing countries lived in rural areas in 1984 (United Nations Environment Programme & United Nations Children's Fund [UNEP & UNICEF], 1990, p. 53). Thus, rural housing forms an important aspect of the total picture of household consumption.

In general, rural housing is likely to be less expensive than urban housing but of poorer quality. In Korea, for example, while about half of the housing did not have electricity in 1970, about three-fourths of the rural housing lacked electricity. The percentage with access to safe water is much lower in rural areas. In developing countries, according to the World Health Organization, less than half (47 percent) of the inhabitants had access in 1985 to "a water supply that was reasonably adequate and could be considered as safe," and only 16 percent had access to an appropriate form of sanitation (WHO, 1988, p. 15). The percentages varied by country and region. The lowest percentages were in Africa, where only 31 percent had access to safe water, and Southeast Asia, where only 7 percent had access to adequate sanitation. The highest percentages for access to safe water and sanitation were in the Western Pacific (Korea, Malaysia, Philippines, Fiji, Macao, and Solomon Islands).

Few rural houses in developing countries have water piped to the house. Thus, water carrying is a regular feature of life in those areas and takes considerable time, depending on the household's needs and distance to water source. Usually laundry is done at the water source—the bank of a stream or pond or at the village well. Bathing may also be done at the water source. Nevertheless, water needed for drinking and cooking remains to be carried. Goldschmidt-Clermont (1987, pp. 81–82) reported that males in Botswana spent about 2 percent of their time and females over 7 percent of their time fetching water. Feachem et al. (1978) estimated that households in Lesotho who relied on springs for their water supply averaged up to an hour and a half a day carrying water. The average for rural women in Nepal was over half an hour per day (Acharya & Bennett, 1982).

Houses in rural areas are likely to be made of inexpensive, locally produced materials, especially in low-income countries. In an Indian village, for example, a 1985 visitor described the houses as follows:

Branching off from [the main] street are lanes along which are houses, many of mud brick covered with plaster, but some of mud and dung over sticks. Many houses have beautifully carved wooden doorways and doors. Their roofs are red tile, made by the village potter and his son. The tiles are laid over tin or sticks. . . . Almost all of the homes are in excellent repair and are kept clean and neat. (Johnson & Bhavnagri, 1987, p. 9)

Most of the houses had floors made of a mixture of mud and cow dung, applied when wet and allowed to dry.

The houses Johnson and Bhavnagri described were generally poorly ventilated. Some of the more modern houses had a chimney to carry away the smoke from the cook stove (*chulah*); in others, the smoke dispersed through the room. Indoor air pollution is a serious problem worldwide. According to a 1989 WHO report (WHSQ, 1989, p. 247), about 800 million people, mostly in rural areas, are exposed to high levels of indoor air pollution.

Many of the houses in the village described by Johnson and Bhavnagri had electricity, but very few had piped water in or adjacent to the house. Water was obtained each morning from wells scattered about the community and carried by the women in earthenware pots to the home for drinking and bathing—sometimes over a considerable distance. Laundry was usually carried to a well or pond and done there.

In that part of India, the main source of water is rainwater. In some villages, the water was used directly from lakes and streams or village ponds. Some other villages were served by public water systems with rainwater collected in reservoirs, purified, and supplied to users (usually at central locations) at certain times each day (Paralikar, 1987). The wells in the village described by Johnson and Bhavnagri were treated with chlorine powder twice a month. Additional purification measures were taken in case of an epidemic (Hart, 1987).

Due to government public health programs, several latrines were available in the village described by Johnson and Bhavnagri; however, most villagers went to the fields to excrete body wastes. Wastewater was poured onto the ground. In some cases, in order to keep the wastewater from making a muddy place in the street or yard, a soak pit would be dug near the bathing area (Paralikar, 1987).

Availability of services is often a problem in rural areas. Wanmali (1985, p. 40) concluded that distance from the service supplier is negatively related to use of the service among rural residents in one section of India. The distance to services for households in the unirrigated section of the district he studied averaged about 9 kilometers for communications (postal, telegraph, or telephone service), 18 kilometers for credit and banking services, 29 kilometers for transportation services (by road, train, or bus), 5 kilometers to vendors of food and personal services, and 17 kilometers to vendors of consumer durables (p. 31). Not all households used the services that were available. Services used by more than 80 percent of the households included bus service, carpenter, cobbler, retail cloth store, tea and coffee shop, chemist or druggist, and vendors of household utensils, glassware and pottery, footwear, fuel, general provisions, vegetables, fruit, and meat (pp. 50–51). Services used by fewer than 20 percent of the households included telephones, telegraphs, credit and banking services, trains, building materials (bricks, tiles, and cement), sales or repair of vehicles (except bicycles), watches, and jewelry.

Urban Housing

About 38 percent of the world's population lived in urban areas in 1975 (WHSQ, 1989b, p. 193). By 1988, the percentage was 42 percent, and by 2000 it is expected that nearly half (47 percent) of the population will live in cities.

Although urban housing generally provides better access to services than rural housing, it also includes some of the worst housing conditions—slums, squatter settlements, and homelessness. A major problem for many poor countries has been the high rate of population growth in cities. While the urban population in the high-income countries shown in Table 6.3 grew at less than 1 percent per year, the rate of growth in poorer countries was 4 or 5 percent—more than four times as rapid as urban population growth in the United States. Lagos, Nigeria, for example, grew from 700,000 to 6 million inhabitants in a twenty-year period (Harden, 1985). São Paulo, Brazil, grew from 2.5 million in 1955 to between 17 million and 20 million in 1989 (*Der Spiegel*, 1989). In 1984, 30 percent of the population in developing countries lived in urban areas. In 2000, 39 percent are expected to be in urban areas (UNEP & UNICEF, 1990, p. 53).

Most of the urban growth in poorer countries is due to migration from rural to urban areas. Even if the migrants had sufficient income to afford adequate housing, construction of new housing could hardly keep pace. In fact, most migrants are seeking jobs and income. Some move in with relatives, some live on the streets, and many move into squatter settlements that spring up on any unoccupied land.

The results of the rapid urban growth can be seen in the increased numbers living on the streets or in squatter settlements and in deteriorating conditions of life in the cities. In some developing countries, one-half to three-fourths of those in urban areas live in slums or squatter settlements (UNEP & UNICEF, 1990, p. 54). From 1965 to 1985, the number of people living in squatter settlements and slums (*favelas*) increased by 300 percent in Rio de Janeiro, while the population outside the *favelas* increased by only 10 percent (Margolis, 1985). It is estimated that in the 1980s, 7 million children lived on the street in Brazil (UNEP & UNICEF, 1990, p. 54).

In Bombay and other cities in India, individuals or family groups are frequently encountered living on the sidewalk. They may have erected a small awning or lean-to to protect them from the weather and perhaps have a cooking fire and utensils. Vacant land is taken over by squatters. Guests in modern luxury hotels may find that their windows overlook a squatter settlement, with its cluster of shacks constructed of waste materials, surrounded by bare dirt or, in the rainy season, mud, and with a few cows and goats wandering among the houses.

Living conditions in burgeoning cities are poor. Squatter settlements are established without arrangements for sewage disposal and may lack water as well as surfaced roads, electricity, and other important services. The World Health Organization (1988, p. 14) estimated that in some countries, over three-fourths of the urban residents lived in substandard housing with inadequate or no services in 1980. Harden (1985) reported that in Lagos, half the city was without sewers or septic tanks and, when it rained, one-third of the city was flooded, contaminating water lines.

Lack of sewage disposal and garbage collection services pose significant health problems in low-income countries, since the amount of waste to be disposed of is not proportionately lower than in high-income countries. In Calcutta, for example, each person generated about half a kilogram of waste per day, in New York 1.8, and in Rome about 0.7 kilograms (Pollock, 1987, p. 9).

The World Health Organization (1988, pp. 38–41) summarized the characteristics of squatter settlements as follows:

• Insecurity of tenure. Because the land has been occupied without the permission of the owner, occupants are subject to eviction at any time.

• Unsuitable land. Often the settlement is located on land that is subject to frequent flooding or landslides or is otherwise unsuitable for habitation. In São Paulo, for example, about two-thirds of those who live in the *favelas* are on land subject to floods or landslides.

• Low-quality houses. Occupants generally have insufficient income to build adequate houses but in any case are discouraged from doing so because they may be evicted at any time.

• Lack of infrastructure, facilities, and services. In Nairobi, for example, in 1978, over one-third of the houses were located in squatter settlements, lacked access to roads, had no sewers or drains, and had no public lighting (WHO, 1988, p. 40). In one city in Central African Republic, according to a 1981 estimate, about three-fourths of the population lived in houses built by the occupants on land to which they had no legal claim and lacked a water supply, sewers, and electricity.

The impact on health, safety, and sanitation is not confined to residents of the squatter settlements and slums. Crime flourishes. Traffic is a problem, partly because of poor planning and the failure of road construction to keep pace with population increases. Many large cities are in locations where geographical configuration and weather lead to buildup of air pollution from industrial emissions and motor vehicle exhausts. According to *Der Spiegel*, "Carbon-monoxide poisoning is one of the most common causes of traffic deaths in São Paulo" (1989, p. 34). Over 600 million people live in urban areas where average sulfur dioxide levels exceed WHO guidelines (WHSQ, 1989a, pp. 246–247). Over a billion people are in areas where suspended particulates—dust and smoke from diesel-burning vehicles or motorscooters—are a hazard. Several studies of children living near sources of lead emissions have found statistical associations between their proximity to the sources of lead emissions and levels of lead in their blood (WHO, 1988, pp. 29–30).

Nigeria provides a specific example of housing conditions in a poor country with high urban growth. Overall, Nigeria experienced a population growth rate of 3 percent per year in the 1980s, slightly higher than the average growth rate for the region and substantially higher than the average of 2 percent for all low-income countries (World Bank, 1989, pp. 230–231). Population growth in urban areas in Nigeria was over 6 percent per year, much higher than the average for the region or the income group. In 1921, less than 5 percent of the Nigerian population lived in urban areas (Salau, 1986); in 1987, one-third were in urban areas (World Bank, 1989). Salau (1986) described conditions in 1983 in small, medium, and large Nigerian cities as follows:

1. Transportation. About 15 to 20 percent of the household heads had to travel more than 5 kilometers to their place of work, while about half were within 2 kilometers. Most households were within 2 kilometers of marketplace and school. Less than half of the streets in large cities were tarred; about 10 percent consisted of footpaths. About one-third of the households in large cities used private automobiles for transportation, 14 percent used a public bus, and 9 percent walked. Motor bikes and taxis were used by about 12 and 30 percent, respectively. In small Nigerian cities only one-fourth of the streets were tarred, and 16 percent were footpaths. In small cities, walking (34 percent) or using a motor bike (28 percent) was more common than driving a private automobile (19 percent).

2. Garbage collection. Even in the large cities of Nigeria, less than one-third of the households had regular garbage pickup, although nearly half reported irregular collection of garbage. About 19 percent of the households in large cities and 60 percent in small cities had no garbage collection service. Asked what they disliked most about the city in which they lived, over half of the respondents in small cities and nearly one-third of those in larger cities complained about the lack of public services and amenities. About one-fourth of those in medium and large cities complained about the dirt and noise.

3. Housing. The materials used for housing construction included cement block (considered the best material), corrugated iron, burned bricks, and mud or sun-dried bricks. Cement block was the most frequently used material, accounting for two-thirds of the houses in large cities and nearly half in small cities. About one-fourth of the houses in large cities and nearly half in small cities were built of mud or sun-dried bricks. Salau pointed out that mud is well adapted to the climate of Nigeria; however, "mud houses invariably lack basic necessities such as pipe-born water, electricity, flush toilets, etc." (p. 198). About one-third of the large-city and one-fourth of the small-city respondents rated their housing as sound. About one-fifth of the large-city and about 30 percent of the medium- or small-city respondents reported that their houses were dilapidated or in need of major repair.

Rapid urban growth is not necessarily associated with poor living conditions. Currie and Thacker (1986) compared residents' satisfaction with their environment in two similar-sized Canadian cities, one a slow-growth and one a rapid-growth city. They found no significant difference in satisfaction.

HEALTH CARE

According to the World Health Organization, over one-fifth of the world's population is seriously sick or malnourished. The incidence of health problems varies among regions, however. In Asia, about 40 percent are sick or malnourished; in sub-Saharan Africa, the figure is about 30 percent. WHO concluded that many of these health problems could be averted by vaccines or treated effectively by drugs (Okie, 1989). Some of the major diseases are:

- Acute respiratory infections. About 4 million die each year (Okie, 1989). In Peru, for example, over 18,000 persons died of respiratory diseases in 1981. Over half of the deaths were of children under 5 years old (WHO, 1988, p. 29).

- Diarrhea caused by viruses, bacteria, and parasites, usually caused by inadequate sanitation. About 4 million children under the age of 5 die each year of dehydration resulting from diarrhea (Okie, 1989). In El Salvador, for example, half of all deaths of children under 5 years old were from feces-related diseases, according to a 1971 report (WHO, 1988, p. 29).

- Vaccine-preventable diseases—polio, tetanus, measles, diphtheria, pertussis, and tuberculosis. About 2.8 million children die of these diseases each year. About 60 percent of children in developing countries receive vaccinations (Okie, 1989).

- Tuberculosis. About 3 million die, and about 10 million persons become infected annually (Okie, 1989).

- Malaria. About 2 million people die, and about 100 million people become infected annually (Okie, 1989).

- Schistosomiasis, a disease caused by a water-borne parasite. About 200 million people are infected annually (Okie, 1989).

- Sexually transmitted diseases, including gonorrhea and herpes. About one-fifth of all teenagers and young adults contract a sexually transmitted disease annually. About 5 million to 10 million people in the world are infected with the virus that causes AIDS (Okie, 1989).

The prevalence of specific diseases varies also by region (Okie, 1989):

- South and East Asia. The commonest diseases are diarrheal diseases, respiratory diseases, dengue, measles, and malaria.

- Sub-Saharan Africa. The commonest diseases are diarrheal diseases, malaria, respiratory diseases, schistosomiasis (a disease characterized by disorders of the liver, urinary bladder, lungs, or central nervous system), sexually transmitted diseases, and measles.

- North Africa and the Middle East. The commonest diseases are diarrheal diseases, respiratory diseases, measles, and tuberculosis.

- Latin America. The commonest diseases are diarrheal diseases, respiratory diseases, malaria, tuberculosis, Chagas disease (a chronic wasting disease caused by a parasite carried by insects), measles, and dengue (an infectious disease transmitted by mosquitos and characterized by severe pains in the joints and back, fever, and rash).

Causes of death differ in frequency between developing and developed countries. Heart disease and strokes, which account for nearly half of the deaths in developed countries, account for 18 percent in developing countries (Chandler, 1984, p. 6). Cancer accounts for 21 percent of deaths in developed but only 8 percent in developing countries. On the other hand, diarrheal infections and parasites cause 17 percent of the deaths in developing countries but only 1 percent of the deaths in developed countries. Respiratory infections also are a more common cause of death in developing than in developed countries.

   Those countries that are most in need of health care, as indicated by incidence of disease, are also those in which the least amount of health care is available. Table 6.4 summarizes indicators of the availability of health care in the eight countries we selected to represent different income levels. In the two highest-income countries, Switzerland and the United States, 100 percent of the population has access to health care. This is true also in Portugal, an upper-middle-income country. In the two lowest-income countries, at least one-fourth of the population lacks access to health care.

   Access to health care is also seen in the number of potential patients per physician, nurse, and hospital bed. There are limits to the number of patients who can be adequately served by a single doctor or who can be accommodated in a single hospital bed. The smaller the number of potential patients, the more likely it is that each has access to health care when needed. Again, the discrepancy between high- and low-income countries is pronounced, especially if considered in the light of statistics on incidence of disease. In India, if patients were divided evenly among physicians, each would have an estimated 1,000 potential patients. In contrast, in the United States, each physician would have fewer than 500 potential patients, only a fraction of whom would be ill.

   As WHO pointed out, much illness can be averted. The percentage of infants (under 1 year old) who were immunized in each of the eight selected countries is shown in Table 6.4. With two exceptions, the higher the income is, the higher the percentage immunized. In Sudan in the lowest-income group, less than one-third of infants had been immunized for measles or diphtheria. In India, although a relatively high percentage had been immunized for diphtheria, only 17 percent had been immunized for measles. Jordan is an exception to the pattern, with nearly 90 percent of the infants immunized. The other exception is immunization for diphtheria in the United States, which is quite low, presumably because risk of the disease is slight.

   Expenditures for health care are influenced by need, importance attached to good health, and ability to pay. Data in Table 6.4 suggest that ability to pay may be the most important factor of the three. In 1987, each of the two highest-income countries spent about 11 percent of their GDP on health care, higher than that of any of the other countries. India, in the lowest-income group, allocated the lowest share—2 percent. Two countries, Jordan and Sudan, allocated a higher percentage than would be expected on the basis of their per capita income (although Sudan ranked among the lowest in access to health care), and Korea allocated a somewhat lower percentage than would be expected.

   Some idea of the adequacy of health care and health conditions generally may be obtained by comparing the excess mortality ratios (EMR) of countries (Uemura, 1989, pp. 33–34). (EMR is number of preventable deaths as a percentage of minimum achievable death rate.) Among the industrialized countries, the United States (EMR equal to 32 percent) ranked about midway in the distribution. Countries with lower EMR include Japan (5 percent), Switzerland (16 percent), Sweden (20 percent), Canada (21 percent), Norway and France (24 percent),

Table 6.4
Indicators of Health Care: Eight Countries

Countries	Health care expenditure as % of GDP	Population per physician	Population per nurse	Population per hospital bed	Population with access safe water	% of population under 12 months immunized for	
						measles	diphtheria
High income:							
Switzerland	11.3	696.1	129.3	-	100	60	90
U.S.	11.2	472.9	73.8	170.8	100	80	37
Upper-middle income:							
Korea	2.9	1,165.8	587.3	600.0	80	89	76
Portugal	4.3	412.4	627.5	200.0	100	66	96
Lower-middle income:							
Ecuador	3.5	826.4	616.3	400.0	-	46	51
Jordan	5.0	1,139.3	1,298.2	1,100.0	80	87	89
Lower income:							
India	2.0	2,520.7	1,699.8	1,300.0	75	17	58
Sudan	6.0	10,108.4	1,248.2	1,112.5	70	22	29

Source: World Bank (1989).

Netherlands (26 percent), and Spain and Greece (27 percent). Countries in Eastern Europe had higher EMRs, ranging from 81 percent in what was then East Germany to 105 in Hungary. In developing countries, EMRs were generally high. Among the highest were Guatemala (300 percent) and other countries in the Caribbean region.

HOUSEHOLD ENERGY, TRANSPORTATION, AND COMMUNICATION

Energy, transportation, and communication play key roles in the lives of households. In Hoyt's terminology, energy is a protective commodity, providing an essential element of household production and consumption. Transportation and communication are expansive commodities, enabling households to strive for higher levels of living.

Energy

The world used energy equal to 163.6 million barrels per day of oil equivalent in 1984, about 28 percent more than was used in 1973. The largest source was oil (35 percent), followed by coal (27 percent) and natural gas (17 percent). Renewable energy sources such as wood accounted for 18 percent and nuclear energy 3 percent (Flavin, 1985, p. 35).

Households use fuels for cooking, heating and cooling the house, transportation, and in various other mechanisms and appliances. Energy is also an input in the production and distribution of goods and services used by households.

Energy can be divided into two types, according to source: commercial energy, which includes coal, lignite, petroleum, natural gas, and hydro, nuclear, and geothermal electricity, and traditional energy, which includes firewood and animal and vegetable wastes. Dunkerly, William, Lincoln, and Cecelski (1981, p. 3) estimated that in 1978, traditional energy comprised about 8 percent of total energy consumption in the world.

Energy consumption is divided unevenly among countries. Low-income countries in 1989 consumed about 324 kilograms of commercial energy per capita, in oil-equivalent units (Table 6.5). The next higher income group consumed nearly three times as much, while the highest group consumed 15 times as much. When traditional fuels are taken into account, the picture is changed only slightly. Dunkerly estimated total per capita energy consumption (in oil-equivalent units) of industrialized countries as nearly eight times that of developing countries. The greatest use of traditional fuels was in Africa, where it comprised two-thirds of total per capita energy consumption. In Latin America and Asia, it comprised about one-fourth of the total, while in industrialized countries it accounted for about 1 percent (Dunkerly et al., p. 3). Although poor countries use much less energy per capita than higher-income countries, it nevertheless accounts for about the same percentage of GDP (Table 6.2).

Table 6.5
Energy Consumption: Eight Countries

Countries	Expenditure on energy as a percentage of GDP	Commercial energy consumption per capita: Kg. of oil equivalent
High income:		
Switzerland	4.2	4,106.4
U.S.	3.0	7,265.3
Upper-middle income:		
Korea	2.8	1,475.3
Portugal	2.4	1,321.5
Lower-middle income:		
Ecuador	0.9	624.9
Jordan	–	749.6
Lower income:		
India	2.3	208.1
Sudan	4.0	58.4

Source: World Bank (1989).

Developing countries have been quick to adopt electricity as a source of energy, although their usage is far less than that in developed countries. In 1982, electricity use in developing countries was six times what it had been 20 years earlier. Electricity consumption in the United States in 1982 was 9,600 kilowatt hours per capita. Per capita consumption in Korea was 12 percent of U.S. consumption, India 2 percent, and Kenya 1 percent (Flavin, 1986, pp. 12–13). In Korea in 1982, 95 percent of the population had electricity, but in Mexico the percentage was only 81, in the Philippines 52 percent, and India 14 percent. Less than 10 percent of the population in Kenya, Nepal, Bangladesh, and Niger had electricity (Flavin, 1986, p. 35).

Patterns of fuel use in poor countries are illustrated by Bowonder, Rao, Dasgupta, and Prasad's study of energy use of farm families in eight rural communities in India (1985). The study was concerned with all end uses of energy, including agricultural uses (both work and fertilizer), commercial and industrial uses, transportation, and domestic uses in cooking and lighting. Traditional fuels included animal waste, agricultural residues, wood, and charcoal. Commercial fuels included electricity, kerosene, coal, gasoline, and diesel fuel. Animal and human energy were also used in transport and to perform work. Nontraditional fuels accounted for well over half of their total energy use (including animal and human energy). In half of the communities, traditional fuels accounted for more than 80 percent of energy used. Use of commercial energy ranged from less than 1 percent to 8 percent of the total. Animal energy accounted for up to 12 percent of the total and human energy (from men, women, and children) about 2 to 4 percent. Domestic uses ranged from 15 to 60 percent of the total. The portion accounted for by lighting was negligible (about 1 percent), but cooking took substantial amounts of energy. The authors believed that the large differences among communities in amounts of fuel used in cooking were due in part to differences in the cereal used as a staple food. Rice, for example, requires less cooking time than wheat or jowar. The cereals were not processed and thus required long cooking. The estimates by Bowonder et al. were consistent with those of Dunkerly, who estimated that traditional fuels accounted for about 80 percent of all energy use in rural India (1981, p. 52). About 64 percent of all energy, according to Dunkerly et al., was used in domestic activities.

George (1987) described fuel use by rural households in Gujarat, India. Almost all of the village households used traditional fuels (wood, dried cow dung, and agricultural wastes) for cooking. A few used coal, sawdust, or liquid petroleum gas. Some households used kerosene as a supplementary fuel for warming milk or making tea. Cooking was generally done on a homemade stove called a *chullah*, formed from mud, cow dung, ash, fine sand, dust, and hay. Homeless families cooked on open fires built within three stones that served to support the cooking pot. Kerosene lamps or, in a few cases, electricity were used for lighting.

Data from other studies of energy use in rural India indicate that fuelwood and human or animal power are the dominant sources of energy, with only small amounts coming from kerosene or electricity (Flavin, 1986, p. 41). Cooking takes the largest share of energy, with lighting and transportation accounting for very small proportions of the total.

A major advantage of traditional fuels in rural areas is that they can be gleaned from the surrounding area without cost. Gathering fuel is, however, a time-consuming activity. Dixon-Mueller (1985, p. 40) reported that women in one part of India spent about an hour per day gathering fuel. Henn (1978) reported that women in Cameroon spent an average of 90 hours per year in gathering firewood. Rural men and women in Nepal averaged about one-third of an hour a day (Acharya & Bennett, 1982).

Total world energy consumption has grown substantially since 1960, with an average annual increase of about 5 percent from 1960 to 1973 (Dunkerly et al., 1981, p. 8). The highest rates of increase were in the developing countries. The oil price shocks of 1973 and 1979 slowed the rate of increase in the industrialized countries but not in the developing countries. Household energy use changed somewhat after 1973 because of higher energy prices and concern for conservation. Schipper and Ketoff (1985) found a decline in household use of oil from 1978 to 1983 among selected industrialized countries. In the United States, for example, household use of oil declined by 40 percent from 1978 to 1982. In 1982 about 6 percent of all homes in the United States were heated with wood. In 1987, wood accounted for about 9 percent of total energy consumed by U.S. households (U.S. Department of Energy, 1989, p. 77).

The increase in total energy consumption has aroused concern not only about dwindling energy supplies but also about the environmental and health impacts of energy exploitation. The United Nations Environment Programme and United Nations Children's Fund issued a 1990 report in which they stated, "Environmental degradation is killing children" (p. 1). They estimated that all children will suffer from atmospheric pollution. An estimated 4.2 million children per year were estimated to die from air pollution in developing countries.

Increased use of traditional fuels has led to deforestation (and hence to soil erosion and floods) and to depletion of soil fertility because these animal and plant wastes are burned rather than returned to the soil (Norman, 1984). In the late 1970s, over 40 percent of the land area in Africa and Asia and 27 percent in South America suffered some degradation (Brown & Young, 1990, p. 60). Reduced food harvests are one consequence of this loss of soil fertility.

Carbon emissions from fossil fuels are another environmental impact (Flavin, 1990, p. 19). Such emissions are partly due to household use of fuels and partly to industrial uses. In 1987, carbon emissions from fossil fuels totaled 5.5 billion tons, more than double that of 1960. Less than one-third came from developing countries; over one-fifth came from the United States.

Transportation and Communication

In general, higher-income countries devote a larger share of their resources to transportation than do lower-income countries. Of our eight selected countries

(Table 6.6), the United States spent the largest share of its GDP on transport and communication; Sudan spent the smallest. The relationship is not perfectly regular, however. Switzerland and Korea, both small countries with more than 60 percent of their populations living in urban areas, allocated relatively low percentages of GDP to transport and communication, while Portugal, which is predominantly rural, allocated a large proportion.

Ownership of private automobiles is relative to income. Number of persons in the population for each passenger car varied from fewer than two in the United States to over 500 in India. The number of private passenger cars in use in the world as a whole increased from 53 million in 1950 to 386 million in 1986 (Renner, 1988, p. 9). Over one-third of these vehicles were in the United States.

Differences in the price of gasoline account for some differences in expenditures for transportation. Gasoline prices in Western Europe are about twice as high as in the United States (Renner, 1988, p. 34).

Public transportation is both cheaper and less energy intensive than private transportation. Intracity rail or bus transport uses less than one-fifth as much energy per passenger as privately owned automobiles (Lowe, 1990a, pp. 13–17). Pollution emissions are also lower. Usage varies among cities, however, People living in Chicago used public transport for an average of 101 trips per person per year; the figure for people in Dallas was 22 trips. Corresponding figures for some other cities were: Moscow, 713 trips; Tokyo, 650; Seoul, 457; and Nairobi, 151.

Bicycles are a low-cost, low-energy alternative to motor transportation. An automobile with one occupant uses 1,153 calories per kilometer, public transportation about 550, and cycling 22. Bicycles have the additional advantage of not adding to air pollution. In the 1980s, China had the highest ratio of bicycles to automobiles—about 250 bicycles to each automobile. India and Korea also had relatively high ratios—30 and 20, respectively. The ratio was low in other developing and developed countries—for example, about one bicycle for each auto—in Tanzania and the United States. In Beijing, China, about half of all trips other than walking were by bicycle; in New Delhi, India, about 22 percent; and in London about 2 percent (Lowe, 1990b, pp. 121–124).

Communication serves not only to inform households about current events and enable them to keep in touch with distant friends and relatives, but it also makes them aware of consumption possibilities and the consumption patterns of households outside their community. Most of these functions are performed by mass media—newspapers and periodicals, movies, radio, and television. In countries and in population groups with high rates of illiteracy, movies, radio, and television are the primary vehicle for mass communication.

Person-to-person communication includes mail, telegrams, and telephones. The need for such communication varies. In industrialized societies, probably all households send and receive mail and use the telephone at least occasionally. In developing countries, especially in rural areas, most person-to-person contacts may occur within the community. Mail is needed only to keep in touch with

Table 6.6
Transportation and Communication: Eight Countries

Countries	Expenditure on transportation & communication as a percentage of GDP	Population per passenger car	Population per telephone
High income:			
Switzerland	6.9	2.5	1.2
U.S.	11.7	1.8	1.3
Upper-middle income:			
Korea	5.6	73.7	4.4
Portugal	9.3	6.7	5.2
Lower-middle income:			
Ecuador	7.9	87.9	26.6
Jordan	5.2	23.1	–
Lower income:			
India	5.1	542.9	188.6
Sudan	2.2	248.8	271.5

Source: World Bank (1989).

family members who have migrated to another location and telephones are used seldom. Wanmali reported that telephones were used by less than 20 percent of the rural Indian households he studied, although purchase of postage stamps was frequent (1985, p. 50). These differences in need and ability to pay are reflected in the data on population per telephone (Table 6.6). In the United States and Switzerland, there are nearly as many telephones as people. In India and Sudan, there is only one telephone per 189 and 272 persons, respectively.

NOTES

1. The Soviet Union and several other countries with centrally planned economies did not report GNP.

2. Data on the distribution of final consumption expenditures were available for only a small fraction of countries.

3. Data on average amounts spent by families in specified categories were requested from the respective governments of 18 countries. Amounts were converted into 1984 U.S. dollar equivalents. Most of the data were for 1984.

Part III

Household Consumption in a
Social Context

7

Household Consumption and Public Policy

The purpose of this chapter is to examine uses of household consumption data in the making of public policy. In focusing exclusively on public policy uses, we do not intend to undervalue the importance of other uses of consumption data, especially in business decision making and in consumer education. Those uses are widespread, diverse, and important.

We have several reasons for limiting our detailed discussion of application to public policy. Applications in business are diverse, are impossible to cover adequately within our page limitations, and are dealt with extensively in publications on business administration and marketing. Applications in consumer education are also diverse but relatively straightforward, at least from the educator's point of view. Consumer education is intended to provide consumers with information—in the case of consumption data, information about the average behavior of other households—from which each individual consumer is expected to draw implications for his or her own situation. Public policy issues are broader in scope than the specific questions dealt with by business firms and consumers. They are important in that their resolution affects large numbers of people. Finally, we believe that the examination of some uses of household consumption data in public policy-making may illustrate the type of applications that are relevant to business and consumer choices.

THE POLICY-MAKING PROCESS

Policy, according to Zimmerman, is "a series of related choices or decisions to support an agreed upon course of action with respect to the pursuit and achievement of a goal or value" (1988, p. 14). A policy issue is a question: Should action be taken? What action should be taken?

Social policy deals with aggregate relationships in society. It may supplement the action of the market by providing goods or services based on status, identity,

or community of the recipient. An example is policies having to do with enti-
tlement programs, such as Medicaid or food stamps. It may be concerned with
the distribution of social costs, for example, tax burden or the costs of environmental cleanup.

Since policy-making is decision making, the process of making public policy
can be conceptualized in terms of decision-making steps: sensing a problem,
formulating a statement of the problem, identifying options, agreeing on characteristics of a good solution (criteria for evaluation of options), identifying
options for dealing with the problem, collecting data on the options, evaluating
options, choosing and implementing an option, and evaluating the impact of the
choice. All of these steps do occur in public policy-making although not necessarily sequentially or in an orderly way.

Public policy-making is more complex than decision making by an individual
or small group because large numbers of persons are involved. Some degree of
consensus, or at least acquiescence, is required in the general public for a public
policy to be adopted and effectively implemented. Even after a policy option
has been adopted and implemented, the process may not be over. Evaluation of
the impacts may result in dissatisfaction and renewed consideration of other
options.

The making of a public policy is a time-consuming process, sometimes lasting
several decades. Information that leads to awareness of a problem must be
disseminated. A consensus must develop to the effect that a problem exists and
that the problem is sufficiently serious as to require public action. Options must
be identified and a consensus reached on the criteria used to evaluate them.
Information must be developed and disseminated on the probable impact of the
options on the original problem and on possible side effects—other impacts that
may need to be taken into account. A consensus must develop within influential
groups regarding which option is best. Legislative, administrative, and perhaps
legal processes must be set in motion to make and implement a decision. Finally,
when the impacts of the policy decision are felt, a new consensus may develop
to the effect that further action is needed to solve the problem or that the selected
option has created a new problem requiring action, either by way of rescinding
or modifying the original policy or taking supplementary actions.

These actions are generally not sequential or in any particular order. Options
may be proposed at any time—perhaps even preceding awareness on the part of
most of the public that a problem exists. Criteria for evaluating options are
usually proposed singly rather than as a comprehensive list and may be proposed
at any time. The options are not necessarily evaluated as a set but may be
evaluated sequentially, as they are proposed. Moreover, the process does not
necessarily move to the point of action. Many issues emerge and are debated
but never resolved, either because a consensus does not develop that is sufficiently
powerful to bring about action or because the importance of the problem declines
as conditions change.

Molitor (1981) analyzed the policy-making process in terms of its elements, which he conceptualized as events, literature, authorities and advocates, organizations, and political jurisdictions. Action by these elements is initiated sequentially but continues concurrently. It begins with the occurrence of events, which at first are not perceived as being related to each other or as symptomatic of a broader problem. The perception of a problem begins when the events attract the attention of authorities and advocates, individuals who collate and analyze data on the events, formulate generalizations, and draw conclusions regarding the existence of a problem. The authorities and advocates may be persons who are victims of the problem, journalists, experts in the area, or simply public-spirited individuals.

At this point, a body of literature begins to develop on accounts of related events, analysis and discussion of the problem, proposals for solutions, calls to action, and so forth. Social scientists collect data regarding the frequency and characteristics of the problem and publish their analysis. Organizations may then become involved as advocates or opponents of action.

Finally, proposals for action are made in governing bodies. Political action, according to Molitor, occurs after a consensus develops, not before. Leadership depends on followership. Politicians prefer to wait until they know the direction in which public affairs are moving before getting out in front. Leaders in public affairs cannot act without sufficient public support.

Data on household consumption behavior are part of the literature that builds up around some issues. Consumption data are used to document the existence and seriousness of problems and as evidence supporting or opposing the adoption of a given policy option. Neutral in itself, the information becomes evaluative in its interpretation.

THE USE OF CONSUMPTION DATA IN POLICY-MAKING

In the remainder of the chapter, we will look at three policy issues that received considerable attention during the 1970s and 1980s. How can we identify the poor? How much should be provided as child support? and Should the taxes paid by households be raised?

Identifying the Poor

Concern of the U.S. government for measuring poverty dates back at least as far as the Great Depression of the 1930s, when President Franklin Roosevelt, declaring that one-third of the nation was ill fed, ill housed, and ill clothed, initiated programs to help the poor. Interest was renewed in the 1960s when President Lyndon Johnson launched his Great Society program and established the elimination of poverty as a goal.

Out of this governmental concern for poverty, and especially with the initiation of programs to eliminate poverty, there arose a need to have an accurate delineation of who was or was not to be regarded as poor. This was needed for at least two reasons: to determine eligibility for receiving government assistance and to enable the government to make accurate counts of the poor in order to assess the success of antipoverty programs and the need for further efforts.

The first official designation of poverty thresholds in the United States came in 1969 when the government adopted a set of income thresholds based on ones developed by Mollie Orshansky for use in preparing a report on the number of children in poverty (Hauver, Goodman & Grainer, 1981). Orshansky used as a base the lowest-cost USDA Family Food Plan. She multiplied the cost of the plan by 3 since the average low-income family at that time spent about one-third of its income on food. Using this method, she developed a set of thresholds, each based on the food plan cost for a given family size and type.

The poverty thresholds have been used to prepare annual reports from the Bureau of the Census on the number and percentage of the population in poverty and have thus enabled that agency to provide information on trends in poverty since 1969. The thresholds have been used as a basis for determining eligibility for food stamps and other benefits. They have also been used in constructing measures of well-being.

In spite of the extensive use of the poverty thresholds, criticism has persisted. Some criticisms are:

• The number in poverty is overstated because noncash income is not counted. Smeeding (1982) demonstrated that the 1979 poverty rate of 11.1 would have been reduced by as much as 42 percent if the value of in-kind income had been added to money income.

• The number in poverty is overstated because the thresholds do not take into account ownership of assets and durables. This especially affects the official poverty status of the elderly, who have a higher rate of home ownership without mortgage than households in general and have low housing expenditures in consequence. Hurd (1990, pp. 581–582) estimated that had capital gains, in-kind transfers, and implicit income from home equity been added to money income of households, the poverty rate in 1986 would have been reduced from 13.8 to 10.9 among those under age 65 and from 12.4 to 5.7 among those aged 65 and over.

• The poverty rate is too low because the multiplier of 3 is no longer representative of actual spending patterns. The decades of the 1960s through the 1980s saw a decline in the percentage spent on food (from 26 to 19 percent) and increases in the percentages spent on shelter (from 13 to 21 percent) and transportation (from 15 to 24 percent) (Jacobs & Shipp, 1990, p. 21). In 1988, food comprised 18 percent of the total expenditures of consumer units in the lowest income quintile (BLS, 1990), implying that the multiplier for the poverty thresholds should be about 5.5 rather than 3.0. Stone (1990) pointed out that if the poverty thresholds were based on percentage of income spent on housing, the poverty rate in 1987 would have been 26.5 (p. 38), nearly twice the Census estimate of 13.5 (U.S. Bureau of the Census, 1989d, p. 1).

Implicit in the definition of poverty is the idea of minimum adequacy of consumption. Thus, a generally accepted criterion for the validity of a poverty income threshold is the notion that it should be the level at which the consumer unit is just able to afford a minimally adequate level of consumption. Hauver, Goodman, and Grainer pointed out that food is the only area in which minimum biological requirements have been specified. However, the theory of utility maximization tells us that if a consumer unit is maximizing its utility, then its allocation of income among consumption categories must be such that the weighted marginal utilities are equal. We can infer that a utility-maximizing household whose food consumption is at an adequate but minimum level will also be consuming at the minimum level of adequacy in other areas. Thus, use of the USDA Family Food Plan, multiplied by a factor representing the average percentage of income allocated to food by families whose food spending is at the level of the food plan, has a theoretical rationale.

The issue regarding what multiplier to use and the issues regarding what should be included as income are, or should be, related. Our theoretical rationale implies that the proper multiplier should be based on the fraction of income (however defined) that is spent on food (however such expenditures are defined). If income were redefined to include in-kind income or implicit value of home equity, or if food expenditure were redefined to include the value of food stamps and donated commodities, then the multiplier should be recalculated as well.

The use of consumption data in establishing a poverty definition involves at least two kinds of data: (1) average amounts of consumption commodities that are required, on the average, to satisfy the needs of a consumer unit of a given size and type at a minimum adequate level, and (2) the average cost to a consumer unit of acquiring that level of consumption. If only one consumption area (food) is used to establish minimum adequacy, data on average allocation of income among commodities are also needed.

Setting Child Support Payments

For some purposes, estimates are needed of amounts consumed (and their cost) by individual family members. This need has been especially urgent with respect to children. Edwards summarized the uses of such data:

Estimates of the cost of raising a child . . . have been used . . . as a budgetary aid for individual families . . . [and] to provide guidelines for judges, attorneys, and expert witnesses in setting support payments for children in divorce cases and in estimating damages arising from personal injury, wrongful death, and malpractice claims. They have been applied by State, county, and municipal social welfare agencies in setting public support levels for families and children, and by educators, financial advisers, and other professionals who work with families or who train those who will. Researchers have used the estimates in analyses on particular family situations, fertility behavior, and other demographic and population topics. (1979, p. 3)

Several questions are implicit in discussions of alternative measures of child rearing costs: What is needed for the health and adequate development of the child? What is fair? What is affordable or collectible? The first question arises from a social concern for the well-being of the child, the second from the fact that the parent or other source of support may have sufficient resources to support the child at a level well above the minimum, and the third from the need to implement awards for child support effectively.

Children provide society with its human capital of the future and with the nonproductive members that society will have to support. It is thus in the interest of society to ensure that all children receive at least the minimum amount of goods and services needed to enable them to become contributing members of society.

The fairness issue can be illustrated with the following questions: Should a father in an upper-income bracket be required to provide no more than poverty-level support for his dependent child? Of course not. Fairness dictates that the level of support be somewhere near the level the father himself enjoys.

The third question is a pragmatic one. How much of the amount awarded is actually paid to the child's caretaker depends as much, perhaps, on what the payer is able or willing to pay as it does on what the child needs or what is fair to the child. In the case of payments to foster parents, government agencies are constrained by taxpayer reluctance and suspicion. In divorce payments, the judge may take into account the low rates of payment on court-awarded child support and the likelihood that low awards are more likely to be paid by the noncustodial parent than higher ones.

Of the three questions, those having to do with fairness and collectibility are likely to receive more weight than need simply because scientifically based standards for consumption (except for food) are lacking. Fairness and collectibility are easier to determine than a defensible standard of need.

Several alternative estimates of child rearing costs are available. The U.S. Department of Agriculture provided estimates based on the 1987 Consumer Expenditure Survey of the Bureau of Labor Statistics (Lino, 1990a) in which child-specific and household expenditures for each commodity area in the budget were first estimated and then child-specific expenditures (such as clothing purchased for an individual in a given age-sex group) were assigned to the child, together with a share of other household expenditures (such as shelter). The share of nonchild-specific expenditures allocated to the child was based on either previous research or a per capita basis. The estimates replaced earlier estimates of the Department of Agriculture based on data from the 1960–1961 and 1973 Consumer Expenditure Surveys. Estimates based on the 1972–1973 survey were made by Espenshade (1984, p. 33) and by Lazear and Michael (1988, p. 122). Beller and Graham (1990, pp. 27–28) developed still another estimate, based on the federal poverty thresholds (essentially the additional income needed by a single mother at the poverty level to maintain a child without changing her poverty status). Although these estimates are based on expenditure data from different years, they can be adjusted to the price level of any given year using the Consumer Price Index.

At the lower level, the four estimates, in 1989 prices, range from $5,680

(Espenshade) to $2,950 (Beller & Graham). Since the Beller and Graham estimate was at the poverty threshold, it is perhaps understandable that it is the lowest. The poverty thresholds are themselves probably too low because of the lower-than-justifiable multiplier. However, there is nearly a $2,000 difference between the lowest and the highest of the remaining three estimates.

Why do estimates of child rearing costs vary so widely? All are based, ultimately, on data from the same series of expenditure surveys, and all are based on an Engel-type function. Although some discrepancies would likely occur because of biases and inaccuracies inherent in use of the Consumer Price Index to adjust the cost estimates to the same price level, the major difference is probably due to differences in the method used to allocate expenditures among family members. The estimates also differ in their selection and use of variables to classify households into socioeconomic groups. Other sources of variability are imperfections in scales or methods for making adjustments for age of child and family size and consumption.

As Lazear and Michael pointed out, there has been little debate over the merit of alternative methods for estimating the allocation of consumption among household members (1988, pp. 1–2). The need for more study of the question was urged by Haddad and Kanbur (1990, p. 880), who studied intrahousehold inequality in nutritional status in the Philippines and concluded that substantial inequality exists.

Raising Taxes

A perpetual issue concerns the type and level of taxes that should be levied on consuming units. Criteria for evaluating tax options include the following:

1. Impact on tax revenues. The primary purpose of a tax is to raise revenues, but tax increases may stimulate tax-avoidance behavior or reduce consumption of the item taxed. Consider the case of an increase in the sales tax on gasoline. Sales taxes are, in effect, additions to the commodity price. If the price elasticity of the commodity is high, the decrease in demand due to a sales tax increase may offset the increase in tax revenues, leaving no revenue increase.

2. Fairness. All would agree that taxes should be fair. However, "fairness" can be interpreted in different ways:

• A tax is fair if everyone is taxed the same amount. This type of tax (called a regressive tax) is not regarded by many people as fair because it takes a higher percentage of the income of low-income than of high-income consumer units. A sales tax on food is an example of a regressive tax. Since low-income consumer units spend a larger proportion of their income on food than do higher-income units, a tax on food takes a larger percentage of their incomes and is thus regressive.

• A tax is fair if everyone is taxed the same proportion of income. This is considered more nearly fair than a regressive tax, but some point out that the marginal utility of income to a wealthy person is much lower than the marginal utility of income to a poor person; hence, the same proportional reduction in income reduces the well-being of the poor person more than that of the rich person.

• A tax is fair if it affects the well-being of all taxpayers equally. A progressive tax would be needed to satisfy this interpretation of fairness. Exact comparisons of utility or well-being are not, of course, possible. Graduated income taxes, with higher rates for the rich, are attempts to make taxes fairer in this sense.

• A tax is fair if it is paid only by those who benefit from the services provided by the tax. User fees on national parks, Medicare premiums, and social security contributions are examples of taxes that are fair in this sense. Such taxes are generally highly regressive and thus unfair in another sense.

3. Impact on consumption levels of vulnerable groups. Some population groups are known to be near the lower limits of consumption adequacy. A tax levy, especially if it were highly regressive for those groups, might push them down into the inadequate consumption range.

4. Impact on other goals of the society, such as the goals of preserving the quality of the environment or conserving nonrenewable resources. Gasoline or fuel taxes are favored by some because they are expected to encourage thrifty and conservative practices and hence reduce total oil consumption.

To assess the impact of a tax increase with respect to fairness (interpreted as regressiveness) or impact on vulnerable groups, data are needed on income elasticities of the commodities taxed, the elasticity of nontaxed commodities with respect to the changes in real income that would result from a tax increase, and the consumption levels of vulnerable groups in relation to standards of minimum adequacy. To assess impact on revenues or on conservation of scarce resources, price elasticities may be needed.

8

Consumption Patterns
of the Future

TRENDS IN FACTORS THAT INFLUENCE CONSUMPTION

Consumption patterns in the United States have changed. The importance of food in the budget has steadily declined, while the importance of housing and transportation has increased. In the 1980s, four basic consumption patterns were apparent. Three of the patterns were dominated by housing, transportation, and basic necessities. The fourth, which was typical of higher-income groups, was a more balanced pattern in which services played an important part.

Will the patterns of the 1980s persist in the rest of the 1990s and into the next century, and will their relative distribution in the population continue at the same level, or will they be replaced in importance by other consumption patterns? The answer depends on trends in factors that influence consumption patterns.

Level and Distribution of Real Income of Households

The 1980s saw little increase in real income at the median but a continuation of the trend toward greater inequality in the distribution of income. At the same time, the level of noncash benefits received by the poor declined (Littman, 1989, p. 16). If these trends continue, we can expect, on the one hand, increased proportions of households with the consumption patterns typical of the very poor, and, on the other hand, continuation and perhaps enhancement of the consumption patterns typical of high-income households.

Price Ratios

Consumer price changes in the 1970s and 1980s were, in large measure, driven by changes in the price of oil, which sharply increased in the 1970s, slumped in the 1980s, and increased again in 1990. Higher oil prices might result in long-term changes in consumer behavior—for example, reduced use of private transportation and shifts to energy-conserving alternatives or use of alternative energy sources.

Environmental Concerns

The 1970s and 1980s saw increased awareness of the environmental impacts of products consumed by households and of consumer and business practices. Legislation was passed to preserve the quality of air and water and clean up hazardous-waste sites. A continuation of this concern would likely result in banning or reduced use of some materials, increased recycling and other types of conservation, and switching from products that cause environmental damage to ones that are less harmful.

New Technologies

The introduction of new or improved products and services changes consumption patterns as consumption of less-favored commodities is cut back to make room for the new. A significant part of the increase in medical costs in the 1980s has been attributed to the availability of new medical technology, such as organ transplants. The discovery and adoption of new technology is largely unpredictable; however, it may be most likely to occur in those areas in which consumers and government policymakers display the greatest interest. Areas of interest in the 1970s and 1980s included medical technology and products for preserving and enhancing health and fitness, communications and information management, alternative energy sources, and products that reduce environmental deterioration from consumption residues.

Demographic Changes

If the trends of the 1980s continue, the 1990s and the next century will see increased proportions of the elderly in the population and well as increased proportions of blacks and other minority groups. If patterns of income distribution continue, this means an increased proportion of low-income households. And unless increased economic pressures (or other factors) change the patterns with respect to divorce and the maintaining of separate households by single persons, there are likely to be increased numbers of one-parent families and single households. Thus, we can expect to see an increased prevalence of the consumption patterns typical of those groups.

Changes in Values

Values determine the tastes and preferences of individuals and hence influence their consumption behavior. By definition, values change slowly; however, differences are observable in the dominant values of different generations and population groups. Consumers who grew up during the Great Depression generally exhibit a greater value for thrift than those who grew up during the affluent 1960s. Older consumers are likely to have a more conservative attitude toward divorce and nontraditional family forms than those reared in the sexually permissive 1960s and 1970s. We can expect those whose values were formed by the War on Poverty and environmental concerns of the 1960s and 1970s to have a different attitude toward personal spending and taxes than those whose values were formed during the self-indulgent 1980s. Differences in values may partially account for the cohort effect found by Heslop (1987). When she analyzed the expenditures pattern of different cohorts of consumer units, she found that age was less important than cohort membership and current environment (represented by the year in which the expenditures were made) as a predictor of expenditures.

CONSUMPTION PATTERN POSSIBILITIES

The expenditure patterns of the future will be influenced by all of the above factors, and not all factors will work in the same direction. Exact and reliable prediction is not possible. We can, however, speculate. Following are some of the possible patterns than might emerge as dominant expenditure patterns in the United States in the 1990s and 2000s.

Haves versus Have-Nots

Because of the increasing inequality of income, it is possible that a strong dichotomy may emerge. At one extreme, we may see the consumption pattern of the haves, characterized by lavish spending on services and luxury goods, and, at the other extreme, the consumption pattern of the have-nots, dominated by basic necessities. This pronounced difference is likely to be exacerbated if the level of noncash benefits to the poor continues the decline begun in the 1980s.

Egalitarian Patterns

The converse of having a strong dichotomy between the haves and the have-nots would be consumption patterns that tended to vary less on the basis of economic factors than because of differences in tastes and preferences. This might result if Americans became concerned about the growing disparity between the rich and poor and decided, as a matter of policy, to redistribute resources in such a way as to increase the middle class as a proportion of the whole.

Conservation-motivated Patterns

Environmental concerns may lead to increased numbers of households whose consumption patterns reflect a strong value on conservation and protection of the natural environment. There have always been a few who practiced voluntary simplicity, whether from religious reasons, concern for the environment, or dislike of waste. The importance of this pattern may increase.

Spendthrift Patterns

One result of the increasing income gap between rich and poor might be to encourage some affluent households to adopt an intentionally wasteful consumption pattern. This behavior was evident in the last part of the nineteenth century in the conspicuous consumption of the very rich that Veblen observed. Conspicuous consumption has never completed disappeared, although it has been less socially acceptable in some decades. The 1990s and 2000s might see a resurgence.

Security-motivated Patterns

Americans in the 1980s became aware of threats to their life-style stemming from the increasing strength of the Japanese and West German economies, negative trade balances, a rapidly increasing national debt financed by foreign lenders, and purchases of real and financial holdings in the United States by foreign investors. American manufacturers have urged consumers to "buy American." It is possible that consumers might react to these threats by changing their consumption behavior. What form the changes might take is a matter for speculation—increased rates of saving, a stronger preference for American-made products, a prejudice against products made in particular countries, or an emphasis on continuing consumption practices that are regarded as distinctively American.

Development-motivated Patterns

An alternative response to the threats of foreign competition and lower rates of income growth might be an increased emphasis on consumption that contributes to the quality of human resources. Such a pattern would certainly include increased expenditures on education but might also include changes to raise the nutritional quality of food intake and housing adequacy of the poor.

References

Abdel-Ghany, M., & Foster, A. C. (1982). Impact of income and wife's education on family consumption expenditures. *Journal of Consumer Studies and Home Economics*, *6*(1), 21–28.

Abdel-Ghany, M., Bivens, G., Keeler, J. P., & James, W. L. (1983). Windfall income and the permanent income hypothesis: New evidence. *Journal of Consumer Affairs*, *17*(2), 262–276.

Acharya, M., & Bennett, L. (1982). *Women and the subsistence sector: Economic participation and household decisionmaking in Nepal.* World Bank Staff Working Papers, No. 526. Washington, DC: World Bank.

Aldenderfer, M. S., & Blashfield, R. K. (1984). *Cluster analysis: Quantitative applications in the social sciences.* Beverly Hills, CA: Sage Publications.

Alderman, H., & Braun, J. von (1984). *The effects of the Egyptian food ratio and subsidy system on income distribution and consumption* (Research Report 45). Washington, DC: International Food Policy Research Institute.

Allen, J., & Gadson, K. (1984). Food consumption and nutritional status of low-income households. *National Food Review*, NFR–26, 27–31.

Anderson, W. T., Jr., & Golden, L. L. (1984). Lifestyle and psychographics: A critical review and recommendation. In T. C. Kinnear (Ed.), *Advances in Consumer Research, Proceedings of the Association for Consumer Research*, *11*, 405–411.

Andorka, R., & Harcsa, I. (1990). Definitions and methods of calculation of social indicators. *Social Indicators Research*, *23*(1–2), 135–151.

Andreasen, A. R. (1975). *The disadvantaged consumer.* New York: Free Press.

Andrews, F. M., & Withey, S. B. (1976). *Social indicators of well-being.* New York: Plenum Press.

Apgar, Jr., W. C., & Brown, H. J. (1988). *The state of the nation's housing 1988.* Cambridge, MA: Joint Center for Housing Studies of Harvard University.

Archibald, R., & Gillingham, R. (1980). An analysis of the short-run consumer demand for gasoline using household survey data. *Review of Economics and Statistics*, *62*(4), 622–628.

Barwise, T. P., & Ehrenberg, A.S.C. (1987). The liking and viewing of regular TV series. *Journal of Consumer Research*, *14*(1), 63–70.

Behlen, P. M., & Cronin, F. J. (1985). Dietary recommendations for healthy Americans summarized. *Family Economics Review*, (3), 17–24.

Behrman, J. R., Deolalikar, A. B., & Wolfe, B. L. (1988). Nutrients: Impacts and determinants. *World Bank Economic Review*, 2(3), 299–320.

Bellante, D., & Foster, A. C. (1984). Working wives and expenditure on services. *Journal of Consumer Research*, 11, 700–707.

Beller, A., & Graham, J. (1990). *The economics of child support: Determinants, trends and consequences*. Unpublished manuscript.

Bettman, J. R. (1979). *An information processing theory of consumer choice*. Reading, MA: Addison-Wesley Publishing Company.

Beutler, I. F., & Owen, A. J. (1980). A home production activity model. *Home Economics Research Journal*, 9(1), 16–26.

Blanciforti, L. (1981). Expenditures on nutritious foods. *National Food Review*, NFR–13, 18–19.

Blaylock, J. R., & Smallwood, D. M. (1986). Projected growth in American food spending. *National Food Review*, NFR–32, 18–21.

Blaylock, J., Elitzak, H., & Manchester, A. (1989). Food expenditures. *National Food Review*, 12(2), 9–16.

Blumberg, R. L. (1988). Income under female versus male control: Hypotheses from a theory of gender stratification and data from the Third World. *Journal of Family Issues*, 9(1): 51–84.

Boissiere, M., Knight, J. B., & Sabot, R. H. (1985). Earnings, schooling, ability, and cognitive skills. *American Economic Review*, 75(5), 6–12.

Bowonder, B., Rao, N. P., Dasgupta, B., & Prasad, S. S. R. (1985). Energy use in eight rural communities in India. *World Development*, 13(12), 1263–1286.

Britton, V. (1973). Clothing budgets for children from the USDA: Annual costs at three levels in four regions. *Home Economics Research Journal*, 1(3), 173–184.

Britton, V. (1975, Fall). Stretching the clothing dollar. *Family Economics Review*, 3–7.

Brodshy, K. A., & Rodrik, D. (1981). Indicators of development and data availability: The case of the PQLI. *World Development*, 9(7), 695–699.

Brown, C. (1987). Consumption norms, work roles, and economic growth, 1918–80. In C. Brown & J. A. Pechman (Eds.), *Gender in the workplace* (pp. 13–59). Washington DC: Brookings Institution.

Brown, L. R. (1990). The illusion of progress. In L. R. Brown (Ed.), *State of the world* (pp. 3–16). New York: W. W. Norton & Company.

Brown, L. R., & Young, J. E. (1990). Feeding the world in the nineties. In L. R. Brown (Ed.), *State of the world* (pp. 59–78). New York: W. W. Norton & Company.

Bryan, W. R., & Linke, C. M. (1988). Value of a college education. *Illinois Business Review*, 45(5), 3–7.

Buckley, J. M. (1983). Attraction toward a stranger as a linear function of similarity in dress. *Home Economics Research Journal*, 12(1), 25–34.

Bunch, K. (1984). Food away from home and the quality of the diet. *National Food Review*, NFR–25, 14–16.

Bunch, K., & Kurland, J. (1984). How America quenches its thirst. *National Food Review*, NFR–27, 14–17.

Burk, M. (1968). *Consumption economics: A multidisciplinary approach*. New York: Wiley.

Caliendo, M. A. (1979). *Nutrition and the world food crisis*. New York: Macmillan.

Cha, S. S. (1991). Consumption patterns of poor households. Unpublished doctoral dissertation, University of Illinois at Urbana-Champaign.

Cha, S. S., Chung, Y. S., & Magrabi, F. M. (1989, October). *Expenditure patterns of poor and non-poor households.* Paper presented at the meeting of the Illinois Economic Association, Chicago.

Chandler, W. U. (1984). *Improving world health: A least cost strategy.* Worldwatch Paper 59. Washington, DC: Worldwatch Institute.

Chandler, W. U. (1985a). *Energy productivity: Key to environmental protection and economic progress.* Worldwatch Paper 63. Washington, DC: Worldwatch Institute.

Chandler, W. U. (1985b). *Investing in children.* Worldwatch Paper 64. Washington, DC: Worldwatch Institute.

Chandler, W. U. (1986). *Banishing tobacco.* Worldwatch Paper 68. Washington, DC: Worldwatch Institute.

Chavez, A., & Martinez, C. (1981). School performance of supplemented and unsupplemented children from a poor rural area. In *Nutrition in health and disease and international development: Symposia from the XII International Congress of Nutrition* (pp. 393–402). New York: Alan R. Liss.

Chung, Y. S. (1990). Expenditure patterns of older and younger consumers. Unpublished doctoral dissertation, University of Illinois.

Chung, Y. S., & Magrabi, F. M. (1990). Age-related changes in expenditure patterns. In M. Carsky (Ed.), *Proceedings of American Council on Consumer Interests* (pp. 200–206).

Cleveland, L. E., & Peterkin, B. B. (1983). USDA 1983 family food plans. *Family Economics Review* (2), 12–21.

Cochrane, W. W., & Bell, C. S. (1956). *The economics of consumption.* New York: McGraw-Hill.

Coe, R. (1978). Dependency and poverty in the short and long run. In G. Duncan & J. Morgan (Eds.), *Five thousand American families—patterns of economic progress* (Vol. 6, pp. 273–298). Ann Arbor: Survey Research Center, University of Michigan.

Congress of the United States. Office of Technology Assessment. (1989). *Facing America's trash: What next for municipal solid waste.* Washington, DC: U.S. Government Printing Office.

Council on Environmental Quality. (1979). *Environmental quality—1979.* Washington, DC: U.S. Government Printing Office.

Courtless, J. C. (1981). Work-related transportation costs. *Family Economics Review* (Winter), 33–35.

Courtless, J. C. (1982a). Home sewing trends. *Family Economics Review,* (4), 19–22.

Courtless, J. C. (1982b). The cost of doing laundry at home. *Family Economics Review,* 4, 17–18.

Courtless, J. C. (1985). Time spent in sewing by employed women. *Family Economics Review* (4), 1–3.

Courtless, J. C. (1988). The employed woman's use of time for wardrobe maintenance. *Family Economics Review,* 1(4), 2–6.

Courtless, J. C. (1989). Households with expenditures for apparel services. *Family Economics Review,* 2(4), 10–14.

Courtless, J. C. (1990). Recent trends in clothing and textiles. *Family Economics Review*, *3*(2), 8–12.

Cravioto, J. (1979). Effects of early malnutrition and stimuli deprivation on mental development. In S. Doxiadis (Ed.), *The child in the world of tomorrow: A window into the future* (pp. 383–385). London: Pergamon Press.

Currie, R. F., & Thacker, C. (1986). Quality of the urban environment as perceived by residents of slow and fast growth cities. *Social Indicators Research*, *18*(1), 95–118.

Dairy Council Digest. (1973). Malnutrition, learning, and behavior. *44*(6), 31–34.

Dairy Council Digest. (1979). Nutrition and behavior. *50*(5), 25–29.

Dardis, R., Derrick, F., & Lehfeld, A. (1981). Clothing demand in the United States: A cross-sectional analysis. *Home Economics Research Journal*, *10*(2), 212–222.

Davis, J. S. (1945). Standards and content of living. *American Economic Review*, *35*, 1–15.

Davis, L. L., Markee, N., Dallas, M. J., Harger, B., & Miller, J. (1990). Dermatological health problems attributed by consumers to contact with textiles. *Home Economics Research Journal*, *18*(4), 311–322.

Deaton, A., & Muellbauer, J. (1980). *Economics and consumer behavior*. New York: Cambridge University Press.

Der Spiegel. (1989, October). Third World metropolises are becoming monsters: Rural poverty drives millions to the slums. Reprinted in *World Press Review*, 32–34.

Development Coordination Committee. (1979, February 1). *Development issues: U.S. actions affecting the development of low-income countries*. First Annual Report of the Chairman of the Development Coordination Committee Transmitted to the Congress, Washington, DC.

Dixon-Mueller, R. (1985). *Women's work in Third World agriculture*. Women, Work and Development, *9*. Geneva: International Labour Office.

Douglas, E. (1980). Changing patterns of consumption expenditures. *Proceedings of American Council on Consumer Interests* (pp. 41–47).

Duesenberry, J. S. (1959). *Income, saving and the theory of consumer behavior*. Cambridge: Harvard University Press.

Duncan, G. J. (1984). *Years of poverty, years of plenty*. Ann Arbor: Survey Research Center, University of Michigan.

Dunham, D. (1986). Food spending and income. *National Food Review*, NFR–34, 28–29.

Dunham, D. (1987). Food spending and income. *National Food Review*, NFR–37, 24–33.

Dunkerly, J., William, R., Lincoln, G., & Cecelski, E. (1981). *Energy strategies for developing nations*. Baltimore: Johns Hopkins University Press.

Durning, A. B. (1989). *Poverty and the environment: Reversing the downward spiral*. Worldwatch Paper 92. Washington, DC: Worldwatch Institute.

Durning, A. B. (1990). Ending poverty. In L. R. Brown (Ed.), *State of the world* (pp. 135–153). Washington, DC: Worldwatch Institute.

Edwards, C. S. (1979, Summer). Users' guide to USDA estimates of the cost of raising a child. *Family Economics Review*, 3–15.

Erickson, G. M., & Johansson, J. K. (1985). The role of price in multi-attribute product evaluations. *Journal of Consumer Research*, *12*(2), 195–199.

Espenshade, T. J. (1984). *Investing in children*. Washington, DC: Urban Institute Press.

Evans, M. D., & Cronin, F. J. (1986). Diets of school-age children and teenagers. *Family Economics Review* (3), 14–21.

Evers, S., & McIntosh, W. A. (1977). Social indicators of human nutrition: Measures of nutritional status. *Social Indicators Research, 4*(2), 185–205.

Family Economics Review. (1983). Journey to work. (3), 23.

Family Economics Review. (1984). Cost of having a baby. (3), 19.

Family Economics Review. (1987). Work schedules of Americans. (4), 26–30.

Family Economics Review. (1988). Cost of food at home. (3), 22.

Family Economics Review. (1990). Reasons for not working: Poor and nonpoor householders. *3*(2), 21–22.

Feachem, R. G. A., Burns, E., Cairncross, S., Cronin, A., Cross, P., Curtis, D., Khalid Khan, M., Lamb, D., & Southall, H. (1978). *Water, health and development: An interdisciplinary evaluation.* London: Tri-med Books. Summarized in L. Goldschmidt-Clermont (1987). *Economic evaluations of unpaid household work: Africa, Asia, Latin America and Oceana* (pp. 93–97). Women, Work and Development, *14*, Geneva: International Labour Office.

Ferber, R. (1973). Consumer economics: A survey. *Journal of Economic Literature, 11*, 1303–1342.

Firat, A. F. (1987). Towards a deeper understanding of consumption experiences: The underlying dimensions. In M. Wallendorf & P. Anderson (Eds.), *Advances in Consumer Research, Proceedings of the Association for Consumer Research, 14*, 342–346.

Flavin, C. (1985). *World oil: Coping with the dangers of success.* Worldwatch Paper 66. Washington, DC: Worldwatch Institute.

Flavin, C. (1986). *Electricity for a developing world: New directions.* Worldwatch Paper 70. Washington, DC: Worldwatch Institute.

Flavin, C. (1990). Slowing global warming. In L. R. Brown (Ed.), *State of the world* (pp. 17–38). New York: W. W. Norton & Company.

Forsythe, S. M., Drake, M. F., & Cox, Jr., C. A. (1984). Dress as an influence on the perceptions of management characteristics in women. *Home Economics Research Journal, 13*(2), 112–121.

French, H. F. (1990). *Clearing the air: A global agenda.* Worldwatch Paper 94. Washington, DC: Worldwatch Institute.

Friedman, M. (1957). *A theory of the consumption function.* Princeton, NJ: Princeton University Press.

Fuchs, V. R. (1986, April 25). Sex differences in economic well-being. *Science*, 459–464.

Gaag, J. van der, & Smolensky, E. (1982). True household equivalence scales and characteristics of the poor in the United States. *Review of Income and Wealth, 28*(1), 17–28.

Gallo, A. E. (1983). Food consumption patterns: Concentration and frequency. *National Food Review*, NFR–22, 5–7.

Gallo, A. E., & Connor, J. M. (1982). Advertising and American food consumption patterns. *National Food Review*, NFR–19, 2–5.

Galster, G. C. (1985). Evaluating indicators for housing policy: Residential satisfaction vs. marginal improvement priorities. *Social Indicators Research, 16*(4), 415–448.

Geistfeld, L. V. (1977). Consumer decision making: The technical efficiency approach. *Journal of Consumer Research, 4*(1), 48–56.

George, R. (1987). Fuel. In F. M. Magrabi & A. Verma (Eds.), *Household resources and their changing relationships: Case studies in Gujarat, India* (pp. 49–51). International Agriculture Publications, General Series No. 3. Urbana: University of Illinois.

Glewwe, P., & Gaag, J. van der (1988). *Confronting poverty in developing countries: Definitions, information, and policies.* Living Standards Measurement Study Working Paper No. 48. Washington, DC: World Bank.

Goldschmidt-Clermont, L. (1987). *Economic evaluations of unpaid household work: Africa, Asia, Latin America and Oceana.* Women, Work and Development, *14.* Geneva: International Labour Office.

Gray, C. W. (1982). *Food consumption parameters for Brazil and their application to food policy* (Research Report 32). Washington, DC: International Food Policy Research Institute.

Gujral, S. (1987a). Meal pattern, nutrient intake, intra-familial distribution of foods, food habits and taboos. In F. M. Magrabi & A. Verma (Eds.), *Household resources and their changing relationships: Case studies in Gujarat, India* (pp. 35–38). International Agriculture Publications, General Series No. 3. Urbana: University of Illinois.

Gujral, S. (1987b). Post harvest conservation of food at the household level. In F. M. Magrabi & A. Verma (Eds.), *Household resources and their changing relationships: Case studies in Gujarat, India* (pp. 38–40). International Agriculture Publications, General Series No. 3. Urbana: University of Illinois.

Haddad, L., & Kanbur, R. (1990, September). How serious is the neglect of intra-household inequality? *Economic Journal, 100,* 866–881.

Hanna, S. (1978). Evaluation of energy saving investments. *Journal of Consumer Affairs, 12*(1), 63–75.

Hannon, B. (1975, July 11). Energy conservation and the consumer. *Science, 189,* 95–102.

Harden, B. (1985, October 21). Oil glut is easing the urban horrors of Lagos. *Washington Post,* pp. A1, A22.

Hart, S. Y. (1987). Water, sanitation, and fuel in Rustumpura—A case study. In F. M. Magrabi & A. Verma (Eds.), *Household resources and their changing relationships: Case studies in Gujarat, India* (pp. 51–53). International Agriculture Publications, General Series No. 3. Urbana: University of Illinois.

Harvey, A. S. (1990). Time use studies for leisure analysis. *Social Indicators Research, 23*(4), 309–336.

Hassoun, V. S. (1984). Portable electric appliance usage by households. *Home Economics Research Journal, 13*(2), 175–183.

Hatfield, K. M. (1981). Changing home food production and preservation patterns. *National Food Review,* NFR–13, 22–25.

Hauser, J. R., & Urban, G. L. (1986). The value priority hypothesis for consumer budget plans. *Journal of Consumer Research, 12*(4), 446–462.

Hauver, J. H., Goodman, J. A., & Grainer, M. A. (1981). The federal poverty thresholds: Appearance and reality. *Journal of Consumer Research, 8*(1), 1–10.

Havlicek, J., Axelson, J. M., Capps, Jr., O., Pearson, J. M., & Richardson, S. (1982). Nutritional and economic aspects of convenience and nonconvenience foods. *Proceedings of the U.S.D.A. Agricultural Outlook Conference* (pp. 539–550).

Hawkes, G. R., Hanson, R. A., & Smith, J. W. (1980). *Quality of life: Perspectives and review*. North Central Regional Research Publication 264. Ames: Agriculture and Home Economics Experiment Station, Iowa State University of Science and Technology.

Hawtrey, R. G. (1925). *The economic problem*. New York: Longmans, Green and Co.

Hayghe, H. (1988). Employers and child care: What roles do they play? *Monthly Labor Review, 111*(9), 38–44.

Hazell, P. B. R., & Roell, A. (1983). *Rural growth linkages: Household expenditure patterns in Malaysia and Nigeria* (Research Report 41). Washington, DC: International Food Policy Research Institute.

Hefferan, C. (1983). Household wealth 1962–81. *Family Economics Review* (3), 2–8.

Hefferan, C. (1985). Employee benefits. *Family Economics Review* (1), 6–14.

Hefferan, C. (1987). Family budget guidelines. *Family Economics Review* (4), 1–9.

Hempel, C. G. (1952). *Fundamentals of concept formation in empirical science*. International Encyclopedia of United Science, 2(7). Chicago: University of Chicago Press.

Henn, J. K. (1978). Peasants, workers, and capital: The political economy of labor and incomes in Cameroon. Unpublished Ph.D. dissertation, Harvard University. Summarized in L. Goldschmidt-Clermont (1987). *Economic evaluations of unpaid household work: Africa, Asia, Latin America and Oceania* (pp. 84–92). Women, Work and Development, *14*. Geneva: International Labour Office.

Herendeen, R., & Tanaka, J. (1976). Energy cost of living. *Energy, 1*, 165–178.

Heslop, L. A. (1987). Cohort analysis of the expenditure patterns of the elderly. In M. Wallendorf & P. Anderson (Eds.), *Advances in Consumer Research: Proceedings of the Association for Consumer Research, 14*, 553–557.

Hill, M. S. (1981). Some dynamic aspects of poverty. In M. S. Hill, H. H. Daniel, & J. N. Morgan (Eds.), *Five thousand American families—patterns of economic progress* (Vol. 9, pp. 93–120). Ann Arbor: Survey Research Center, University of Michigan.

Hogarth, J. M. (1989). Saving and dissaving in retirement. *Family Economics Review, 2*(2), 13–17.

Hoyt, E. E. (1938). *Consumption in our society*. New York: McGraw-Hill.

Hoyt, E. E. (1959). A new approach to standards of living. *Journal of Home Economics, 51*, 83–86.

Huntley, S., with Bronson, G., & Walsh, K. T. (1984, April 16). Yumpies, YAP's, yuppies: Who they are. *U.S. News & World Report*, p. 39.

Hurd, M. D. (1989a). The economic status of the elderly. *Science, 244*, 659–664.

Hurd, M. D. (1989b). The poverty of widows: Future prospects. In D. A. Wise (Ed.), *The economics of aging* (pp. 201–229). Chicago: University of Chicago.

Hurd, M. D. (1990, June). Research on the elderly: Economic status, retirement, and consumption and saving. *Journal of Economic Literature, 28*, 565–637.

Jacobs, E., & Shipp, S. (1990). How family spending has changed in the U.S. *Monthly Labor Review, 113*(3), 20–27.

Jacobs, E., Shipp, S., & Brown, G. (1989). Families of working wives spending more on services and nondurables. *Monthly Labor Review, 112*(2), 15–23.

Johnson, C. M., Sum, A. M., & Weill, J. D. (1988). *Vanishing dreams: The growing economic plight of America's young families*. Washington, DC: Children's Defense Fund and Center for Labor Market Studies, Northeastern University.

Johnson, E.C.K., & Bhavnagri, N. (1987). Visitors view a village. In F. M. Magrabi

& A. Verma (Eds.), *Household resources and their changing relationships: Case studies in Gujarat, India* (pp. 9–18). International Agriculture Publications, General Series No. 3. Urbana: University of Illinois.

Johnson, E.C.K., & Shukla, S. (1987). Village households. In F. M. Magrabi & A. Verma (Eds.), *Household resources and their changing relationships: Case studies in Gujarat, India* (pp. 18–26). International Agriculture Publications, General Series No. 3. Urbana: University of Illinois.

Johnson, K.K.P., & Roach-Higgins, M. E. (1987). The influence of physical attractiveness and dress on campus recruiters' impression of female job applications. *Home Economics Research Journal, 16*(2), 87–95.

Jolly, R. (1988). A UNICEF perspective on the effects of economic crises and what can be done. In D. E. Bell & M. R. Reich (Eds.), *Health, nutrition, and economic crises: Approaches to policy in the Third World* (pp. 81–102). Dover, MA: Auburn House.

Jordan, M. (1987, June 3). 18 million homeless seen by 2003. *Washington Post*, p. A8.

Juster, F. T., Courant, P. N., & Dow, G. K. (1981). A theoretical framework for measurement of well-being. *Review of Income and Wealth, 27*(1), 1–31.

Kaneko, Y., & Nidaira, K. (1988). Towards basic human needs in relation to public health and nutrition. In D. E. Bell & M. R. Reich (Eds.), *Health, nutrition, and economic crises: Approaches to policy in the Third World* (pp. 241–263). Dover, MA: Auburn House.

Katona, G. (1975). *Psychological economics*. New York: Elsevier Scientific Publishing Co.

Keeler, J. P., James, W. L., & Abdel-Ghany, M. (1985). The relative size of windfall income and the permanent income hypothesis. *Journal of Business & Economic Statistics, 3*(3), 209–215.

Kelley, A. C. (1988, December). Economic consequences of population change in the Third World. *Journal of Economic Literature, 26*, 1685–1728.

Kelley, E., Gray, J. K., & Blouin, D. (1980). Consumers' priorities for flame retardant protection. *Home Economics Research Journal, 9*(2), 105–115.

Kerr, R. L., Peterkin, B. B., Blum, A. J., & Cleveland, L. E. (1984). USDA 1983 thrifty food plan. *Family Economics Review* (1), 18–25.

Keynes, J. M. (1936). *The general theory of employment, interest and money*. London: Macmillan.

Khan, M. E., Anker, R., Dastidar, S.K.G., & Bairathi, S. (1988). Inequalities between men and women in nutrition and family welfare services: An in-depth enquiry in an Indian village. *Social Action, 38*(4), 398–417.

Kim, J. O., & Mueller, C. W. (1978). *Factor analysis*. Beverly Hills, CA: Sage Publications.

Kimbrell, A. (1989, September 3). Car culture: Driving ourselves crazy. *Washington Post*, p. C3.

Kinsella, K. (1988). *Aging in the Third World*. U.S. Bureau of the Census, International Population Reports Series P–95, No. 79. Washington, DC: U.S. Government Printing Office.

Korb, P. (1987). Comparing international food expenditures. *National Food Review*, NFR–38, 18–21.

Korb, P., & Cochrane, N. (1989). World food expenditures. *National Food Review, 12*(4), 26–29.

Kristensen, T. (1982). *Development in rich and poor countries*. New York: Praeger.

Kyrk, H. (1923). *The theory of consumption*. New York: Houghton Mifflin.

Kyrk, H. (1933). *Economic problems of the family*. New York: Harper & Brothers.

Lancaster, K. (1971). *Consumer demand: A new approach*. New York: Columbia University Press.

Lazear, E. P., & Michael, R. T. (1988). *Allocation of income within the household*. Chicago: University of Chicago Press.

Lennon, S. J. (1990). Effects of clothing attractiveness on perceptions. *Home Economics Research Journal, 18*(4), 303–310.

Leonard, P. A., Dolbeare, C. N., & Lazere, E. B. (1989). *A place to call home: The crisis in housing for the poor*. Washington, DC: Center on Budget and Policy Priorities and Low Income Housing Information Service.

Leonard-Barton, D., & Rogers, E. M. (1980). Voluntary simplicity. In J. C. Olson (Ed.), *Advances in Consumer Research, Proceedings of the Association for Consumer Research, 7*, 28–34.

Levy, F. S. (1980). *The intergenerational transfer of poverty*. Washington, DC: U.S. Department of Labor, Employment and Training Administration.

Levy, S. J. (1981). Interpreting consumer mythology: A structural approach to consumer behavior. *Journal of Marketing, 45*, 49–61.

Linden, F., Green, Jr., G. W., & Coder, J. F. (1989). *A marketer's guide to discretionary income*. Joint study by the Consumer Research Center & U.S. Bureau of the Census. New York: Conference Board.

Lino, M. (1990a). Expenditures on a child by husband-wife families. *Family Economics Review, 3*(3), 2–18.

Lino, M. (1990b). Factors affecting expenditures of single-parent households. *Home Economics Research Journal, 18*(3), 191–201.

Lipton, M. (1988). *The poor and the poorest: Some interim findings*. World Bank Discussion Papers 25. Washington, DC: World Bank.

Littman, M. S. (1989). Poverty in the 1980s: Are the poor getting poorer? *Monthly Labor Review, 112*(6), 13–18.

Lovingood, R. P., & McCullough, J. L. (1986). Appliance ownership and household work time. *Home Economics Research Journal, 14*(3), 326–335.

Lowe, M. D. (1990a). *Alternatives to the automobile: Transport for livable cities*. Worldwatch Paper 98. Washington, DC: Worldwatch Institute.

Lowe, M. D. (1990b). Cycling into the future. In L. R. Brown (Ed.), *State of the world* (pp. 119–134). New York: W. W. Norton & Company.

McCall, S. (1975). Quality of life. *Social Indicators Research, 2*, 229–248.

McCracken, G. (1988). *Culture and consumption*. Bloomington: Indiana University Press.

McCracken, V. A., & Brandt, J. A. (1990). Time value and its impact on household food expenditures away from home. *Home Economics Research Journal, 18*(4), 267–285.

McCullough, J. S., & Morris, M. A. (1980). Development of a model for quality grading of textile products. *Home Economics Research Journal, 9*(2), 116–123.

McNeal, J. (1990, September). Children as customers. *American Demographics*, 36–39.

McNeil, J. M. (1985). In-kind income—Effect on poverty. *Family Economics Review* (2), 14–19.

Magrabi, F. M. (1984). Establishment of family economics as a conceptual field. In M. East & J. Thomson (Eds.)., *Definitive themes in home economics and their impact on families 1909–1984* (pp. 45–50). Washington, DC: American Home Economics Association.

Margolis, M. (1985, October 20). Favelas. *Washington Post*, p. A24.

Marks, S. M., & Yetley, M. J. (1987). *Global food demand patterns over changing levels of economic development* (ERS Staff Report No. AGES870910). Washington, DC: Economic Research Service, U.S. Department of Agriculture.

Matsumoto, M., & Smith, M. (1989). Food assistance. *National Food Review*, *12*(2), 33–39.

Meuller, E. (1984). The value and allocation of time in rural Botswana. *Journal of Development Economics*, *15*(1–3), 329–360. Summarized in L. Goldschmidt-Clermont (1987). *Economic evaluations of unpaid household work: Africa, Asia, Latin America and Oceana* (pp. 79–83). Women, Work and Development, 14. Geneva: International Labour Office.

Minshall, B., Winakor, G., & Swinney, J. L. (1982). Fashion preferences of males and females, risks perceived, and temporal quality of styles. *Home Economics Research Journal*, *10*(4), 369–379.

Mitchell, A. (1983). *The nine American lifestyles: Who we are & where we are going*. New York: Macmillan.

Modigliani, R., & Brumberg, R. (1962). Utility analysis and the consumption function: An interpretation of cross-section data. In K. Kuribara (Ed.), *Post-Keynesian economics* (pp. 388–437). New Brunswick, NJ: Rutgers University Press.

Molitor, G. T. T. (1981). Consumer policy issues: Global trends for the 1980s. In K. B. Monroe (Ed.), *Advances in Consumer Research*, Proceedings of the Association for Consumer Research, *8*, 458–466.

Monroe, D. (1974). Pre-Engel studies and the work of Engel: The origins of consumption research. *Home Economics Research Journal*, *3*(1), 43–65.

Morgan, J. N. (1978). Multiple motives, group decisions, uncertainty, ignorance, and confusion. *Psychology and Economics*, *11*(2), 58–62.

Morgan, K. J. (1988). Socioeconomic factors and food usage patterns. *Family Economics Review* (1), 19–25.

Morgan, K. J., Peterkin, B. B., Johnson, S. R., & Goungetas, B. (1985). Food energy and nutrients per dollar's worth of food from available home food supplies. *Home Economics Research Journal*, *14*(2), 241–251.

Morganosky, M. (1984). Aesthetic and utilitarian qualities of clothing: Use of a multidimensional clothing value model. *Home Economics Research Journal*, *13*(1), 12–20.

Mork, L. F. (1975, Fall). The cost of doing laundry at home. *Family Economics Review*, 32–33.

Morris, E. W., & Eichner, M. M. (1986). Health and safety in the residential environment: Air quality. In R. E. Deacon & W. E. Huffman (Eds.), *1887–1987 Proceedings, Human Resources Research* (pp. 103–111). Ames, IA: College of Home Economics.

Murdoch, W. W. (1980). *The poverty of nations: The political economy of hunger and population*. Baltimore: Johns Hopkins University Press.

National Center for Education Statistics. (1988). *Digest of education statistics*. Washington, DC: U.S. Department of Education, Office of Educational Research and Improvement.

National Center for Health Statistics. (1988). *Current estimates from the National Health Interview Survey: United States, 1987* (Publication No. [PHS] 88–1594). Data from the National Health Survey Series 10, No. 166. Washington, DC: U.S. Government Printing Office.

National Center for Health Statistics. (1989). *Health, United States 1989*. Washington, DC: U.S. Government Printing Office.

National Center for Health Statistics. (1990). *Health, United States, 1990*. Washington, DC: U.S. Government Printing Office.

National Food Review. (1987). Foodservice trends. NFR–37, 10–15.

National Law Center on Homelessness and Poverty. (1990). *Shut out: Denial of education to homeless children*. Washington, DC.

National Research Council. (1989). *Recommended dietary allowances* (10th ed.). Washington, DC: National Academic Press.

Nickols, S. Y., & Fox, K. D. (1983). Buying time and saving time: Strategies for managing household production. *Journal of Consumer Research, 10*, 197–208.

Nightingale, R. W. (1990). Is the world facing a food crisis? *National Food Review, 13*(2), 1–5.

Norman, C. (1984, November 9). No panacea for the firewood crisis. *Science, 226*, 676.

Norum, P. S. (1989). Economic analysis of quarterly household expenditures on apparel. *Home Economics Research Journal, 17*(3), 228–240.

Okie, S. (1989, September 25). 1.3 billion said to need health care: 20% of mankind sick or malnourished, U.S. report says. *Washington Post*, p. A1.

Overton, C. E. (1990). Trends in world food consumption. *National Food Review, 13*(2), 6–12.

Pao, E. M., & Mickle, S. J. (1981). Problem nutrients in the United States. *Food Technology, 35*(9), 58–69.

Paralikar, K. R. (1987). Water. In F. M. Magrabi & A. Verma (Eds.), *Household resources and their changing relationships: Case studies in Gujarat, India* (pp. 46–49). International Agriculture Publications, General Series No. 3. Urbana: University of Illinois.

Parsons, T., & Smelser, N. J. (1956). *Economy and society*. New York: Free Press.

Pearce, D. W. (1986). *The MIT dictionary of modern economics* (3d ed.). Cambridge, MA: MIT Press.

Peskin, J. (1982). Measuring household production for the GNP. *Family Economics Review*, (3), 16–25.

Peterkin, B. B., & Rizek, R. L. (1984). National nutrition monitoring system. *Family Economics Review* (4), 15–19.

Pinstrup-Andersen, P. (1988). Assuring food security and adequate nutrition for the poor. In D. E. Bell & M. R. Reich (Eds.), *Health, nutrition, and economic crises: Approaches to policy in the Third World* (pp. 147–175). Dover, MA: Auburn House.

Pleck, J. H. (1985). *Working wives/working husbands*. Beverly Hills, CA: Sage Publications.

Poduska, B. (1988). A comparative study of family budget: An international perspective. *Journal of Home Economics, 80* (2), 16–23.

Pollock, C. (1987). *Mining urban wastes: The potential for recycling*. Worldwatch Paper 76. Washington, DC: Worldwatch Institute.

Polyzou, A. (1979, Spring). Energy consumption for textiles and apparel. *Family Economics Review*, 3–10.

Popkin, B. M. (1978). Nutrition and labor productivity. *Social Science and Medicine*, *12*(3), 117–125.

Popkin, B. M., & Lim-Ybanez, M. (1982). Nutrition and school achievement. *Social Science and Medicine*, *16*, 53–61.

Postel, S. (1985). *Conserving water: The untapped alternative*. Worldwatch Paper 67. Washington, DC: Worldwatch Institute.

Price, C. (1985). Eating "natural" gains popularity. *National Food Review*, NFR–28, 14–18.

Price, C. (1988). Take-out food in convenience stores. *National Food Review*, *11*(4), 14–17.

Purchase, M. E., Berning, C. K., & Lyng, A. L. (1982). The cost of washing clothes: Sources of variation. *Journal of Consumer Studies and Home Economics*, *6*(4), 301–317.

Putnam, J. (1989). Food consumption. *National Food Review*, *12*(2), 1–8.

Raab, C. A., Holyoak, A., & Raff, L. G. (1988). Bridging the hunger gap. *Journal of Home Economics*, *80*(3), 3–8.

Ratchford, B. T. (1975). The new economic theory of consumer behavior: An interpretive essay. *Journal of Consumer Research*, *2*(2), 65–75.

Redman, B. J. (1980). The impact of women's time allocation on expenditure for meals away from home and prepared foods. *American Agricultural Economics Association*, *62*(2), 234–237.

Reid, M. (1934). *Economics of household production*. New York: John Wiley & Sons.

Renner, M. (1988). *Rethinking the role of the automobile*. Worldwatch Paper 84. Washington, DC: Worldwatch Institute.

Rhodes, P. (1979). Prenatal factors in child health. In S. Doxiadis (Ed.), *The child in the world of tomorrow: A window into the future* (pp. 383–385). London: Pergamon Press.

Rich, S. (1988, November 4). Urban Institute study puts number of U.S. homeless at close to 600,000. *Washington Post*, p. A10.

Rich, S. (1989, August 9). Millions of families said to be on the brink of homelessness. *Washington Post*, p. A19.

Richardson, S., Pearson, J. M., & Capps, Jr., O. (1985). Convenience and nonconvenience food use in single-person and multi-person households. *Home Economics Research Journal*, *14*(1), 11–20.

Riesman, D., & Rosebourough, H. (1960). Careers and consumer behavior. In N. Bell & E. F. Vogel (Eds.), *A modern introduction to the family*. New York: Free Press.

Ritzmann, L. J. (1982). Household size and prices paid for food. *Family Economics Review* (4), 27–31.

Roberts, S. D., & Dant, R. P. (1988, Winter). *Societal antecedents of contemporary American resource allocation*. Paper presented at the meeting of the American Marketing Association.

Robine, J. (1989). Estimation de la Valeur de l'Esperance de Vie Sans Incapacité (EVSI) pour les Pays Occidentaux au Cours de la Dernière Decennie: Quelle Peut-Etre l'Utilité de ca Nouvel Indicateur de l'Etat de Santé? *World Health Statistics Quarterly*, *42*(3), 141–147.

Robinson, J. P. (1977). *How Americans use time: A social-psychological analysis of everyday behavior*. New York: Praeger.

Rossi, P. H., Wright, J. D., Fisher, G. A., & Willis, G. (1987, March 13). The urban homeless: Estimating composition and size. *Science, 235,* 1336–1341.

St. John, C., & Clark, F. (1984). Racial differences in dimensions of neighborhood satisfaction. *Social Indicators Research, 15*(1), 43–60.

Salathe, L., & Buse, R. (1978, January). The relationship between household food expenditures and household size and composition. *National Food Review,* 25–28.

Salau, A. T. (1986). Quality of life and city size: An exploratory study of Nigeria. *Social Indicators Research, 18*(2), 193–203.

Samuelson, P. A. (1961). *Economics: An introductory analysis* (5th ed.). New York: McGraw-Hill.

Sawhill, I. V. (1988, September). Poverty in the U.S.: Why is it so persistent? *Journal of Economic Literature, 26,* 1073–1119.

Schipper, L., & Ketoff, A. N. (1985, December 6). The international decline in household oil use. *Science, 230,* 1118–1125.

Schultz, T. W. (1961). Investment in human capital. *American Economic Review, 51,* 1–7.

Schwenk, F. N. (1984). Developments in consumer product standards. *Family Economics Review* (3), 10–13.

Schwenk, F. N. (1988). Household expenditures for education and reading. *Family Economics Review, 1*(3), 6–8.

Schwenk, F. N. (1988). Housing expenditures. *Family Economics Review* (1), 1–7.

Schwenk, F. N. (1989). Households with expenditures for housekeeping services, including child care. *Family Economics Review, 2*(4), 15–20.

Schwenk, F. N. (1990). Households with expenditures for health insurance. *Family Economics Review, 3*(1), 2–6.

Scitovsky, T. (1976). *The joyless economy.* New York: Oxford University Press.

Scoon, L. M. (1989). Utility expenditures of homeowners. *Family Economics Review, 2*(2), 2–4.

Scoon, L. M. (1990). Vehicle insurance expenditures. *Family Economics Review, 3*(1), 7–11.

Selowsky, M., & Taylor, L. (1973). The economics of malnourished children: An example of disinvestment in human capital. *Economic Development and Cultural Change, 22,* 17–30.

Seneca, J. J., & Taussig, M. K. (1971). Family equivalence scales and personal income tax exemptions for children. *Review of Economics and Statistics, 53,* 253–262.

Sharif, M. (1986). The concept and measurement of subsistence: A survey of the literature. *World Development, 14*(5), 555–577.

Silvestri, G. T., & Lukasiewicz, J. M. (1987). A look at occupational employment trends to the year 2000. *Monthly Labor Review, 110*(9), 46–63.

Smallwood, D. (1989). Consumer demand for safer foods. *National Food Review, 12*(3), 9–11.

Smeeding, R. M., & Torrey, B. B. (1988, November 11). Poor children in rich countries. *Science, 242,* pp. 873–877.

Smeeding, T. M. (1982). Alternative methods for valuing selected in-kind transfer benefits and measuring their effect on poverty. *Technical Paper 50.* U.S. Department of Commerce, Bureau of the Census. Summarized in *Family Economics Review* (1983), (2), 22–23.

Smith, A. (1937). *The wealth of nations.* New York: Modern Library.

Stampfl, R. W. (1978). The consumer life cycle. *Journal of Consumer Affairs*, *12*(2), 209–219.

Stone, M. E. (1990). *One-third of a nation: A new look at housing affordability in America*. Washington, DC: Economic Policy Institute.

Strober, M. H. (1977). Wives' labor force behavior and family consumption patterns. *American Economic Review*, *67*(1), 410–417.

Strober, M. H., & Weinberg, C. B. (1977). Working wives and major family expenditures. *Journal of Consumer Research*, *4*, 141–147.

Strober, M. H., & Weinberg, C. B. (1980). Strategies used by working and nonworking wives to reduce time pressures. *Journal of Consumer Research*, *6*, 338–348.

Sun, T. Y. (1982, Winter). Three kinds of frankfurters: Retail demand. *National Food Review*, 20–21.

Suranyi-Unger, T. Jr. (1977). *Identification of standard classes in the United States* (NSF/RA 77–0205). Washington, DC: National Science Foundation, Research Applied to National Needs.

Swoboda, F. (1990, December 6). Third World said to be hard hit by workers' exodus from Gulf. *Washington Post*, p. A44.

Tarrant, J. R. (1980). *Food policies*. Chichester, England: John Wiley and Sons.

Tippett, K. S., & Ruffin, M. D. (1975, Summer). Service-life expectancy of household appliances. *Family Economics Review*, 3–6.

Tippett, K. S., Magrabi, F. M., & Gray, B. C. (1978). Service life of appliances: Variations by selected characteristics of owner households. *Home Economics Research Journal*, *6*(3), 184–191.

Tippett, K. S., Mickle, S. J., & Roidt, L. (1990). Food and nutrient intakes of low-income women and children, in metro/nonmetro areas, 1985/1986. *Family Economics Review*, *3*(1), 12–15.

Trostle, R. G. (1989). Food aid needs during the 1990s. *National Food Review*, *12*(1), 31–33.

Turner, A. (1980). Planning and development standards. In A. Turner (Ed.), *The cities of the poor* (pp. 218–249). London: Croom Helm.

Uemura, K. (1989). Excess mortality ratio with reference to the lowest age-sex-specific death rates among countries. *World Health Statistics Quarterly*, *42*(1), 26–41.

United Nations Department of International and Social Affairs. (1986). *Economic recession and specific population groups*. New York.

United Nations Environment Programme & United Nations Children's Fund. (1990). *Children and the environment: The state of the environment—1990*. Geneva.

United Nations Statistical Office. (1988). *Women's indicators and statistics data base (WISTAT)*. New York.

U.S. Bureau of the Census. (1986). *Projections of the number of households and families: 1986 to 2000*. Current Population Reports, Series P-25, No. 986. Washington, DC: U.S. Government Printing Office.

U.S. Bureau of the Census. (1989a). *Characteristics of persons receiving benefits from major assistance programs*. Current Population Reports, Series P-70, No. 14. Washington, DC: U.S. Government Printing Office.

U.S. Bureau of the Census. (1989b). *Child care costs estimated at $14 Billion in 1986* (Reports CD89–119). Washington, DC: U.S. Government Printing Office.

U.S. Bureau of the Census. (1989c). *Earnings of married-couple families: 1987*. Current

Population Reports, Series P-60, No. 165. Washington, DC: U.S. Government Printing Office.

U.S. Bureau of the Census. (1989d). *Money income and poverty status in the United States: 1988*. Current Population Reports, Series P-60, No. 163. Washington, DC: U.S. Government Printing Office.

U.S. Bureau of the Census. (1989e). *Projections of the population of the United States, by age, sex, and race: 1988 to 2080*. Current Population Reports, Series P-25, No. 1018. Washington, DC: U.S. Government Printing Office.

U.S. Bureau of the Census. (1989f). *Studies in marriage and the family*. Current Population Reports, Series P-23, No. 162. Washington, DC: U.S. Government Printing Office.

U.S. Bureau of the Census. (1990a). *Average child support payments increased in 1987* (Reports CB90–138). Washington, DC: U.S. Government Printing Office.

U.S. Bureau of the Census. (1990b). *Children's well-being: An international comparison*. International Population Reports Series P-95, No. 80. Washington, DC: U.S. Government Printing Office.

U.S. Bureau of the Census. (1990c, November 9). *College degrees mean higher incomes*. News release, CB90–204. Washington, DC: U.S. Government Printing Office.

U.S. Bureau of the Census. (1990d). *Household wealth and asset ownership: 1988*. Current Population Reports, Series P-70, No. 22. Washington, DC: U.S. Government Printing Office.

U.S. Bureau of the Census. (1990e). *Measuring the effect of benefits and taxes on income and poverty: 1989*. Current Population Reports, Consumer Income Series P-60, No. 169-RD. Washington, DC: U.S. Government Printing Office.

U.S. Bureau of the Census. (1990f). *Money income and poverty status in the United States 1989*. Current Population Reports, Consumer Income Series P-60, No. 168. Washington, DC: U.S. Government Printing Office.

U.S. Bureau of the Census. (1990g). *Statistical abstract of the United States* (110th ed.). Washington, DC: U.S. Government Printing Office.

U.S. Bureau of the Census. (1990h). *Trends in income, by selected characteristics: 1947 to 1988*. Current Population Reports, Series P-60, No. 167. Washington, DC: U.S. Government Printing Office.

U.S. Bureau of the Census, jointly with the Department of Agriculture (1989). *Rural and rural farm population: 1988*. Current Population Reports, Series P-20, No. 439. Washington, DC: U.S. Government Printing Office.

U.S. Bureau of the Census & U.S. Department of Housing and Urban Development. (1989). *American housing survey for the United States in 1987*. Current Housing Reports H-150–87. Washington, DC: U.S. Government Printing Office.

U.S. Bureau of Labor Statistics. (1964). *Consumer expenditures and income*. Washington, DC: U.S. Government Printing Office.

U.S. Bureau of Labor Statistics. (1977). *The Consumer Price Index: Concepts and content over the years* (Report 517). Washington, DC: Government Printing Office.

U.S. Bureau of Labor Statistics. (1983). *The CPI detailed report*. Washington, DC: Government Printing Office.

U.S. Bureau of Labor Statistics. (1988). *Consumer Expenditure Survey: Interview survey, 1988*. Public use tapes.

U.S. Bureau of Labor Statistics. (1989). *Consumer Expenditure Survey: Integrated survey data, 1984–1986*. Washington, DC: U.S. Government Printing Office.

U.S. Bureau of Labor Statistics. (1990). *Consumer Expenditure Survey: Integrated survey data, 1988*. Washington, DC: U.S. Government Printing Office.

U.S. Department of Agriculture. (1988). *Food program update for August 1988*. Washington, DC: Food and Nutrition Service, PID/PRAB.

U.S. Department of Agriculture, Consumer Nutrition Division, Human Nutrition Information Service. (1983). *Food intakes: Individuals in 48 States, year 1977–78* (Report No. I–1). Washington, DC: U.S. Government Printing Office.

U.S. Department of Agriculture & U.S. Department of Health and Human Services. (1985). *Nutrition and your health: Dietary guidelines for Americans* (2d ed.). Washington, DC: U.S. Government Printing Office.

U.S. Department of Energy, Energy Information Administration. (1989). *Household energy consumption and expenditures 1987, part 1: National data* (DOE/EIA–0321/1, 87). Washington, DC: U.S. Government Printing Office.

U.S. House of Representatives. (1990). *Economic report of the president* (House Document No. 101–121). Washington, DC: U.S. Government Printing Office.

Uusitalo, L. (1980). Identification of consumption style segments on the basis of household budget allocation. In J. C. Olson (Ed.), *Advances in Consumer Research, Proceedings of the Association for Consumer Research, 7*, 451–459.

Veblen, T. (1953). *The theory of the leisure class*. New York: Mentor.

Vemury, M., & Levine, H. (1978). *Beliefs and practices that affect food habits in developing countries*. New York: Care.

Volker, C. B., & Winter, M. (1989). Primary household production of food, food expenditures, and reported adequacy of food. *Home Economics Research Journal, 18*(1), 32–46.

Volker, C. B., Winter, M., & Beutler, I. F. (1983). Household production of food: Expenditures, norms and satisfaction. *Home Economics Research Journal, 11*(3), 267–279.

Wagner, J. (1986). Expenditures for household textiles and textile home furnishings: An Engel curve analysis. *Home Economics Research Journal, 15*(1), 21–31.

Walker, K. E., & Woods, M. E. (1976). *Time use: A measure of household production of family goods and services*. Washington, DC: American Home Economics Association.

Wanmali, S. (1985). *Rural household use of services: A study of Miryalguda Taluka* (Research Report No. 48). Washington, DC: International Food Policy Research Institute.

Weagley, R. O., & Norum, P. S. (1989). Household demand for market purchased, home producible commodities. *Home Economics Research Journal, 12*(1), 6–18.

Weinberg, C. B., & Winter, R. S. (1983). Working wives and major family expenditures: Replication and extension. *Journal of Consumer Research, 10*, 259–262.

Wells, W. D., & Cosmas, S. C. (1977). Life styles. In *Selected Aspects of Consumer Behavior* (pp. 299–316). Washington, DC: National Science Foundation.

Whorton, J. W., & Moore, A. B. (1984). Summative scales for measuring community satisfaction. *Social Indicators Research, 15*(3), 297–307.

Winakor, G. (1975). Household textiles consumption by farm and city families: Assortment owned, annual expenditures, and sources. *Home Economics Research Journal, 4*(1), 2–26.

Winakor, G., & Lubner-Rupert, J. (1983). Dress style variation related to perceived economic risk. *Home Economics Research Journal. 11*(4), 343–351.

Winakor, G., & Thomas, L. (1978). Standard budgets for household textiles: Farm and city families at two income levels and three family sizes. *Home Economics Research Journal, 7*(1), 2–19.

Wolfe, B. A., & Abdel-Ghany, M. (1981). Residential electric applications: Determinants of ownership. *Journal of Consumer Studies and Home Economics, 5*, 339–348.

Wood, P. H. N. (1989). Measuring the consequences of illness. *World Health Statistics Quarterly, 42*(3), 115–121.

World Bank. (1989). *Social indicators of development 1989*. Baltimore: Johns Hopkins University Press.

World Bank. (1990). *World development report 1990: Poverty*. New York: Oxford University Press.

World Health Organization. (1988). *Urbanization and its implications for child health: Potential for action*. Geneva: World Health Organization.

World Health Statistics Quarterly. (1989a). Availability of health care. *42*(4), 235–254.

World Health Statistics Quarterly. (1989b). Global socioeconomic development trends (1985–1988). *42*(4), 190–196.

Yang, S. (1991). The effects of wife's employment on family expenditures: Gross effect, work-related effect, and net income effect. Unpublished doctoral dissertation, University of Illinois.

Yang, S., & Magrabi, F. M. (1989). Expenditures for services, wife's employment, and other household characteristics. *Home Economics Research Journal, 18*, 133–147.

Zimmerman, S. L. (1988). *Understanding family policy: Theoretical approaches*. Beverly Hills, CA: Sage Publications.

Author Index

Subject Index

About the Authors

FRANCES M. MAGRABI is professor of consumption economics in the Consumer Sciences Division of the School of Human Resources and Family Studies, University of Illinois at Urbana-Champaign. She received a Ph.D. in economics from Iowa State University in 1962 and held positions at Michigan State University and the Agricultural Research Service, U.S. Department of Agriculture. During her employment with the Department of Agriculture, she served on delegations to the Food and Agricultural Organization of the United Nations and the World Food Council and was detailed to the White House staff during the Carter administration as an expert on international nutrition policy. Dr. Magrabi was a Fulbright scholar in India in 1985 and has also traveled in Europe and Latin America. She is the author of more than 100 papers that have been published in research journals or been presented at national and international scholarly meetings.

YOUNG SOOK CHUNG did her undergraduate work at Taegu University, Korea. She received an M.S. and Ph.D. from the University of Illinois at Urbana-Champaign and is now an assistant professor at Taegu University, teaching in the areas of research methods and home management and conducting research on household expenditures. She has presented papers at meetings of the Korean Home Economics Association, the Eastern Economic Association, the American Council on Consumer Interests, the American Home Economics Association, and the International Federation for Home Economics, and she has published in the *Journal of Housing and Society*.

SANGHEE SOHN CHA received a B.A. and M.S. at Seoul National University, Korea, and a Ph.D. from the University of Illinois at Urbana-Champaign. During her graduate study, she received several honors and awards, including the Omicron Nu Research Fellowship, the Illinois Home Economics Association Research Award, the Wright Fellowship, the Alice and Charlotte Biester Graduate Fellowship, and a summer university fellowship. She has reported her research at meetings of the American Home Economics Association, the Beatrice Paolucci Symposium, and the Illinois Economic Association.

SE-JEONG YANG did her undergraduate work at Korea University, Korea. She received an M.S. and Ph.D. from the University of Illinois at Urbana-Champaign. Her research interests have focused on consumption patterns of employed-wife families. She has presented her research at scholarly meetings of the American Home Economics Association and the American Council on Consumer Interests and has published in the *Home Economics Research Journal*.